REPRESENTING PEOPLE WITH
Autism Spectrum Disorders

A Practical
Guide for Criminal
Defense Lawyers

ELIZABETH KELLEY, EDITOR

AMERICAN**BAR**ASSOCIATION

ABA Publishing

Cover by ABA Design.

Printed in the United States of America.

24 23 22 21 20   5 4 3 2 1

ISBN: 978-1-64105-634-2

Cataloging-in-Publication Data is on file with the Library of Congress

Discounts are available for books ordered in bulk. Special consideration is given to state bars, CLE programs, and other bar-related organizations. Inquire at Book Publishing, ABA Publishing, American Bar Association, 321 N. Clark Street, Chicago, Illinois 60654-7598.

www.shopABA.org

Contents

Introduction

If you as a criminal defense lawyer tell the court or the prosecutor that your client is on the autism spectrum, what images likely come to their mind? Perhaps Raymond, the character played by Dustin Hoffman in *Rain Man*? Perhaps Adam Lanza, the young man who shot and killed the children and a teacher at Sandy Hook? Perhaps nothing. Your challenge as a criminal defense lawyer is to give an accurate portrait of your client while humanizing him or her. In addition, you must show the nexus between autism spectrum disorder (ASD) and the alleged conduct; argue that prison is the wrong place for your client while proposing a probationary sentence that makes sense for your client; or if prison is mandatory, arguing for as short a term as possible with the best accommodations available. This is a monumental challenge, and this book attempts to help you meet it.

Representing People with Autism Spectrum Disorders: A Practical Guide for Criminal Defense Lawyers, is modeled on my earlier book, *Representing People with Mental Disabilities: A Practical Guide for Criminal Defense Lawyers*. The reason for this book is twofold: first, there is a growing recognition that people with ASD are involved in the criminal justice system and need vigorous, informed advocacy; and second, there is a need for practical, easily digestible information for lawyers.

This book is meant to cover the complete anatomy of a criminal case, from the initial encounter with law enforcement, through the bond hearing, through the use of experts, through plea bargaining or dismissal, through resolution, including a sentencing hearing to prison or probation.

Theoretically, you can open this book to any chapter. However, the material in that chapter may necessarily overlap with material in one or more other chapters. Whenever possible, cross-references are provided. You also may want to read chapters in sets. For instance, you might read Dr. Elliot Atkins's chapter on working with experts in conjunction with Federal Public Defender Melanie Gavisk's chapter on the same topic. Similarly, you may want to read Nicolas Dubin's chapter about how he dealt with his own case alongside that written by his father, Lawrence Dubin, about what it was like—as a father and as a law professor—to have a son indicted, subjected to zealous prosecution, and despite marshalling every defense, sentenced and placed on the sex offender registry.

Although you can open the book to any chapter, the chapters do not have detailed definitions and explanations of autism spectrum disorder. Instead, the authors dive right into the topic of their chapter. My chapter at the beginning of the book, "The Intersection of Autism Spectrum Disorders and the Criminal Justice System," is intended to give a brief, working introduction to ASD. Certainly, many of the works cited in the "Suggested Works" section can provide a deeper treatment, and there are additional and abundant resources online.

The chapters are relatively short (as far as legal works go). Although the chapters lack the footnotes traditionally seen in legal writing, attribution is given when appropriate, and complete citations are available by contacting the author or authors. The back of the book contains a list of Suggested Works arranged by chapter heading if you would like to further explore a topic. As with the chapters, the works cited may overlap with one another in terms of content.

I have written a brief introduction to each chapter to put the topic in context or to raise a point not covered by the author. As editor, this is my attempt to weave together the different voices and perspectives of a diverse group of writers.

Thanks are due to a host of people. First and foremost, I appreciate the contributions of my authors. I am grateful that they shared their expertise and embraced the parameters of this project. I also acknowledge the individuals who peer-reviewed chapters: Dr. Mary Cohen; Dr. Eric Y. Drogin; Andrea George, Esq.; Dr. Joette James; Ilene Jaroslaw, Esq.; Jennifer K. Johnson, Esq.; Professor Daniel J. Morrissey; and Dr. Lauren Persing. Thanks, also, to John Palmer, my editor at the ABA, for his support on this project.

The human brain has long fascinated me. It is a wondrous organ, yet also fragile. It can sometimes cause people to do awful things, or to behave in ways that are an affront to societal norms and laws. When this happens, too many people find out that the criminal justice system is the worst place in the world to deal with mental disabilities, whether mental illness or intellectual and developmental disabilities such as autism spectrum disorders. Still, the situation must be resolved, and the criminal defense lawyer is pressed into action. We can't solve every problem, and indeed, some clients and their families ignore our advice. But this book is an attempt to provide knowledge and to give courage.

—Elizabeth Kelley, Editor

1

The Intersection of Autism Spectrum Disorders and the Criminal Justice System

Elizabeth Kelley

If you are a criminal defense lawyer, it is inevitable that you will represent someone on the autism spectrum. Indeed, the Centers for Disease Control and Prevention estimate that one in fifty-nine children is on the spectrum—and because autism is a lifelong condition, these children will become adults on the spectrum. Moreover, because of the changes in how autism is defined and society's greater awareness of it, many adults we now consider to be on the spectrum were never diagnosed as children.

But what is autism spectrum disorder (ASD)? How will you recognize it in a client? Why is it relevant to the criminal justice system, and why do people with ASD get ensnared in the criminal justice system?

What Is ASD?

The fifth edition of the *Diagnostic and Statistical Manual (DSM-V)*, commonly regarded as the "bible" of the mental health profession, defines ASD as a "neurodevelopmental disorder." This means that it is a brain disfunction affecting emotion, learning ability, self-control, and memory.

Specifically, ASD manifests itself in "severe and pervasive impairments in reciprocal social communication and interaction (verbal and nonverbal)" and "restricted, repetitive patterns of behavior, interests, and activities."

It is important to emphasize that ASD is *not* a mental illness, although some people may have a diagnosis of a mental illness separate from and independent of ASD. Also, some people with ASD may suffer from depression related to bullying and social ostracism or anxiety because of the criminal charges.

How Will You Recognize ASD?

The term "spectrum" is broad, and that in itself poses a challenge. At one end of the spectrum, you may have a client with a low IQ (below 70) with poor living skills. Indeed, he/she may have an intellectual disability. On the other end of the spectrum, your client may have a high IQ but still struggle with skills of daily living. Hence, what has now become a cliché: "if you've met one person on the autism spectrum, you've met one person on the autism spectrum."

If your client or his/her family says that there has been a prior diagnosis of ASD, then you can check off that box. However, your task as a lawyer has only begun. For example, you will still have to obtain a thorough forensic evaluation, present to the court/prosecutor that your client may not have had the ability to form the intent to commit the conduct alleged, and advocate for the appropriate resources.

Note that even if your client is being treated in some fashion, you will still have to obtain an independent forensic evaluation. Generally, it would be a conflict of interest and violation of confidentiality for a person treating an individual to render a forensic evaluation. However, the forensic evaluator may very well note that an individual is in treatment and describe the course of treatment.

If your client or his/her family says that there has been a prior diagnosis, ask what terminology they prefer. Broadly speaking, attorneys should use person-centered language: that is, first say "person," and then add the appropriate term, such as "with bipolar disorder." In the case of people with ASD, ask if they prefer "a person with ASD" or "on the spectrum." Some people on the spectrum use the term "autistic" to describe themselves. In particular, although the *DSM-V* no longer uses the term

"Asperger's syndrome," many people and their families prefer it. Also, many object to the terms "low-functioning" and "high-functioning."

If there has not been a prior diagnosis, your task is more difficult. If there are resources available, you will have to convince the client and/or the client's family that an evaluation is in order. If resources aren't available, you will have to request an evaluation from the court. If your client is older, it could be that he/she is from an era when parents and educators were not as aware of a potential diagnosis. Similarly, if your client is from an environment where he/she does (or did) not have access to good schools, educators may not have had the opportunity to notice the constellation of symptoms that comprise ASD.

There is no bright-line test you as an attorney can follow. At the end of the day, an attorney is just that, an attorney, not a doctor or other mental health expert. The CDC's site is a good place to start. Although some of the signs and symptoms are phrased in terms of children (e.g., child not responding to his/her name by twelve months of age), much is applicable to adults (e.g., echolalia or the repetition of words and phrases).

How Is a Diagnosis of ASD Relevant in the Criminal Justice System?

Your challenge as an attorney is to make a diagnosis of ASD relevant to the prosecutor and the court. This is often easier said than done. You can't just assert that one in fifty-nine Americans has ASD. You may have to explain why your client's ASD will make him vulnerable in jail. For example, his rocking back and forth (stimming) may make him the butt of inmates' jokes, or upset the corrections officers, resulting in punishment. You, along with the evaluation from your expert, must emphasize to the court that your client's downloading of child pornography was not done to satisfy any deviant interest but rather was a result of his spending hours and hours online as his only social outlet, and his viewing of the images was a result of curiosity.

Make no mistake, as with any mental disability, you are not using ASD as an excuse but rather as a reason and a mitigator. Certainly, though, if you have a case of factual innocence, or your expert opinion is strong enough to refute intent, that is a different matter.

Why Do People with ASD Get Ensnared in the Criminal Justice System?

At the risk of being repetitive, I will restate two points I made earlier: the term "spectrum" is tremendously broad, and "if you've met one person on the autism spectrum, you've met one person on the autism spectrum." It is important to keep these two points in mind because the reasons people with ASD get involved with the criminal justice system are individualized and multilayered. Nonetheless, some common themes and common narratives emerge.

For example, people with ASD are often implicated in sexually oriented offenses, particularly ones involving the internet. Many kids with ASD are bullied while growing up because they are "different." Others simply do not make friends. They are not invited to other kids' birthday parties, and as teenagers they get little dating experience. Thus, young adults with ASD might spend an unusually large amount of time online. In a society in which virtually everyone (including neurotypicals) spends a lot of time online, what makes this unusual is that the internet is frequently the only social outlet for a person with ASD. Moreover, if you forced a neurotypical person into a social situation, he/she could adapt, whereas someone with ASD could not, or would find it painful, or could adapt only after being coached.

A person with ASD often gets into trouble because he/she lacks the judgment or social sophistication to avoid potentially dangerous situations online, or even in person. He may stumble upon child pornography and obsessively download, not because of a deviant interest but because of an obsession to organize or curiosity. Indeed, the images could be of anything and not provoke any particular interest response. Or someone with ASD may be lonely and go into a chat room or other forum. There, she could be vulnerable to someone's demands (that they meet for sexual contact) or naïve about her needs (that the online contact needs money or rescue from an abusive environment). Unfortunately for someone with ASD, much of this conduct is basically a strict liability crime at the federal and state levels, carrying mandatory jail time or onerous probation in addition to registration as a sex offender.

People with ASD may be vulnerable to interaction with law enforcement in other ways. Someone with ASD may be in a public place and acting in a way that might be thought of as strange. A police officer might approach, but the person would not be responsive to the officer's request for information. Indeed, the encounter could escalate, particularly if the officer is in uniform. To avoid such situations, which (like some others) can escalate to resulting in fatal consequences, some states have enacted programs in which people with ASD can carry cards identifying that they have this issue; law enforcement personnel should conduct themselves accordingly and make appropriate accommodations.

Media accounts about people with mental illness involved in the criminal justice system routinely cite a 2017 Bureau of Justice Statistics report stating that approximately half the people in U.S. jails and prisons have a mental illness. However, no such data exists for people with intellectual and developmental disabilities in general or ASD in particular. Also, any collection of reliable data is predicated on diagnosis.

What we do know is that people on all points of the autism spectrum are a distinct and sizeable portion of the population; that their characteristics are easily misunderstood (sometimes frustrating, but often valuable and endearing); and that their vulnerabilities make them particularly susceptible to becoming involved in the criminal justice system.

● ● ●

Elizabeth Kelley, Esq., is a criminal defense lawyer with a nationwide practice focused on representing people with mental disabilities. She co-chairs the Criminal Justice Advisory Panel of The ARC's National Center on Criminal Justice and Disability. She is the editor of *Representing People with Mental Disabilities: A Practical Guide for Criminal Defense Lawyers* published by the American Bar Association (ABA) in 2018. She is active in the ABA, serving on the Editorial Board Criminal Justice Section Magazine and Council of the Criminal Justice Section, as well as on the Commission for Disability Rights. She recently served as a Non-Governmental Observer on behalf of the ABA of the Military Commission Hearings at Guantanamo.

Ms. Kelley served three terms on the board of the National Association of Criminal Defense Lawyers (NACDL), chaired its Mental Health as well as Membership Committees, and is a Life Member. She served on the Problem-Solving Courts Task Force and Body Camera Task Force. She traveled to Liberia in 2009 and 2014 as part of a delegation sponsored by the UN Commission on Drugs and Crime and NACDL to train that country's criminal defense bar.

She speaks and writes widely on the subjects of the intersection of mental disabilities and the criminal justice system, as well as on attorney wellness. She has completed her 500-hour Yoga certification through Semperviva Studio in Vancouver, B.C.

2

Competency

Stephen Greenspan

"Is my client competent?" is the threshold inquiry for any criminal proceeding. As this chapter by Dr. Stephen Greenspan points out, this question is particularly complicated when representing clients with ASD. Application of the two prongs of the competency standard—the client's understanding of the proceedings and the client's ability to assist counsel—may be affected by the unique characteristics of a client with ASD, such as social deficits. However, the initial impression of the client and even the use of testing instruments may not accurately gauge these deficits. This, combined with the fact that as a practical matter the legal standard for competency is low and the vast majority of defendants are eventually found competent, makes representation of a client with ASD particularly challenging.

Although Dr. Greenspan's article does not provide easy answers, it does encourage the attorney to take a deep dive into the questions surrounding the capacity of a client with ASD to comprehend the gravity of the legal situation and make decisions that are in the client's best interest.

●　　●　　●

In criminal jurisprudence, the term *incompetence* typically means incompetence to stand trial. In the field of neurodevelopmental disorders—two examples of which are autism spectrum disorder (ASD) and intellectual disability (ID)—*incompetence* refers to the defining elements of such disorders. Although this chapter is in a book on legal aspects of ASD, I mention ID for the simple reason that a large percentage (a quarter to more than a half, depending on how one defines either disorder) of people with the disorder category of ASD also qualify for the disability category of ID. Moreover, ID has stronger legal standing in criminal precedents and statutes (an example, but not the only one, being the death penalty exemption under *Atkins v. Virginia*, 593 U.S. 304 (2002)).

A *disorder* is a medical classification reflecting some underlying biological vulnerability or disease. In contrast, a *disability* is a functional category used by bureaucracies to determine eligibility for services or protections. ASD is a quasi-medical category reflecting documented or presumed brain abnormalities, whereas ID is a bureaucratic disability category determined by meeting arbitrary performance criteria, such as full-scale IQ scores. With regard to both ASD and ID, the distinction is not absolute: ASD has some qualities of a functionally determined disability, and ID is a bureaucratic disability status often treated as a biological disorder, even when (as is usually the case) etiology is unknown. An obvious conclusion to be drawn from these two somewhat separate sides of the classification coin is that not everyone with a particular label will be found legally incompetent, even when the person has qualities (such as low IQ) that are strongly correlated with legal incompetence. It should also be noted that forensic experts who make such determinations differ widely in their approaches, and that the criteria and methods for determining competence are not as developed, universal, or adequate as one might like.

A problem facing any lawyer representing someone who might have ASD (or ID, for that matter) is that within the universe of people captured by this diagnostic label, competence levels vary substantially, and a previous diagnosis may not have been made accurately or at all. Five complicating factors are present in higher-functioning individuals (which is the subpopulation of ASD or ID most likely to be facing criminal charges):

- Co-occurring psychiatric conditions are often—in fact, usually—present (*see* Chap. 4, Co-Occurring Disorders).

- Incompetence is not consistent across the board; a person may have areas of relative normality and still qualify appropriately for a diagnosis of ASD or ID.

- Every person with ASD or ID (or any other psychiatric label) is unique (some shy, others less shy, etc.) and may differ in small or large ways from diagnostic stereotypes or prototypes.

- Limitations may be masked by the existence of "benefactors" (parents, spouses, co-workers, prison pod-mates) who help an individual do things (write letters, fill out forms, secure medical help, handle money, etc.) that the person may be unable to do on his or her own.

- As a rule, people with high-functioning ASD or ID make an effort to appear more competent and "normal" than they are, meaning that the self-presentation they provide regarding their accomplishments and "normality" can be very misleading.

This last consideration flies in the face of the usual assumption made by forensic psychologists, which is that defendants in criminal cases are motivated to make themselves appear less competent than they actually are. In fact, the opposite is more often the case for people with ASD or ID, for three reasons: (1) those who have a lifetime of pain stemming from feelings of academic and social failure are very motivated to appear more competent than they are, regardless of whether it is in their interest to do so; (2) according to the Dunning-Kruger effect (Kruger & Dunning, 1999), people who are cognitively incompetent are poor judges of their own competence; and (3) understanding of the consequences of poor test performance for one's legal case requires more reasoning ability than people with ASD or ID generally possess.

This chapter has two purposes: (a) to provide a general treatment of the topic of "personal competence," with some discussion of how it relates to people with ASD; and (b) to provide a discussion of legal competence of people with ASD, focusing primarily on competence to stand trial. One thing to note is that my focus is mainly on acts allegedly committed by adults or youths involved in court settings; I have little or nothing to say about children or the settings in which they are found. One potential exception (which I just briefly touch on) involves retrospective assessments, such as of "adaptive behavior" (a construct related to competence), where information about such things as past special education placements is important in establishing age of onset for ID.

The Nature of Personal Competence

The term *competence* refers to the extent to which someone is able to perform activities or roles that are typical for that person's age, gender, and cultural-familial upbringing. Intelligence (measured by IQ but also other indices) is a common measure of competence that is obtained and used in many forensic cases, but it is hardly the only important indicator of competence. For example, it is increasingly understood, as stated in *DSM-5*, that measures of "executive functioning," which include skills such as planning, reasoning, and causal understanding, are often better measures of intelligence than full-scale IQ. Although competence in many spheres is a common target of psychological assessments, the selection and use of psychological tests has generally not been guided by the use of a comprehensive competence model, in large part because no such model is in widespread circulation. Figure 2.1 depicts a model of personal competence developed by Dr. John M. Driscoll and Elizabeth Kelley in 1997, as part of an effort to locate intelligence in a wider framework. Their model

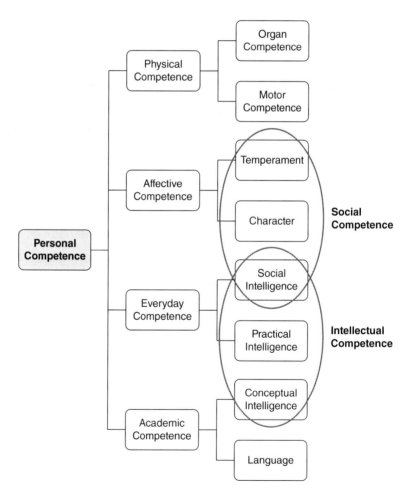

FIGURE 2.1 Content model of personal competence.

built on other competence modeling efforts, including my earlier, less comprehensive efforts.

In the next few pages, I illustrate the utility of the model in explaining the diagnostic features of ASD.

Application of the Competence Model to ASD

All of the eight variables in the model are briefly described here, with some discussion of whether and how each applies diagnostically to people who may have ASD. Keep in mind that our understanding of ASD has evolved over time (Rutter, 2007) and that there are multiple causal pathways to ASD. As an example, my younger brother's autism—diagnosed by Leo Kanner, the coiner of the term—likely was caused by being dropped on his head at age two days.

Organ competence (sensation): This refers to relative "abnormality" in sensory modalities and perceptions such as touch, taste, sight, hearing, and smell. In terms of outcomes, it is common for caregivers to report that individuals with ASD, especially when young, exhibited unusual sensory symptoms, such as appearing to be deaf, being very sensitive to (and avoidant of) touch, having a very highly developed sense of smell, and finding certain visual stimuli (such as wallpaper with busy patterns) to be aversive. In terms of inputs, it is usually not the case that formal tests of these sensory modalities are applied; these apparent abnormalities are more in the realm of "unusual" rather than deficient (or enhanced) processing of sensory stimuli. Furthermore, the extent of these sensory abnormalities has not really been determined empirically. The possession of sensory abnormality is hardly universal, differing in nature across individuals, and thus is not an established diagnostic indicator.

Motor competence (motoricity): This refers to movements that are voluntary as well as involuntary, and the quality of control, coordination, effectiveness, and normality of such movements. Motor movements are neurologically controlled; thus, as ASD is a brain-based disorder, it is to be expected that motoricity would be abnormal. As with sensation, the motoricity outcome that is associated with ASD is less in the realm of impaired limbs or motoric ability and more in the self-regulatory realm of bizarre or unusual movements. In ASD, these manifest in repetitive and stereotypic motoric rituals that are in fact part of the ASD diagnostic phenotype.

Temperament: This has to do with self-regulatory competence. The two main aspects of temperament are attention focus and emotion regulation. People with ASD often (but not always) have attentional problems, as is true of people with brain-based disorders generally. Because attention issues are so widespread, they are not diagnostically specific to ASD. Emotion regulation (primarily excessive emotional responses) is, however, a universal problem for people with ASD and is a diagnostic indicator.

Character: This refers to how empathic one is toward others. ASD has been termed an "empathy deficit disorder" (Baron-Cohen, 2011), which in the case of ASD refers not to how intentionally nasty someone is but to how able a person is to experience what others are feeling. People with ASD are unable to experience empathy, which in their case is at least partially related to an absence of role-taking (social intelligence) ability.

Social intelligence: This refers to one's ability to "read" people and social situations and, consequently, to exhibit adequate judgment in addressing problematic or routine social situations. All definitions of ASD start by mentioning a failure in "social reciprocity," which is another term for poor social intelligence. Thus, an inability to demonstrate good social intelligence must be considered a central defining characteristic of ASD.

Practical intelligence: This refers to one's ability to understand and cope with physical and mechanical tasks and challenges. Examples are finding one's way within a city or neighborhood, operating a machine, dealing with daily living challenges, and so on. Although people with ASD, especially those with very low IQ, often have limitations in this domain, poor practical intelligence is not in itself a defining characteristic of ASD.

Conceptual intelligence: This refers to academic functioning and potential, as indicated by outcomes such as grades and school retention, and input measures such as full-scale IQ, executive functioning (implied by *DSM-5* to be as good as IQ as an indicator of intelligence), and academic achievement. People with ASD almost always have depressed IQ scores, but these typically are above the threshold for legal or clinical definitions of ID. In terms of executive functions (planning, reasoning, etc.), however, people with ASD always have significant deficits (as is true also of those with other brain-based disorders), although the specific nature of the deficits (determined by specific location, timing, and severity of brain insult) varies across individuals. Thus, ASD is a condition marked by deficits in conceptual intelligence, broadly defined.

Language: This has to do with the ability to communicate, both expressively and receptively. As with motoricity, the language impairments of people with ASD are found more in the oddness or unusualness of their language (echolalia, nonsense, failure to understand or communicate clearly, delays in acquiring literacy) than in any physical or linguistic inability to make speech sounds or use symbols (although for very low-functioning individuals with ASD, muteness is not uncommon). Such a "sociolinguistic" approach to language impairment addresses an important aspect of the language deficits in ASD, again one that is partly reflective of the condition's core deficiency in social intelligence.

Diagnostic Applicability of the Model to Two Other Categories

As an illustration of the competence model for purposes of differential diagnosis, in Figure 2.2 I have depicted three "ideal type" comparative profiles: one for ASD, one for ID, and one for a new *DSM-5* category, Social-Pragmatic Communication Disorder (SCD). The reason for using ID as a comparison is obvious: namely, the fact that a sizable number of people with the disorder category of ASD also qualify for the disability category of ID (which is not an exclusionary diagnosis; therefore, a person with ASD can also qualify for ID). As mentioned, SCD is a new category, created in 2013 in *DSM-5*, to address a portion of people formerly considered to have ASD who no longer qualify given the dropping of Asperger disorder from *DSM-IV*.

Competence Domains	Organ	Motor	Temperament	Character	Social Intelligence	Practical Intelligence	Conceptual Intelligence	Language
Autism	—	Impaired	Impaired	Impaired	Impaired	—	Impaired	Impaired
Intellectual Disability	—	—	—	—	Impaired	Impaired	Impaired	—
Social Communication (Pragmatic) Disorder	—	—	—	—	Impaired	—	—	Impaired

FIGURE 2.2 Aspects of competence affected in three disorders.

The new category of SCD has not really caught on and, at this point, does not appear to be much in use. Figure 2.2 reveals that the difference between SCD and ASD is that although the core symptoms of SCD (as with ASD) are reduced social intelligence and social communication, the other cognitive, affective, and motoric problems associated with ASD are not present.

Legal Competence and ASD

In the balance of this chapter, I turn from the general topic of personal competence as it applies to people with ASD to a more specific examination of legal competence. The main focus is on competence to stand trial, followed by a brief mention of other forms of legal competence.

Competence to Stand Trial

The basic concept of competence to stand trial was established in a landmark U.S. Supreme Court decision, *Dusky v. United States*, 362 U.S. 402 (1960), and further articulated in subsequent cases such as *Drope v. Missouri*, 420 U.S. 162 (1975). The defendant, Milton Dusky, was a thirty-three-year-old man with schizophrenia charged with being an accomplice in the kidnapping and rape of an underage female. His attorneys argued that, in light of his condition, he had a right to have his competency evaluated. The *Dusky* court (and other later courts) established that defendants with a mental illness or developmental disability are entitled to have their competence determined. ASD is a developmental disability that at one time was considered a mental illness, and many individuals with ASD also have a history of being labeled with a mental illness. Consequently, defendants with ASD often exhibit behaviors (such as not seeming to understand what is going on) that could cause their attorneys to request that a competency evaluation be conducted.

Dusky requires that the defendant have a "sufficient present ability to consult with his lawyer with a reasonable degree of rational understanding" and possess a "rational as well as factual understanding of the proceedings against him." On the surface this seems fairly clear, but what exactly is meant by the word "rational"? I would wager that if I asked ten experts (or judges) to define "rational," there would be more than half a dozen different answers, with only one or two even coming close to being adequate. The vagueness of the term "rational" is reflected in the fact that in a recent widely reviewed book on the philosophy of irrationality the author provided not a single statement of what he or other authorities mean either by *irrationality* or its opposite. A related source of confusion has to do with what the *Dusky* court meant by "a reasonable degree" of rational understanding. In practice (given that there are many experts who almost never find a defendant incompetent), a reasonable degree might include things as minimal as knowing what a lawyer does and being able to state the charge against oneself.

I have written a book on human foolishness (a concept closely related to irrationality), in which I also addressed the phenomenon of "common sense" (a concept closely related to rationality). Based on my analysis of these concepts, I believe rationality reflects two qualities: the use of logical reasoning and being grounded in reality. Of the two, the second—being grounded in reality—is undoubtedly the more important quality.

The *Dusky* opinion required that a competence evaluation be more than cursory and should involve some in-depth assessment. Specifically, the opinion stated that "it is not enough for the district judge to find that 'the defendant [is] oriented to time and place and [has] some recollection of events'" (both of which are covered in a mental status exam); instead, the judge must address the two earlier-stated rationality questions. However, it is my experience that competency evaluations are often little more than "drive-by" assessments that have no depth whatsoever. This seems especially to be the case when the assessment is handled by a single expert on a court panel who is being paid a small flat fee. Because the base rate for such legal competency determinations is more than 75 percent "competent," and because experts who find too often for a petitioner might find themselves without future referrals from prosecutors, in my experience, it is safe for a lazy or corrupt expert to use any excuse to find a defendant competent, even when there is substantial evidence to the contrary.

A key to knowing why legal competency assessments are often superficial is to be found in another word that appears in both of the *Dusky* criteria: that word is "understanding." This term refers to the ability to describe and make inferences about an object such as a person, situation, or message sufficient to make intelligent decisions regarding that object. Understanding can occur at multiple levels, which I term "shallow," "medium," and "deeper" (*see* Figure 2.3). These levels of understanding are analogous to Jean Piaget's cognitive development stages, with shallow understanding corresponding to pre-operations (roughly ages three

Modes	Levels of Understanding		
	Shallow	Medium	Deeper
Knowledge of Actors	X		
Knowledge of a Case		X	
Legal Reasoning and Judgment			X

FIGURE 2.3 Levels of understanding involved in legal competence assessments.

to seven), medium understanding (roughly ages seven to eleven) corresponding to concrete operations, and deeper understanding (roughly ages twelve on) corresponding to formal operations. In terms of the elements of a legal competence determination, a shallow understanding would be reflected in something like knowing who the actors are in a legal proceeding, a medium understanding would be reflected in something like knowing the relative sentencing severity of different plea options, and a deeper understanding would be reflected in something like being able to follow the stream of testimony in a trial and know what kind of evidence is likely to benefit or harm one's case. It is my contention that much of what passes for meeting the legal competence threshold, as assessed by psychologists and psychiatrists, rises only to the level of shallow understanding, with some forays into medium understanding, and with almost no effort to determine someone's level of deeper (or abstract) understanding.

As a rule, competency assessments do not use a formal instrument or follow a standard protocol. Some efforts have been made to correct that problem, with the two best known ones being the MacArthur Competence Assessment Tool–Criminal Adjudication (MacCAT-CA) (Hoge, Bonnie, Poythress, & Monahan, 1999) and the Evaluation of Competency to

Stand Trial—Revised (ECST-R) (Rogers, Tillbrook, & Sewell, 2003). These evaluation methods are semi-structured interviews relying mainly on hypothetical situations, which are used in an effort to determine a defendant's level of factual and rational understanding of legal concepts and processes. Because I am more familiar with the MacCAT-CA, my comments focus mainly on that instrument.

The MacCAT-CA uses a hypothetical situation: Two men are playing pool in a bar when they get into an altercation and one of the men hits the other over the head with a pool cue and knocks him down, appearing to do some damage. The assaulter is arrested and is facing criminal charges that could involve either simple or aggravated assault. A number of questions are presented verbally by the examiner, most requiring a choice between two alternatives. In each question pair, there is one obviously right answer pointing to something useful to the defendant or his attorney (e.g., that the victim had a history of violence, that the assaulter was the one who called 911, that the assaulter had no criminal history, that the men had been drinking); the other choice involves something irrelevant and slightly absurd (for example, that before the pool game the assaulter had taken his girlfriend to a baseball game).

In addition to picking the right or wrong answer, a subject is also asked to explain why he or she made that choice. The hypothetical is also used as a take-off point for questions (again mainly framed as a choice) about the nature and severity of the possible charges, the identity and functions of various actors in the judicial drama, and the desirability of pleading to the lesser charge, given the risk involved in going to trial. Subjects are also asked a few questions about their own case, although that is a small part of the assessment. The use of a structured interview method such as the MacCAT-CA, with comparison norms for various clinical and adjudicated (competent vs. incompetent) groups, is a big advance in legal competence assessment. Nevertheless, it should not be the sole method used because there are aspects (such as understanding one's own case and expressive communicative issues) that are not fully assessed. Furthermore, as indicated in Figure 2.3, of the three legal competence domains tapped (I have renamed them), only one, "legal reasoning," comes close to addressing the "rationality" requirement in the *Dusky* decision.

In terms of defendants with ASD, in Figure 2.4 I address (a) the level of understanding required for the three MacCAT-CA domains plus three other skills (receptive processing of testimony, expressive ability to testify,

	Levels of Understanding Required	Affected in ASD	Ease of Restoring Competence
Knowledge of Actors	Shallow	Not affected	Easy
Knowledge of Case	Medium	Somewhat affected	Easy
Legal Reasoning and Judgment	Deeper	Affected	Difficult
Receptive Processing of Testimony	Medium	Affected	Difficult
Expressive Ability to Testify	Medium	Likely affected	Difficult
Ability to Resist Undue Influence	Medium	Likely affected	Difficult

FIGURE 2.4 Impairments and restorability of skills involved in ASD legal competence.

and ability to resist undue influence from others) relevant to competence to stand trial but not covered by the MacCAT-CA instrument; (b) the extent to which I believe defendants with ASD are likely to be affected (i.e., to be incompetent) in those six domains; and (c) the ease with which someone initially found incompetent to stand trial could be restored to competence if the prosecution and court (as they often do) seek such a restoration.

Because ASD (along with ID) is essentially an intellectual disorder (if one considers social intelligence an important aspect of intelligence), and because the understanding and rationality required for a person to be found legally competent essentially constitute a form of social and conceptual intelligence (combined with emotional stability, which is also usually lacking in ASD), there is reason to believe that a substantial majority of people with ASD (and ID) should be found incompetent to stand trial. In reality, getting someone with ASD to be found incompetent is usually an uphill battle for the simple reason that most assessments (especially the majority that never utilize an instrument such as the MacCAT-CA or ECST-R) never go beyond the shallow level of understanding required for knowledge of actors and the shallow-to-medium level of understanding required for concrete knowledge of a case. Legal reasoning (which is an abstract form of understanding requiring something close to rationality) is typically not addressed at all.

People with ASD can demonstrate competence in concrete tasks involving the first two skills, and thus many of them will be found competent in an assessment limited (as is typically the case) just to those skills. Furthermore, as these skills are also the main focus of restoration efforts, it is likely that people with ASD who are initially found incompetent will eventually be found restorable as a result of being constantly drilled on concrete aspects of the criminal justice process and their own legal situation. Other aspects of competence to stand trial (such as ability to communicate expressively, or to resist undue influence regarding legal decisions) are much more difficult for people with ASD and are much more challenging to change but are also typically not assessed. It is for these reasons that many experienced criminal defense attorneys will not seek a competency determination even when they feel their client is incompetent. This is both because it is likely to be a waste of time given the expected outcome, and also because it often involves involuntary incarceration (considered treatment, and thus not credited toward a sentence), sometimes for as long as a year, in a forensic psychiatry institution where a client with a neurodevelopmental disorder stands a substantial chance of being sexually or otherwise abused.

Other Forms of Legal Competence

Although competence to stand trial remains the bedrock of legal competence, other aspects have been raised and clarified in court decisions and legal guidelines. These include decisional competence, especially competence to plead guilty (*Godinez v. Moran*, 509 U.S. 389 (1983)), competence to waive counsel for the purpose of representing oneself (*Indiana v. Edwards*, 554 U.S. 164 (2008)), competence to refuse treatment (*Perry v. Louisiana*, 498 U.S. 38 (1990)), competence to refuse an insanity defense

(*Frendak v. United States*, 408 A.2d 364 (D.C. 1979)), competence to testify (Fed. R. Evid. Rule 601), competence to consent to a search or seizure (*Florida v. Rodriguez*, 469 U.S. 1 (1984)), competence to be executed (*Panetti v. Quarterman*, 551 U.S. 930 (2007)), and competence to commit a crime (partly covered by an insanity claim).

Given the global and intellectual incompetence involved in ASD and related developmental disorders such as ID, defendants with these labels should have a strong chance of being found incompetent on many of these matters. As illustrated earlier in this chapter, however, the field of forensic mental health has a long way to go in developing adequate procedures for determining such forms of competence in a way that is scientifically valid, satisfies evidentiary requirements, and does justice to the needs and qualities of people with autism spectrum disorder.

● ● ●

Stephen Greenspan, PhD, recently relocated to Northern California. He is an emeritus professor of educational psychology at the University of Connecticut. His work on social and personal incompetence in children and adults with developmental disorders has been heavily cited, in particular, his books on the related topics of foolishness (general risk-unawareness) and gullibility (social risk-unawareness). For approximately forty years, Dr. Greenspan has served as a forensic psychologist in criminal cases and has published influential papers aimed at educating practitioners and attorneys on matters pertaining to defendants with developmental disorders. Dr. Greenspan's email is stephen.greenspan@gmail.com and his website is stephen-greenspan.com.

Complete citations are available from the author upon request.

3

Criminal Responsibility

Nancy Kaser-Boyd

It is a bedrock principle of our criminal justice system that people cannot be held responsible when they do not understand what they are doing or cannot control their actions. Nonetheless, large numbers of people with mental disabilities, including autism spectrum disorders, are routinely prosecuted. Why? As this chapter by Dr. Nancy Kaser-Boyd shows, the answers are complex. Whatever the jurisdiction, the legal standard for insanity at the time of the act (the most common form of criminal responsibility) is extremely high. Furthermore, there is no such medical term as insanity. *ASD is not a mental illness, although some people with ASD do have a co-occurring mental illness that is independent of the ASD diagnosis. Similarly, people with ASD do not necessarily have an intellectual disability, but instead, most have a developmental disability of some sort. Thus, people with ASD do not always have insight into their behaviors and, depending on the nature of the offense, may have been powerless to control their actions. This chapter dives into the complexities of the relationship between ASD and criminal responsibility and also explains the forensic interview, standard testing instruments used for sanity evaluations, and the similarities and differences between ASD and anti-social personality disorder.*

• • •

Garrett (not his real name) was a nineteen-year-old man who carried the diagnosis of autism spectrum disorder (ASD) from the time he was eight years old. His mother was convinced that he had this disorder. She spent many hours reading about autism, and she eventually enrolled at a community college to study child development, with the ultimate goal of becoming a specialist in autism. She took Garrett to a number of local mental health clinics and ended up at a university medical center, where the chart notes reflect her list of Garrett's many symptoms. Garrett's home life with his mother was tortured. His sister recalled that their mother was very abusive to Garrett, often beating him and calling him names. His sister said that during these incidents Garrett would run to a corner and cower "like a whipped dog." Garrett ran away from home as a teenager, and he told his friends that he was afraid of his mother. The police would bring him back home, and his mother would tell them that he was very mentally ill. For much of his childhood and adolescence, he was on psychotropic medications: Seroquel to keep him calm and Ritalin to address attention deficits. Sometimes his mother would take his Ritalin.

Police were called to the family home after a woman was seen lying in the street outside her house, bleeding. A delivery man noticed her and called 911. When police arrived, she was barely able to speak, but when asked who did this to her, she said "My son." Garrett was located several miles away, running, and taken into custody. The careful homicide investigation uncovered a schoolmate who said that, several days before, Garrett had said that if his mother hit him again, he was going to kill her. In the forensic psychological examination, Garrett said that his mother was angry that he had not done his chores and began chasing him around the house. As he ran through the kitchen, he grabbed a knife off the counter and stabbed her as she ran toward him. Garrett was charged with first-degree murder.

It is important first to note that individuals with autism spectrum disorder are not overrepresented in the criminal justice system compared to individuals without ASD (King & Murphy, 2014), and that individuals with ASD are much more likely to be victims than perpetrators of crime (National Research Council, 2001). Compared to adults without ASD, adults with ASD report similar rates of being charged with crimes but report experiencing more victimization as children (ranging from verbal bullying to sexual assault and property crime) and experiencing more emotional bullying and sexual contact victimization as adults (Weiss & Fardella, 2018). However, by age twenty-one, one in five youths with ASD has been stopped and questioned by police, whereas only one in six individuals in the general population has had police encounters. Furthermore, almost one in twenty youths with ASD has been arrested by age twenty-one (Rava et al., 2017). Individuals with ASD who have experienced a police encounter are also at higher risk for school disciplinary action and psychiatric hospitalization (Tint et al., 2017). They are generally older, live outside the family home, have a history of aggression, and have parents with higher rates of caregiver stress and financial burden. Taken together, police encounters for individuals with ASD may not occur in isolation; these encounters are frequently accompanied by significant traumas and stressors, which may ultimately lead to involvement in the criminal justice system.

The involvement of individuals with ASD in the criminal justice system may be partially attributable to tendencies that are observed more frequently in males, with or without ASD. ASD disproportionately affects males at approximately three times the rate of females (Werling & Geschwind, 2013). This sex bias is in part due to behavioral differences in how males present with ASD compared to how females present with ASD. Specifically, males with ASD show more externalizing behaviors, including restricted and repetitive behaviors, hyperactivity, and aggression, than females with ASD. Males with ASD also have more difficulties with "blending in" in social environments compared to their female counterparts (Hattier et al., 2011; Berger et al., 2013). Females are acculturated differently and do not always present noticeable behaviors. They often learn different coping skills that include social initiation (Halladay et al., 2015). Thus, males with ASD may tend to demonstrate particularly disruptive behaviors that, in certain contexts, may lead them to become involved in the criminal justice system. Indeed, males with ASD, particularly those who demonstrate externalizing behaviors, are more likely to be involved in the criminal justice system than females with ASD (Rave et al., 2017). Externalizing of ASD symptoms may thus be particularly apparent in individuals with ASD who require criminal defense.

A defendant demonstrating ASD symptoms may be perceived negatively by judges and jurors who have not been presented with adequate information to help them understand how the defendant's behaviors are affected by ASD. In evaluating a defendant whose offense and interview behaviors are consistent with high-functioning ASD, the majority of mock jurors provided with a diagnosis and background information about ASD reported that the defendant's legal responsibility should not generally be affected by the ASD diagnosis but considered the diagnosis to be a mitigating factor in assessing the defendant's responsibility and legal consequences (Maras, Marshall, & Sands, 2019). Similarly, when provided with a case study of a defendant with high-functioning ASD, judges were likely to consider ASD as both a mitigating and an aggravating factor and to consider alternatives beyond prison sentences for an individual with ASD (Berryessa, 2016). These attitudes are consistent with the finding that youths with ASD are ultimately more likely to be funneled into pre-trial interventions and are less likely to be prosecuted than youths without ASD (Cheely et al., 2012). In summary, the thorough presentation of information about ASD may assist the defense in cases of defendants with ASD. (*See* Chap. 6, The Bond Hearing; Chap. 14, Vulnerabilities of Defendants with ASD and Strategies for Improving Outcomes; and Chap. 15, Perception of Defendants with ASD by Judges and Juries.)

Criminal Responsibility

Criminal responsibility in the most general sense revolves around the mental state of the individual at the time of the crime. This includes, but is not limited to, the insanity defense. Other mental-state defenses exist in some U.S. states. For example, in California, there is a doctrine of imperfect self-defense, which requires that the defendant had a subjective belief in the need to defend himself/herself. Some mental states address whether the defendant has the requisite intent to commit the crime. This chapter discusses ASD and the insanity defense, as well as how features of ASD may allow the use of other defenses to charges of criminal conduct.

Autism and Criminal Conduct

Criminal charges can result from the specific impairments in autism, which are:

1. Difficulty interpreting social cues and understanding what others are thinking and feeling. Difficulty anticipating and understanding the actions of others and the emotional impact of their actions on others.
2. Poor emotional regulation, with impulsivity, difficulty controlling strong emotions or urges and possible "meltdowns."
3. Difficulty with moral reasoning. Moral reasoning requires a degree of abstract thinking, and individuals with ASD tend to be concrete in their reasoning.
4. Intense restricted interests (i.e., fixations).
5. Repetitive behaviors, compulsivity.

Difficulty interpreting social cues and the actions of others can lead a person with autism to overreact or react inappropriately. In social and sexual relationships, for example, this can result in unwanted sexual aggression, or perhaps in stalking. Difficulty managing emotions may result in an emotional outburst that frightens or even injures others. Fixations, which often have the strength of an obsession, can result in trespassing or stealing. The need to repeat actions and the compulsion to collect may put ASD individuals at risk to repeatedly visit illegal websites or collect pornographic images of children (Attwood, Henault, & Dubin, 2014). However, deliberate violence in individuals with autism is not common. A number of studies have concluded that, when an individual with ASD acts purposely to harm another, there is likely to be comorbid psychiatric illness (e.g., depression or bipolar disorder) or substance abuse. (*See* Chap. 4, Co-Occurring Disorders.)

The Insanity Defense

The legal definition of insanity differs state by state. Twenty-five states have adopted the *M'Naughten* standard or some variation of it. Under the *M'Naughten* test, the defendant must have a mental disorder or defect that renders him/her unable to understand the nature and consequences of his/her act and distinguish right from wrong. Individual states that have adopted the *M'Naughten* standard have variations in the meaning of "right from wrong." In California, "right from wrong" can be legal or moral; that is, the defendant may have an awareness that the act is legally wrong, but he/she felt it was morally necessary, as in the defendant who felt God ordered him to kill but turned himself over to authorities shortly after killing. Four of the twenty-five states add "irresistible impulse" to *M'Naughten*. Irresistible impulse must be the result of mental disease or defect. Twenty-one states use the American Law Institute (ALI) Standard, also called the Model Penal Code Test. This standard has a "knowing" leg and a volitional leg. The defendant satisfies this standard if he/she lacks substantial capacity either to appreciate the wrongfulness of his/her conduct or to conform his/her conduct to the requirements of the law. Three states use only "guilty but mentally ill." One state, New Hampshire, uses the *Durham* rule. The *Durham* standard states that the defendant cannot be convicted of a crime if the act was the result of a mental disease or defect, but does not require an actual diagnosis of mental illness or disorder. Legal and psychological/psychiatric practitioners must be familiar with the precise wording of the standard for insanity in their state.

Individuals on the autism spectrum may have difficulty meeting the "knowing" requirement of *M'Naughten* because often they are not impaired in knowing right from wrong. ASD individuals are typically not psychotic, and thus would not have the hallucinations or delusions that are common in defendants who plead not guilty by reason of insanity (NGRI). At higher levels of severity of ASD, it is conceivable that they may not know right from wrong. ASD individuals may meet the volitional leg of the ALI standard, also known as the irresistible impulse standard, if they are found unable to conform their conduct to the requirements of the law. These standards might apply, for example, in the midst of a "meltdown" in which another or others are injured or killed. It is also conceivable, before a consideration of NGRI, that the ASD defendant would be found not competent to stand trial, due to impairments in social cognition or fixations. (*See* Chap. 2, Competency.)

For investigating mental states short of insanity, the evaluation can range more broadly, instead of focusing on whether the defendant knew right from wrong or was able to control his/her emotions and impulses. For example, in claiming "imperfect self-defense," the ASD defendant may have believed that his/her life was in danger. This might have been wrong from an objective viewpoint. But the defendant's difficulty with social cues and understanding the motives of others, or his/her history as a victim of bullying, or perhaps from child abuse or other trauma, can cause the defendant to have an honest belief in the need to defend himself/herself. "In defense of another" is also a conceivable defense. Suppose that an ASD defendant, with a documented history of naïveté, had been talked into killing his friend's parents after she convinced him that she was being molested. Emotional meltdowns, if the case is brought in a state where the ALI or irresistible impulse standards are not applicable, could form the basis of an argument that the defendant lacked the necessary "specific intent(s)" for the crime. For clients under the age of twenty-five, the defense attorney might also argue that the adolescent brain causes the adolescent or young adult to be, in contrast to adults, more impulsive, more powerless over environmental circumstances, more subject to peer pressure, and less able to anticipate the consequences of behavior.

The Forensic Psychological Evaluation

Identifying the evaluator as a psychologist rather than a psychiatrist stems from the necessity of psychological testing to document ASD. For defendants who have a comorbid psychiatric disorder (such as bipolar disorder), a psychiatrist may, however, be a consultant on those focused issues. The forensic psychological evaluation begins with an introduction to the case. This means providing the expert with all relevant materials about the crime. It is not good to hold back material in the discovery phase of a case: it is not a good day when an expert is confronted on the witness stand about materials he/she didn't review.

One crucial piece of discovery is the confession, if there is one. Most investigation interviews are now videotaped, and the taped interview can provide valuable clues about the presence of symptoms of ASD, and the defendant's mental state near the time of the crime charged. The interview also furnishes critical information regarding the defendant's understanding of his/her actions and may reflect extremely flawed or limited social awareness, an inability for perspective-taking, and even delusional thinking. The police reports and witness statements also provide clues to the ASD defendant's behavior before and during the crime(s) charged. Early on in a case where ASD is suspected, the defense attorney should begin a records search to document the ASD diagnosis and treatment(s). This should include:

1. School records and Individualized Education Plans.
2. Developmental history provided by a parent or caregiver (siblings if parents are deceased or unable to be interviewed).
3. Psychoeducational evaluations (often done every three years for students in Special Education).
4. Records from the Regional Center, if any.
5. Medical/Psychiatric records. This includes pediatrician evaluation of developmental milestones, records of acute or chronic medical issues, diagnostic work-ups that document ASD, and psychiatric treatment (e.g., medications for ADHD, agitation, or comorbid psychiatric conditions). If the ASD individual has suffered accidental brain trauma and received brain scans, then neurologists' reports should be sought.
6. Psychological treatment records, which include the progress notes and diagnostic conclusions of the treatment provider.
7. Custody evaluations, if parents are divorced and fought for custody.
8. Dependency court records, if any.
9. Criminal history records for parents, if any.

The direct evaluation of the ASD defendant should include a face-to-face interview, ideally on more than one occasion so that comfort and rapport can be established. This is especially important with ASD defendants, who may be particularly anxious around people they have just met. The evaluation should include a battery of tests that are both broad-band and narrow-band. The broad-band tests are those such as the Wechsler Adult Intelligence Scale (WAIS-IV), which surveys an array of cognitive strengths and deficits and gives standardized scores for various abilities (verbal comprehension, perceptual reasoning, working memory, processing speed, and full-scale IQ). A broad-band test for evaluating "adaptive abilities" is the Adaptive Behavior Assessment System (ABAS-III). The ABAS-III evaluates adaptive behavior and related skills in multiple skill areas and compares them to chronological age. The skill areas encompass the practical, everyday skills required to function and meet environmental demands, including those needed to effectively and independently care for oneself and interact with others. The ABAS-III is completed by the defendant ("self-report") and by parents and/or teachers. Results are presented as standard scores, or T-scores, where 100 is "average," that is, like the average same-aged person. They are also presented as a percentile rank and as a qualitative range (e.g., "below average," "extremely low.") Broad-band instruments that test for comorbid disorders include the Minnesota Multiphasic Personality Inventory (MMPI-2), the Personality Assessment Inventory (PAI), and the Millon Clinical Multiaxial Inventory. It is important to note that the research on ASD individuals' performance on these personality tests is not well-developed; nevertheless, each test might provide important information about clinical depression, bipolar disorder, delusional disorder, or other comorbid disorders, as well as personality disorders such as anti-social personality disorder (ASPD). ASPD may be present, in addition to ASD, but it is often the case that an opposing expert will identify the behavioral aspects of the ASD individual as anti-social personality disorder. (See the more complete discussion of this danger later in this chapter.)

Narrow-band tests are those that focus more specifically on the symptoms or impairments of ASD. Accepted and commonly used tests include:

- *The Social Responsiveness Scale—Second Edition (SRS-2)*. The SRS-2 identifies social impairment associated with autism spectrum disorders and quantifies its severity. The defendant completes the SRS, and versions are given to parents and/or teachers. Subscales parcel results into social awareness, social cognition, social communication, social motivation, and restricted interests/repetitive behaviors. Results are presented as standard scores or T-scores. For example, the SRS-2 was completed by Garrett's sister and the following helpful description was generated: "Garrett sometimes behaves in ways that may seem bizarre to others. He does not join group activities or social events unless he is forced to do so. He becomes upset in situations with lots of things going on. He frequently can't get his mind off something once he starts thinking about it."

- *Behavior Rating of Executive Functioning (BRIEF-A).* The BRIEF-A assesses nine aspects of executive functioning organized into two main categories: Behavioral Regulation and Metacognition Index. Behavioral Regulation reflects the ability to maintain appropriate control over one's thoughts, behaviors, and emotions. The Metacognition Index reflects the ability to manage one's attention and problem-solving. The BRIEF-A also has forms for the defendant, parents, or teachers. Results are presented as T-scores, with 50 as the mean. Percentile scores are also available. Garrett's sister completed the BRIEF-A, from which the following description of his executive functioning was generated: "Garrett often does not notice when he causes others to feel bad or get angry. He talks at the wrong time. He does not understand why people seem upset with him. He says things without thinking, and he does not think about the consequences of his actions. He becomes upset and disturbed by unexpected changes in routine. He over-reacts to small problems. His anger can be intense but ends quickly."

- *Autism Diagnostic Observation Schedule—Second Edition* (ADOS-2). This instrument is a measure of social communication and social behavior in adults with fluent speech. It surveys the core issues related to ASD, specifically the issues in social communication and repetitive behaviors and interests. The ADOS-2 for Garrett yielded a finding that "Garrett demonstrated repetitive speech typical of individuals on the Autism Spectrum with frequent references to highly restricted interests. He lacked social reciprocity and appeared to be childlike and naïve. He was markedly impaired in social communication."

- *Autism Diagnostic Interview-Revised* (ADI-R). When evaluating adult clients suspected to be on the autism spectrum, it is extremely important to have a comprehensive developmental history. Many adults do not exhibit the overt symptoms of autism seen in younger children such as hand flapping, rocking, or idiosyncratic language. These behaviors diminish through childhood and may be totally absent in ASD adults. The ADI-R is an extended interview with a parent or caregiver who is familiar with the developmental history and current behavior of the individual. The scoring of responses produces the Diagnostic Algorithm, which focuses on the full developmental history of the assessed individual to produce a diagnosis.

It is possible that diagnostic testing will have been done by school psychologists or during the ASD individual's sojourn through diagnosis and treatment. Still, it may be beneficial to update the testing, with the forensic psychologist thereby getting firsthand knowledge about how the individual responds. (It is always recommended to have current, up-to-date testing that reflects the individual's present state of mind, including cognitive and social/emotional functioning.)

The awareness that the ASD defendant may have experienced trauma is a recent development. Many ASD adults have trauma histories due to their lack of social awareness, which puts them at risk for many types of abuse at home, school, and in their community. If there is a history of trauma in the defendant in the form of bullying, child abuse, or institutional abuse, trauma inventories should be added to the test battery. Two widely accepted trauma inventories are the *Detailed Assessment of Posttraumatic Stress* and *The Trauma Symptom Inventory*. A child/adolescent version (for ages eight to sixteen) is the *Trauma Symptoms Checklist for Children*.

Ultimately, the forensic psychological evaluator will need to understand whether the ASD defendant is competent, and what he/she was perceiving, thinking, and feeling at the time of the offense. There are times when the evaluator will encounter ASD defendants who can't say what they were thinking or feeling. Because language impairment is a common effect of ASD, it is possible that the ASD defendant will not have the verbal communication skills to respond to this line of questioning. This will certainly affect competency to stand trial. As for mental state inquiries, in such cases the evaluator will likely rely on the behavioral clues and observations by witnesses, family members, teachers, or others who had contact with the defendant in and around the time of the crimes charged.

Autism Spectrum Disorder or Anti-social Personality Disorder

The opposing expert is inclined to adopt one of two strategies: (1) To admit that the defendant has ASD but argue that it is mild and does not meet the legal standard for insanity, or qualify the defendant for a claim of imperfect self-defense, or render the defendant unable to form the intent necessary for the crime; or (2) to opine that the defendant actually has anti-social personality disorder (ASPD) rather than autism spectrum disorder, and that the offense was the result of anger, vengeance, sadism, or some other anti-social purpose. Persons with ASPD lack a conscience. They are callous and manipulative in relationships. Typically, they lack empathy for others and assume no guilt for wrongful behavior.

However, there are distinctions between a person with autism spectrum disorder and a person with an anti-social personality disorder. For the person with ASD, the criminal behavior is often impulsive, as in the explosion of emotion commonly known as a "meltdown." In contrast, in the ASPD individual, the criminal behavior is often planned and predatory. The lack of empathy and perceived detachment of the ASD individual can be mistakenly seen as the callousness of the sociopath. Individuals with ASD have affective empathy (the drive to respond appropriately to other's thoughts/feelings). However, they lack cognitive empathy (the ability to imagine other's thoughts/feelings). This can make them appear unfeeling when they really cannot form an appropriate emotional response. It should be noted that this is reversed in sociopaths who are adept at reading people's emotions and understanding their motivations. They then use this information to deceive because they lack true affective empathy. The lack of remorse for wrongful behavior that can be observed in ASD defendants may stem from deficits in moral reasoning. The best antidote to a diagnosis of ASPD is a file replete with diagnostic evaluations from other professionals who documented symptoms of ASD.

Epilogue

Garrett was tried for the murder of his mother. He was found competent to stand trial. There were abundant records of his diagnosis with autism spectrum disorder. His sister and grandmother testified in detail about the abuse he suffered at the hands of his mother (who, incidentally, had a criminal record). The forensic expert testified that he also had posttraumatic stress disorder and was hypervigilant to danger, anticipating real harm from his mother. In the final moments of her anger that day, he picked up a knife even though she had no weapon. Nevertheless, because of years of physical and emotional abuse, he perceived the need to defend himself. He was convicted of voluntary manslaughter.

● ● ●

Nancy Kaser-Boyd, PhD, ABAP, is a Clinical Professor of Psychiatry and Biobehavioral Sciences at the David Geffen School of Medicine at UCLA, where she teaches advanced psychodiagnostic assessment and violence risk assessment. She is a consultant to the USC Gould School of Law on the effects of trauma and on adolescent brain functioning. She serves as a forensic psychological consultant to the Superior Courts of Los Angeles County in child abuse and neglect, delinquency court, and criminal court, conducting forensic psychological evaluations and testifying as an expert witness. She is co-author of *Forensic Psychological Assessment in Practice* (Routledge, 2015) and numerous book chapters and articles. Dr. Kaser-Boyd can be reached at nkbforensics@gmail.com and her website is http://www.nancykaser-boyd.com.

Complete citations are available from the author upon request.

Chapter

4

Co-Occurring Disorders

Clare S. Allely

Trying to get inside the mind of someone with autism spectrum disorder (ASD) can be a fascinating, but sometimes complex, experience. As this chapter by Dr. Clare Allely shows, a significant number of people with ASD have co-occurring disorders: that is, other conditions such as sleep disorders, attention deficit/hyperactivity disorder (ADHD), obsessive-compulsive disorder (OCD), schizophrenia, anxiety, depression, and/or an intellectual disability. Thus, when interviewing a client with ASD, you will need to be sensitive to additional behaviors. Furthermore, you will need to be open to additional diagnoses from your expert. Finally, when advocating for your client, presenting the evidence of ASD is not enough; the other conditions that accompany and perhaps are a result of the ASD all coalesce to form the unique portrait of your client.

● ● ●

As pointed out by Lever and Geurts (2016), among individuals with autism spectrum disorder (ASD), at least 69 percent are considered to have co-occurring psychiatric disorders and symptoms (*see* Buck et al., 2014). However, in individuals with both ASD and intellectual disability (ID), the prevalence of co-occurring psychiatric disorders and symptoms is lower (Howlin & Moss, 2012; Matson & Cervantes, 2014). Studies have found that the presence of co-occurring disorders is associated with a lower quality of life, increased demands for professional help and support, poorer prognosis, greater interference with everyday life, and more negative outcomes (e.g., Matson & Goldin, 2013; Matson & Cervantes, 2014; Seltzer et al., 2004; Vannucchi et al., 2014; Wood & Gadow, 2010). Matson and colleagues have also highlighted that the cumulative effects of these core symptoms and disorders are significant obstacles in development and everyday adjustment (Matson et al., 2009). In adults with ASD, there are significantly increased rates of all major psychiatric disorders, such as depression, anxiety, obsessive–compulsive disorder, sleep problems, schizophrenia, and attention-deficit/hyperactivity disorder (ADHD) (*see*, e.g., Matson & LoVullo, 2008). Also, the prevalence of ID has been found to be more prevalent in individuals with ASD.

This chapter discusses some of the key co-occurring disorders in individuals with ASD. First, though, I review the importance of considering these co-occurring disorders in individuals with ASD who are involved in the criminal justice system. There are many other disorders and symptoms that are more prevalent in this particular group (e.g., suicidal ideation), but coverage of all would be too lengthy. The key ones are covered in this chapter.

The Importance of Considering Co-Occurring Disorders in Individuals with ASD

It is crucial that co-occurring disorders in individuals with ASD be recognized and identified as soon as possible during the criminal justice process. The role that these co-occurring disorders have in contributing to offending behavior can be significant. For instance, in a review carried out by Newman and Ghaziuddin (2008), the researchers identified studies that had examined the possible role that psychiatric factors/co-occurring disorders play in contributing to offending behavior in individuals with ASD. They identified seventeen publications that met the inclusion and exclusion criteria they established prior to carrying out their review. They found that the majority of the papers were single case reports. Across the seventeen publications identified, a total of thirty-seven cases was reviewed. Interestingly, they found that at the time the offense occurred, a definite psychiatric disorder was found in eleven of these thirty-seven cases (29.7 percent). Additionally, probable psychiatric disorder was found in twenty of the thirty-seven cases (54 percent). Newman and Ghaziuddin (2008) found that the majority of the studies on violent offenders with

ASD indicate that these individuals were also experiencing a range of co-occurring psychiatric disorders, including conduct disorder, depression, and schizoaffective disorder. It is crucial to emphasize here that by themselves these psychiatric disorders (conduct disorder being the exception) (Hodgins et al., 2008) do not confer a significant additional risk of engaging in violent offending behavior (Newman & Ghaziuddin, 2008).

Wachtel and Shorter (2013) have also recognized that simply having a diagnosis of ASD does not make a person more likely to engage in violent behavior when compared to the general population. What they hypothesize, however, is that the additional co-occurrence of psychotic disorder in individuals with ASD may result in what they call a one-two "vulnerability punch." It is suggested that in some individuals with ASD, there may be an increased propensity to act on psychotic impulses when compared to individuals without ASD. They also suggest that, in individuals with ASD, there is a baseline higher risk of psychiatric disorders, not infrequently including psychosis.

Obsessive-Compulsive Disorder in ASD

Obsessive-compulsive disorder (OCD) has been found to have a lifetime prevalence of between 2 and 3 percent. OCD is characterized by time-consuming obsessions and/or compulsions that cause significant levels of distress and anxiety (American Psychiatric Association, 1994). "Lifetime prevalence" refers to the proportion of a population that at some point during their lifetime (up until the point of assessment) have experienced the condition or disorder in question. It has been emphasized that the compulsive behaviors exhibited by individuals with OCD can appear similar in presentation to the restrictive and repetitive behaviors exhibited in individuals with ASD (Cath et al., 2008). These similarities may be unsurprising given the studies that have indicated a neurobiological overlap between these two disorders (e.g., Carlisi et al., 2017). An increasing number of studies investigates the prevalence of compulsions in individuals with ASD. For instance, in a 1985 study, Rumsey, Rapoport, and Sceery found that as many as 86 percent of individuals with ASD exhibited compulsions including handwashing, arranging objects, repetitive tapping, phonic tics, and stereotyped touching of clothes and other objects at some stage during the course of their lifetime. Looking at it from the other side of the coin, one study found that 20 percent of individuals with OCD exhibited significant autistic traits (Bejerot, Nylander, & Lindstrom, 2001).

Some studies have compared symptom characteristics between ASD and OCD. McDougle and colleagues (1995) found that, when compared to the obsessive-compulsive group, the individuals in the ASD group were significantly less likely to experience thoughts with aggressive, contamination, sexual, religious, symmetry, and somatic content. In the individuals with ASD, repetitive ordering; hoarding; telling or asking; touching, tapping, or rubbing; and self-mutilating occurred significantly more frequently than in the individuals with OCD. Also, cleaning, checking, and counting were found to be less frequent in the individuals with ASD than in the individuals with OCD.

Even more interesting, this study also identified a specific subset of seven obsessive-compulsive variables from the Yale-Brown Obsessive Compulsive Scale and Symptom Checklist that were found to reliably predict membership in the ASD group. Specifically, the study identified seven variables that predict the correct classification of individuals in the ASD group in 85 percent of cases (e.g., the presence of hoarding, touching, tapping, and self-damaging behavior and the absence of checking, counting, and aggressive and symmetry-related repetitive thoughts). The findings from this study indicate that the repetitive thoughts and behaviors that are characteristics of ASD differ significantly from the obsessive-compulsive symptoms exhibited in individuals with OCD.

In another study, Russell and colleagues (2005) administered the Yale-Brown Obsessive-Compulsive Scale and Symptom Checklist to a group of adults with high-functioning ASD (sample size of forty). They compared this group with a gender-matched group of adults with a primary diagnosis of OCD (sample size of forty-five) who also completed the same checklist. OCD symptoms were very carefully distinguished from the stereotypic behaviors and interests typically exhibited by individuals with ASD. Findings from the study revealed that there were similar frequencies of obsessive-compulsive symptoms between the two groups. Only somatic obsessions and repeating rituals were found to be more frequent in the OCD group. *Somatic obsessions* refers to intrusive thoughts that call the individual's attention to processes such as awareness of breathing, blinking, swallowing, body positioning, physical sensations, ringing in the ears, or heightened awareness of normal occurrences such as itching, being full, or having a pulse. Moreover, higher obsessive-compulsive symptom severity ratings were found in the OCD group. Interestingly, at least moderate levels of interference from their symptoms were reported by 50 percent of the ASD group. Overall, the findings from this study indicate that both obsessions and compulsions are common in adults with high-functioning ASD. The study also revealed that these obsessions and compulsions are associated with significant levels of distress in individuals with ASD.

Co-Occurring Intellectual Disabilities

It is important to highlight some examples from the well-established literature that has identified a high comorbidity between ASD and ID (*see* Matson & Shoemaker, 2009). Studies have investigated the prevalence of ID in the ASD literature. For instance, Fombonne (2003) carried out a systematic review comprising more than thirty epidemiological surveys of ASD and other pervasive developmental disorders. The findings from the systematic review showed that ID is associated with about 70 percent of individuals on the spectrum (among whom 30 percent experienced mild to moderate levels of intellectual impairment, with relevant disorders such as fragile X, Down syndrome, and tuberous sclerosis). Studies have also explored the prevalence of ASD in the ID literature. As highlighted by van Dooren and colleagues (2016), studies have found the prevalence of ASD among those with ID to be between 8.8 percent and 30 percent. Additionally, Postorino and colleagues (2016) emphasized that studies investigating the comorbidity between ID and ASD have consistently found that females with ASD have a tendency to exhibit lower average cognitive ability when compared to males with ASD, and have also found that the male to female ratio in ASD is highest when there is no ID (e.g., Fombonne, 2009).

Co-Occurring Attention Deficit/ Hyperactivity Disorder

Attention deficit/hyperactivity disorder (ADHD) is a neurodevelopmental disorder characterized by inattention, disorganization, and/ or hyperactivity-impulsivity. The three ADHD presentations are: (1) combined presentation, characterized by both inattention and hyperactivity-impulsivity; (2) inattentive presentation, characterized primarily by inattention symptoms; and (3) hyperactive-impulsive presentation, characterized primarily by hyperactive and impulsive symptoms

(American Psychiatric Association, 2013). According to the *Diagnostic and Statistical Manual of Mental Disorders, Fifth Edition* (*DSM-5*; American Psychiatric Association, 2013), the prevalence of ADHD across the majority of cultures is about 5 percent among children.

Prior to the publication of the *DSM-5* in 2013, clinicians were not able to diagnose an individual with ADHD if that individual had a diagnosis of ASD (Antshel & Russo, 2019). It was presumed that any symptoms of inattention and/or hyperactivity-impulsivity were secondary to ASD and not due to an additional ADHD condition (American Psychiatric Association, 2000). This is surprising given that ASD and ADHD co-occur at very high rates (e.g., Tureck, Matson, May, Davis, & Whiting, 2013). The estimated prevalence of ADHD found within the ASD population across studies is high, ranging from 20 to 70 percent (e.g., Charnsil & Sriapai, 2011).

Studies have found that the most common ADHD diagnosis in individuals with ASD is Inattentive type, followed by Combined, and then Hyperactive type (Reiersen, Constantino, & Richard, 2008). Research has also shown that co-occurring ADHD in individuals with ASD is associated with ASD severity, social deficits, lower cognitive functioning, delays in adaptive functioning, and overall internalizing and externalizing symptoms (e.g., Rao & Landa, 2014). Additionally, numerous studies have found evidence of an overlap between challenging behaviors and social deficits in individuals with ASD and those with ADHD (e.g., Clark, Feedhan, Tinline, & Vostanis, 1999). Executive function (EF) is a broad term that refers to a variety of domains of function, including inhibition, cognitive shifting, planning, working memory, and concept formation. ADHD and ASD may share overlapping executive function profiles; however, they are still unique (Karalunas et al., 2018). The findings indicate an additive nature for the co-occurrence of ASD and ADHD (Lukito et al., 2017).

Matson and colleagues (2013) pointed out that there are studies showing that not only is there a frequent co-occurrence between ASD and ADHD but also that the co-occurrence of these two disorders increases the risk of other conditions in the individual. For instance, tic disorders, trichotillomania (hair pulling), anxiety, and depression are frequently found in individuals with both ASD and ADHD (Simonoff et al., 2008). Furthermore, Hofvander and colleagues (2009) also found that individuals with both ASD and ADHD exhibited high rates of both depression and anxiety. Gargaro and colleagues (2011) have also argued that, in individuals with co-occurring ASD and ADHD, the symptom expression is additive in nature when compared to either ASD or ADHD alone. The theory that there is an additive effect is supported by the findings of Goldstein and Schwebach (2004), who found greater impairment of daily functioning in individuals with co-occurring ASD and ADHD compared to individuals with either disorder alone.

Co-Occurring Sleep Problems

Deliens and colleagues (2015) have noted that there is a range of studies investigating sleep disturbances in adults with ASD. Biological, psychological, and/or social/environmental factors can all contribute to sleep problems/disturbances in individuals with ASD. In individuals with ASD, co-occurring medical conditions also may predispose this group to sleep problems. Some of these co-occurring medical conditions include ADHD (Liu et al., 2006), asthma (Liu et al., 2006), epilepsy (Liu et al., 2006), pain (Tudor et al., 2014), and gastrointestinal problems (Mannion et al., 2013). Carmassi and colleagues (2019) have pointed out that a number of studies have found a high frequency of sleep problems and alterations of circadian sleep rhythmicity in individuals with ASD across all ages (e.g., Irwanto, Rehatta, Hartini, & Takada, 2016). The most commonly reported sleep disturbances in individuals with ASD include difficulties in being able to fall asleep, frequent night-time awakenings, and a shorter sleep duration (e.g., Verhoeff et al., 2018). Individuals with ASD who exhibit hypersensitivity to tastes or textures (commonly found in this group) may experience more feelings of anxiety around bedtime (such as when they brush their teeth), which has a negative impact on their ability to go to sleep (Stein et al., 2011).

Research has also found that the likelihood of sleep dysfunction is increased in individuals with ASD when in the presence of anxiety, higher symptom severity, communication and social interaction deficits, sensory sensitivities, developmental regression, and gastrointestinal problems (Hollway et al., 2013). This has led researchers to conclude that the occurrence of sleep problems in individuals with ASD involves "complex and multiple risk markers" (Deliens, Leproult, Schmitz, Destrebecqz, & Peigneux, 2015).

It has also been shown that poor sleep worsens daytime functioning to a greater extent in adolescents with high-functioning ASD than it does in typically developing adolescents (Richdale et al., 2014). Both adolescents and adults with ASD with moderate to severe sleep dysfunction were found to be more likely to exhibit aggressive behaviors. In adolescents and adults with ASD who experienced mild sleep problems, researchers found that they were more likely to exhibit eccentric types of problem behaviors, such as unusual play with objects and inappropriate sexual behavior (Matson et al., 2008). Another study found an association between poor sleep quality and sustained attention and impairments in working memory, in addition to impaired performance in sensory motor and cognitive procedural memory (i.e., prolonged sleep latency, increased light sleep) in a group of ASD young adults with intelligence levels in the normal range (Limoges et al., 2013).

Significantly, Carmassi and colleagues (2019) pointed out that there have been numerous studies demonstrating that a correlation may exist between sleep disturbances and the severity of ASD symptomology, particularly repetitive behaviors and deficits in verbal communication and/or social reciprocity (Cornish, Conduit, Rajaratnam, & Rinehart, 2015). One study found that night waking was a strong predictor for social interaction deficits (Tudor et al., 2012). Also, they found that sleep-onset delay was predictive of communication difficulties, stereotyped behavior (repetitive actions with no apparent purpose), and the severity of ASD symptomology (Tudor et al., 2012). Evidence appears to show that sleep problems exacerbate the severity of ASD symptomology and vice versa (Adams et al., 2014).

Co-Occurring Mood Disorder (e.g., Anxiety and Depression)

In individuals with ASD, mood disorders such as anxiety and depression are one of the most frequently reported co-occurring psychiatric disorders (Skokauskas, Gallagher, Skokauskas, & Gallagher, 2010). This reported co-occurrence is particularly noteworthy given that any changes in mood tend to go undetected in many individuals with ASD. One of the explanations for this is the impaired language/verbal abilities of some individuals with ASD, which results in an inability to express their feelings and describe changes in mood. There may also be impaired reporting of the presence of these symptoms even in individuals with ASD who are not verbally impaired, due to their deficits in socioemotional communication. Additionally, some of the features characteristic of ASD are also commonly found in individuals with depression, including social withdrawal, limited facial expression, and flattened affect (Skokauskas & Frodl, 2015).

Compared to the general population, depression is more commonly reported in individuals with ASD (e.g., Mazzone et al., 2013; Bekhet & Zauszniewski, 2013). Pouw, Rieffe, Stockmann, and Gadow (2013) studied sixty-three people with ASD and compared them to typically developing peers. Consistent with previous studies, depressive symptoms were found to correlate with negative factors related to social difficulties and victimization (e.g., Cappadocia, Weiss, & Pepler, 2012). One study found that young adults with ASD are at significantly increased risk for mood and anxiety disorders. Lugnegård, Hallerbäck, and Gillberg (2011) investigated the presence of comorbid psychiatric disorders in young adults with a clinical diagnosis of Asperger syndrome (twenty-six men and twenty-eight women, mean age twenty-seven years). The Structured Clinical Interview for DSM-IV Axis I Disorders was used to assess psychiatric comorbidity. The Wechsler Adult Intelligence Scale, Third Edition, was used to assess intelligence quotient (IQ). The Diagnostic Interview for Social and Communication Disorders was used to confirm ASD diagnosis. Findings revealed that the experience of at least one episode of major depression was found in 70 percent and recurrent depressive episodes had been experienced by 50 percent. Approximately 50 percent of the sample had experienced anxiety disorders. Psychotic disorders and substance-induced disorders were not common (Lugnegård, Hallerbäck, & Gillberg, 2011).

The Co-Occurrence of and Symptom Overlap Between ASD and Schizophrenia Spectrum Disorders

Schizophrenia and psychotic disorders are characterized by abnormal behavior, including delusions, hallucinations, disorganized speech and/ or motor behavior, and/or negative symptoms including flat emotional expression and avolition (American Psychiatric Association, 2013). In the general population, the estimated prevalence of schizophrenia is 1 percent (Bradley et al., 2011). It has been posited that ASD is one of the potential risk factors for schizophrenia or psychosis, although this hypothesis requires more investigation (e.g., Nylander, Lugnegärd, & Hallerback, 2008). The relationship between ASD and schizophrenia and other psychotic disorders is complex. Nevertheless, a number of researchers have highlighted the significant degree of symptom overlap between these two disorders (Kurita, 1999; King & Lord, 2011). Indeed, Kincaid, Doris, Shannon, and Mulholland (2017) stated that there is evidence in support of a symptomatic overlap, in addition to the recognition of the clinically significant rate of co-occurrence between ASD and psychotic disorders such as schizophrenia (e.g., Solomon et al., 2011). However, the exact nature of this relationship remains unknown; further research is needed to explore this important relationship.

Research has found that ASD and psychosis share common neuro-biology (e.g., Sporn, Addington, Gogtay, et al., 2004). It has been argued that the negative symptoms (e.g., decline in social functioning, passivity, and withdrawn behavior) of psychosis may be the common ground (over-lapping symptomology) between these two disorders (Eussen et al., 2015). It has even been suggested that the diagnostic distinction may be based on the diagnosing clinician's experience and preference (Bejerot, 2007; Nylander, Lugnegärd, & Hallerback, 2008). Kincaid, Doris, Shannon, and Mulholland (2017) have noted that, although there is a relatively small number of studies indicating a high degree of comorbidity between schizophrenia and ASD, there has been little systematic research (e.g., Chisholm et al., 2015).

Conclusion

It is important that lawyers know about some of the frequently co-occurring conditions or disorders in individuals with ASD. Numerous studies have found co-occurring conditions or disorders in individuals with ASD who have engaged in offending behavior. In a key review carried out by Newman and Ghaziuddin in 2008, studies that explored the potential role of psychiatric factors in contributing to offending behavior in individuals with ASD were examined. Most of the seventeen publications that the researchers identified (which met their review's inclusion and exclusion criteria) were single case reports. A total of thirty-seven cases was covered across the seventeen identified publications. At the time of the offense, a definite psychiatric disorder was found in eleven of those thirty-seven cases (29.7 percent). Further, probable psychiatric disorder was found in twenty of the thirty-seven cases (54 percent). Most of the studies that the researchers identified on violent offenders with ASD suggest that these individuals also had a variety of co-occurring disorders, including conduct disorder, depression, and schizoaffective disorder. Nevertheless, it is important for lawyers to be aware that, by themselves, these co-occurring conditions or disorders (conduct disorder being an exception) (Hodgins, Cree, Alderton, et al., 2008) do not cause a substantial additional risk of violent offending behavior in an individual (Newman & Ghaziuddin, 2008). In sum, research indicates that co-occurring disorders are a likely factor when individuals with ASD engage in offending behavior.

● ● ●

Clare S. Allely, PhD, is a Reader in Forensic Psychology at the University of Salford in Manchester, England, and is an affiliate member of the Gillberg Neuropsychiatry Centre at Gothenburg University, Sweden. She holds a PhD in Psychology from the University of Manchester and previously graduated with a Master's in Psychology from the University of Glasgow, a Master's in Psychological Research Methods from the University of Strathclyde, and a Master's in Forensic Psychology from Glasgow Caledonian University. Dr. Allely is an Honorary Research Fellow in the College of Medical, Veterinary, and Life Sciences, as well as being affiliated with the Institute of Health and Wellbeing at the University of Glasgow. Her primary research projects and interests include the pathway to intended violence in mass shooters, serial homicide, investigating how autism symptomology can contribute to different types of offending behavior, and autism in the criminal justice system.

Dr. Allely's email is C.S.Allely@salford.ac.uk and her website is https://www.researchgate.net/profile/Clare_Allely.

Complete citations are available from the author upon request.

5

Adults with ASD

Eric Endlich

In the book In a Different Key: The Story of Autism, *by John Donovan and Caren Zucker (a magnificent study of the history of autism), many individuals with ASD are profiled. In the most tragic cases, children with ASD were banished to institutions. In the best situations, they lived at home or in the community, where family and neighbors included them and sometimes delighted in their apparent eccentricities. It was only relatively recently that the terms "autism" and "Asperger's syndrome" were coined and that parents and educators became aware of the telltale signs of these conditions.*

As the following chapter from Dr. Eric Endlich shows, there is still a significant number of adults of a certain age who were never formally diagnosed with ASD. When such adults become involved in the criminal justice system, the attorney must ensure that the expert spends time with the client's family, friends, and neighbors in order to assemble a complete history. This chapter also provides several suggestions about working with a client with ASD. This chapter has particular credibility because Dr. Endlich was not diagnosed as being on the spectrum until his middle years.

● ● ●

You might assume that the topic of autism interests me because I'm a psychologist, but it's actually much more personal. My son—now a young adult—was diagnosed with autism in 1999. The moment of his diagnosis was life-changing; my wife and I knew our future had been forever altered. We immersed ourselves in the autism world, reading, learning, and meeting with professionals. Sixteen years later, while attending an Asperger/Autism Network (AANE) conference in 2015, she and I simultaneously realized that I am on the spectrum too.

Learning that I'm autistic led me to reevaluate my past; for example, it gave me a better understanding of why I approach things with such a single-minded intensity. (One of the core features of autism is a restricted focus on one thing: a "deep interest" or "special interest.") My diagnosis of Asperger's syndrome (now considered part of autism spectrum disorder, or ASD) also led me to change my future, becoming a college admissions consultant to provide a brighter future for students on the spectrum—a job that, naturally, I also pursued with a singular focus.

Middle-aged and older adults on the spectrum like me grew up at a time when autism was little understood. The work of Hans Asperger was not translated into English until 1991, and the diagnosis of Asperger's syndrome (or Asperger's disorder) didn't appear in the standard American psychiatric diagnostic manual until 1994. Many adults currently over the age of forty had long been out of school by then. As a result, "higher functioning" autistic individuals (those with normal or higher IQs) were routinely overlooked by teachers, parents, researchers, and psychotherapists. I myself didn't recognize my autism until I was in my late fifties, and I know a number of other adults who weren't diagnosed until their sixties or seventies. There are undoubtedly many older "Aspies" who still don't know they're on the spectrum. This may explain why someone in his/her forties or beyond who is charged with a crime does not have a formal diagnosis.

Because many ASD adults learned early in life how to camouflage their autism, and few clinicians are expert at late diagnosis, "the longer we delay our diagnosis, the higher the probability that the diagnostic 'opinion' will be incorrect" (Wylie, 2014, p. 54). But without the diagnosis, "others may incorrectly think that the ASD individual behaves in a certain way because he doesn't care about the feelings of others" (Regan, 2016, p. 16). Women are more likely to be overlooked for diagnosis for a number of reasons, one being that they seem to camouflage more effectively (Dean, Harwood, & Casari, 2017).

Going through much of your life with undiagnosed autism has a number of potential effects. *The Nine Degrees of Autism* (Wylie, Lawson, & Beardon, 2016) proposes a model of stages we go through before and after diagnosis, beginning with "being born on the spectrum" (first degree) and "knowing we are different without knowing why" (second degree).

The strain of the second degree—being aware of being different without really understanding it—leads to the third degree, "developing other health problems." The longer one goes before reaching the fourth degree ("self-identification"), the more intractable these problems tend to be.

Being different in childhood often leads to mistreatment by others: teasing, bullying, or exclusion. As a result, spectrum youth who have the ability to mask or camouflage their autism frequently do so. Although this behavior may lead youth to feel more accepted, what's accepted is a façade rather than the true inner self. Constant camouflaging has been associated with anxiety, depression, and fatigue (Hull et al., 2017).

Studies of Older Autistic Adults

When it comes to older autistic adults, the research is scant. The few studies that have been conducted report fairly discouraging findings: one study described 80 percent of the subjects as suicidal (Wylie & Heath, 2013); another found that 100 percent of the adults surveyed were single and never married (Kats et al., 2013). A third study stated that adults with Asperger's syndrome "rarely succeed in having relationships with others" (Tantam, 2000, p. 390). Researchers emphasize the importance of obtaining a diagnosis—even if it occurs later in life—to ensure access to needed treatment and services, and to avoid receiving inappropriate treatments (Howlin, 2000).

Because of this paucity of information, my colleagues Wilma Wake, Rob Lagos, and I undertook a study of autistic adults over age fifty, a group to which all three of us also belong (Wake, Endlich, & Lagos, 2019). We distributed a 124-item survey that was completed by 150 adults worldwide. Most of the adults were in their fifties, although slightly more than a third were in their sixties (and about 5 percent were seventy or older). Respondents were about equally split between the United States and the United Kingdom, with 8 percent residing in other countries (including Canada and Australia). Here are some of our notable findings:

- The sample was 57 percent male, 43 percent female. Other autism studies find a male-female ratio ranging from 2:1 to 10:1. We don't know the significance of the relatively high number of females in our survey, but it's possible that women are disproportionately represented in the support groups and social media groups from which we drew our sample.

- More women than men reported having posttraumatic stress disorder (41 percent vs. 21 percent), and both rates were higher than what is reported in the general population (around 8 percent). This is not entirely surprising, given that more than half felt ignored or abused by their families, and 83 percent were bullied or teased in childhood. For comparison, the national average for children being bullied is around 30 percent (Nansel et al., 2001).

- More women than men reported having self-identified their autism (24 percent vs. 10 percent) as opposed to receiving a professional diagnosis. Clinicians may be biased against diagnosing females, which in turn would lead women to avoid seeking professional diagnosis, perpetuating the cycle of autistic women being overlooked. A number of the women reported having negative experiences interacting with clinicians when pursuing an autism evaluation.

- 78 percent of the sample reported being heterosexual, versus a 97 percent rate in the general population (Ward et al., 2014). Males were more likely to report being heterosexual than were females (85 percent vs. 68 percent), which is consistent with other findings (Gilmour et al., 2012).

- 34 percent of our group described themselves as atheist or agnostic, compared with 7 percent in the general population (Pew Research Center, 2014). It's fair to say that our survey takers were less likely to follow social conventions.

- Almost everyone in the group was diagnosed after age forty.

- In childhood, more than 90 percent attended mainstream schools and received no special services. This is to be expected given that they were not diagnosed in childhood.

- Most survey takers were "bored a lot in classes" and performed above average in science, reading, and language, but below average in team activities (e.g., sports) and social situations.

- Although many felt nurtured and supported by their families, more than half felt ignored or abused at home. Nearly 90 percent experienced communication difficulties such as being misunderstood or finding it hard to understand others. Ninety-four percent felt "different from other children and teens." Examples of some comments from respondents include: "I felt on the outside looking in . . . they were like an utterly baffling different species. . . . I could not relate to almost anyone. . . . I always felt like I was two steps behind. . . . I always felt different, left out, misunderstood. . . . I felt like an outcast I felt very much an outsider."

It is common for autistic individuals to suffer from multiple co-occurring conditions (comorbidity). (*See* Chap. 4, Co-Occurring Disorders.) In our study, more than 80 percent of adults reported one or more mental disorders, such as depression, anxiety, obsessive-compulsive disorder (OCD), and/or posttraumatic stress disorder (PTSD), supporting the notion that "most Aspergic adults who are diagnosed late in life have already developed some form of mental illness" (Wylie, 2014, p. 39). Although some of these conditions might involve an inherited predisposition, growing up different and being bullied probably contributes to their development in many instances.

Relationships

Forty-three percent of survey takers were currently married, but 26 percent in our study endorsed the statement, "I've really never been close to anyone."

In 2018, the Asperger/Autism Network conducted a survey of 461 adults in neurodiverse relationships. "Neurodiverse" means that one or both partners has an autism profile. The survey found the following:

- More than 90 percent agreed that it's important or very important to recognize that you're in a neurodiverse relationship.
- About 90 percent experienced being in a neurodiverse relationship as difficult or very difficult.
- Virtually all respondents agreed that neurodiverse relationships have unique challenges.
- More than 90 percent reported communication difficulties, especially in seeing each other's perspectives, problem-solving together, making plans together, and emotional and physical intimacy.
- About 90 percent felt that working with a couples therapist experienced in treating neurodiverse couples was important or very important—and nearly half felt that the therapist's lack of such experience could make therapy harmful or very harmful (Grace Myhill, Asperger/Autism Network, personal communication, 2018).

Realizing that one partner is on the spectrum can be a critical "aha" moment for a couple. Conflicts that may have felt very personal before can now be seen as a result of neurological differences. Finally understanding the true reason for longstanding marital issues can sometimes save a marriage that was on the brink of dissolution, especially if the couple finds competent help.

Employment

Most of our study participants felt that autism had made employment difficult, but 25 percent felt that "autism has helped my work." Although many of them held graduate degrees, unemployment or underemployment was disconcertingly common. Some studies have found that more than 80 percent of autistic adults are unemployed.

Finally, though, there are signs that the times are changing. A number of companies—notably Auticon, SAP, and Microsoft—proactively recruit employees on the spectrum, recognizing their unique contributions. Autism@Work is a collaboration of several employers with autism-focused hiring initiatives, including EY, the FMAC, Ford, IBM, Travelers, J.P. Morgan Chase, and Willis Towers Watson. The Auticon website proclaims that autistic employees often exhibit:

- Distinctive logical and analytical abilities
- Sustained concentration and perseverance even when tasks are repetitive
- Conscientiousness, loyalty, and sincerity
- An exceptional eye for details, deviations, and potential errors
- Continuously thorough target/actual comparisons and a genuine awareness for quality
- A strong interest in factual matters and comprehensive technical expertise.

Integrate Advisors, a New York-based nonprofit, helps college graduates on the spectrum transition to the world of work, coaching them as well as employers on how to have a successful partnership. Many autistic tendencies, such as avoidance of eye contact and sensory sensitivities, can interfere with job interviews and integration into the workplace. Prospective employees need to learn to advocate for themselves by requesting accommodations such as a quieter or dimmer workspace, if needed. Disclosing one's condition may reduce the chance of getting an interview, but perhaps it's just as well for applicants to know at the outset if a company isn't autism-friendly. Employers can bring in trainers to educate the workforce on what autism looks like and how to be more inclusive. A National Autistic Society study found that more than one-third of autistic adults have experienced bullying or discrimination at work, and 43 percent reported losing a job because of their autism. Clearly, there is still a need for additional training.

Adjusting to the Diagnosis

As noted earlier, the adults we studied were diagnosed after age forty, in some cases decades later. The number one reaction they experienced upon learning they were autistic was relief. The next most common feeling (besides "other") was excitement. Some participants reported feeling grief, disappointment, sadness, regret, or isolation.

A minority of our study participants seem to have become "stuck" in their development, exhibiting negative, bitter attitudes about their experiences. These adults were more likely to experience career challenges and to not feel accepted by their family or the autism community.

Here's an example of a rather "stuck" respondent: Jonathan, a 54-year-old British man, complained of "low levels of academic/clinical/interactional understanding of ASD amongst health professionals outside the autism field." He felt that "discrimination is rampant" and that for the "much milder forms such as Asperger's and high-functioning autism, there is very little support out there, except to just get on with it." Sadly, he seems to have given up on seeking support: "At the moment, I am minimizing/eliminating any form of human contact." Such isolation, however, may only worsen his situation.

Others react to a late diagnosis much more positively. "In general, those who have been diagnosed later in life have been very pleased to have that diagnosis as a means of explaining being different" (Wylie, 2014, p. 26). In our research, 77 percent felt relief and 29 percent felt excitement.

In *The Nine Degrees of Autism*, degrees five through seven are "considering all the options," "crisis of identity/resolution to deal with autism," and "self-acceptance" (Wylie, Lawson, & Beardon, 2016). Many of our participants seem to have successfully navigated these stages. Just over two-thirds of our survey takers were now comfortable with being on the spectrum and considered it a positive part of their lives. It would seem that they have reached the seventh degree of autism, self-acceptance.

Since diagnosis, the adults who felt better (the majority of our survey takers) reported better self-understanding, confidence, and self-acceptance; more understanding by family and peers; and more involvement in the autism community. The final degrees of autism in the Wylie et al. model are unconditional service (eighth degree) and recognition, mastery, unity (ninth degree). Temple Grandin and Stephen Shore are examples of well-known autistic adults who seem to have reached the ninth degree. Temple Grandin is a professor of animal science at Colorado State University, a prolific author, a frequent speaker about her experiences as a person on the spectrum, and the subject of an HBO film titled *Temple Grandin* (starring Clare Danes). Stephen Shore is a professor of special education at Adelphi University, the author of three books, and a past president of AANE.

Some of our research participants talk about how their autism has enhanced their connections with others:

- "I feel that my autism enables me to identify, more than others can, with people who are marginalized."
- "I was able to use my own diagnosis and life experience positively to help youngsters going through the school system and to support their parents from an unusually informed perspective."
- "Accepting that I am autistic and neurologically different gives me a greater understanding of humanity."

For my own part, recognizing my autism has increased my sensitivity to neurodiversity and strengthened my commitment to help fellow individuals on the spectrum through writing, presenting, and consulting, as well as leading support groups and hosting events. After feeling alienated or excluded for many years, giving back to the autism community can be vital, "because by helping others we heal ourselves" (Wylie, 2014, p. 41).

Here are some guidelines that may be helpful when you are working with a client on the autism spectrum:

- *Respect sensory sensitivities.* These may involve vision (e.g., certain types of lighting), touch (e.g., dislike of constricting clothes or certain fabrics, discomfort with physical contact such as handshakes), sound (e.g., office machines), or smell (e.g., perfumes, air fresheners). Personally, I am bothered by fan noises and a wide variety of odors.
- *Communicate with care.* Clients may have difficulty understanding sarcasm, figurative speech (e.g., idioms), tone of voice, and body language.

Do not expect them to "read between the lines" (or even know what that saying means). Be as clear, literal, and explicit as possible. They may be anxious and have difficulty processing what you're saying, so ask them to summarize what you've said to ensure that they understood correctly. Visual aids may be helpful in the event that they are visual thinkers. Follow up with a summary in writing to be on the safe side. Don't assume that someone will recognize your face just because you've met before.

- *Stick to the plan.* People on the spectrum tend to prefer things to be routine and predictable. If there is a change in plan (e.g., meeting time or place), provide notice and rationale, and be patient if someone is upset by the change.

- *Stay calm.* Your clients are likely to be anxious, and as noted may become upset by unexpected events. Many aspects of social interactions are baffling to people on the spectrum. The more you can remain calm, the quicker they can settle down as well. Providing rational explanations for events (when applicable) may help too.

- *Don't take things personally.* Your autistic clients may not smile at you or make eye contact. They may not wish to engage in social pleasantries such as discussing the weather before getting down to business. They may express themselves in a manner that seems blunt, curt, or pedantic. They may struggle to understand another's point of view or the impact of their words and actions on others. These tendencies are no reflection on you, so try to take them in stride.

- *Maintain perspective.* People on the spectrum often focus on details and may "miss the forest for the trees." Make sure they understand not just the details of a situation, but the overall implications.

For additional suggestions on dealing with people on the spectrum who are accused of crimes, I recommend a piece available on AANE's website titled "Asperger's Syndrome and the Criminal Justice System" by Judge Kimberly Taylor (retired), Dr. Gary Mesibov, and Dennis Debbaudt. Although it focuses on people with Asperger's syndrome, much of the information is applicable to any adult on the spectrum who is involved in the criminal justice system.

Of course, these are only broad generalizations; autistic adults are as varied as nonspectrum adults. They may prove challenging at times, but working with them can also be a very rewarding experience.

● ● ●

Eric Endlich, PhD, is a clinical psychologist dedicated to working with individuals on the spectrum. He holds a BA from the University of California, Berkeley; an MA from New York University; and a PhD from Boston University. He is the co-author of *Older Autistic Adults: The Lost Generation* (Shawnee, KS: AAPC, 2019), a book based on an international study of 150 older autistic adults.

As founder of Top College Consultants, he helps spectrum teens successfully transition from high school and promotes the development of college autism support programs.

Dr. Endlich is an Advisory Team Member for the Friedman Neurodiverse Couples Institute and a Clinical Advisory Group member of the Asperger/Autism Network (AANE). He has also led support groups at AANE and presented at several of their conferences. Additionally, he has presented at the Harvard Medical School Continuing Education Autism Conference, the Southern Maine Autism Conference, and the Massachusetts Psychological Association Annual Conference.

He has taught psychology courses at Suffolk University, Tufts University, Boston College, and University of Massachusetts/Boston, and has supervised doctoral students from William James College. Dr. Endlich is also a senior writer and wellness advisory board member for Personal Best Publishing.

Dr. Endlich is an autism father and an autistic adult. His email is eedlich1@gmail.com and his website is http://www.topcollegeconsultants .com.

Complete citations are available from the author upon request.

6

The Bond Hearing

David Daggett

Often, jail is the worst possible place for any defendant awaiting disposition of his/her case. In particular, jail is a heinous experience for someone with autism spectrum disorder (ASD). Depending on the nature of the condition, the person may be sensitive to the loud noises, be resistant to following orders, and have personal characteristics such as stimming or repetitive speech patterns that could make him/her the target of others' jokes or hostility. The bond hearing is your first chance as an attorney to get your ASD client out of that environment.

As the following chapter from David Daggett points out, the bond hearing can be fraught with challenges. However, it can also provide the opportunity to show the court and prosecutor your client's unique behavioral traits as well as educate them about ASD. Attorney Daggett includes a link to a video about a client with ASD who is arrested. Readers are strongly encouraged to watch this, not only to see a demonstration of a bond hearing, but also to hear the attitude by the court and law enforcement toward the accused. Although this video is several years old as of the publication of this book, you should be alert to these attitudes, spoken and unspoken, concerning your client.

• • •

Over the years it has been my pleasure to work with, represent, and volunteer for many people with disabilities, including autism spectrum disorders. Certainly, those circumstances present a host of challenges. At the same time, they have also rewarded me with great internal gratification and satisfaction. It is my pleasure to share with you some tips I have learned in more than thirty years of practice.

The bond hearing is one of the first, if not *the* first, court appearance for an arrestee, and thus often defines the entire case. In some circumstances, particularly for public defenders or appointed lawyers, the bond hearing is the first opportunity for the lawyer to meet the individual facing criminal charges. As with all clients, pay attention to specific behavioral patterns. Certainly, when a family member is in the courtroom and you as the lawyer have time to talk with that person, if you are told that there is a diagnosis of ASD, you should present that information to the court. If you are retained and have more time to meet with the client and his/her family, take time to learn about the client: habits, personality, vulnerabilities, and treatment regime.

The bond hearing is also the first step in educating the prosecution, judge, and other members of the judicial system. Moreover, the lawyer will face presentation opportunities as well as challenges at the bond hearing. The purpose of this chapter is to help the practitioner best advocate for the autistic individual.

General Principles of Bond

In every jurisdiction, the basic goal of a bond is to ensure that a criminal defendant will appear in court at a future date. The history and character of the defendant will be examined by the court to consider the risk that the defendant will not appear. Generally, the court will examine any evidence that helps evaluate the risk of nonappearance, injury to any person, destruction of evidence, or intimidation of or influence on any witness. The primary factors the court will look at include the nature and circumstances of the charge, the defendant's history, the defendant's mental condition, and the defendant's family and ties to the community. The substantive law and procedure of the hearing may vary from jurisdiction to jurisdiction. Accordingly, this chapter does not center on the substantive aspects of the law and procedure; rather, it focuses on dealing with the special circumstances presented in representing an autistic individual.

Setting Bond

Many criminal defendants receive initial conditions of bond, or bail, from a magistrate immediately following arrest or at the jail facility in the hours following their arrest. It is here or shortly following this time that the attorney is typically engaged for representation. The bond hearing, or first appearance hearing, typically follows within a matter of hours or just a few days. In most states, this is regulated by statute. For example, in North Carolina where I practice, the first appearance must occur within ninety-six hours after the defendant is taken into custody, or at the first regular session of district court in the county, whichever occurs first. This moves very quickly. The attorney has a very short period of time in which to become familiar with the circumstances of the charges and the specific considerations regarding the client.

To illustrate how quickly the individual moves to the bond hearing, I have had occasions in which I met the client for the first time at the courthouse holding cell immediately prior to heading into the courtroom for the bond hearing. Knowing the system is a great advantage. Furthermore, learning and being exposed to the various aspects of handling the client and the hearing all contribute to your personal body of knowledge and, therefore, to the best possible representation of the client. Add in nuanced factors such as a client on the autism spectrum, and it is clearly understandable that preparation, experience, and advance knowledge of potential issues are extremely valuable.

Release Conditions

At the bond hearing, the judge or magistrate will determine any pretrial release conditions. Remember that the purpose of this hearing is to determine the flight risk of the criminally accused and any potential danger to the public from a pretrial release. Depending on the severity of the charges, the defendant could be held without bail, released on a monetary bond (secured or unsecured), or released on personal recognizance. Additionally, state and federal laws also provide for a number of conditions that may be imposed on any pretrial release.

In addition to a monetary or unsecured release, a court may impose release conditions that range from travel and employment to possession of firearms, substances, or tools/technology associated with the alleged offenses. Furthermore, the court may require some sort of examination of the defendant, including medical and/or psychological.

Either the defendant or the government can appeal a bond decision. The scope of review is usually limited to abuse of discretion by the judge or magistrate. So, unless the bond or release provisions are clearly unreasonable or arbitrary on the facts or law, the appellate court will not alter the outcome.

The Hearing

Many years ago, the North Carolina judicial system produced an educational video about ASD and the criminal justice system. It can be found at https://www.youtube.com/watch?v=dYj6acMLJuY. This video provides a great overview of the challenges a person with ASD faces when interacting with the legal process, including the process of arrest and charging. At about sixteen minutes, there is an example of a bond hearing for a person with ASD. This video shows skepticism, misunderstanding, and even outright hostility toward people with ASD. Unfortunately, although the video was made many years ago, these attitudes are still held by some law enforcement and court personnel. (*See* Chap. 14, Vulnerabilities of Defendants with ASD and Strategies for Improving Outcomes; and Chap. 15, Perception of Defendants with ASD by Judges and Juries.) Accordingly, it is incumbent on the attorney to fully understand the client's condition and to take affirmative steps to educate the court.

Understand the Client's Condition

In my experience, relationships are everything. They help give the lawyer perspective and understanding. Relationships with autistic clients are just as important as any other client relationship, if not more so. It is essential for the attorney to learn about the client's disability and the client's unique behavior patterns. Learning about and becoming comfortable interacting with people with autism makes you, the attorney, more comfortable and effective in the representation. With experience, you can do an effective job in representing your autistic client.

If an attorney's practice is going to involve representing persons with disabilities, it is helpful to spend time around people with various disabilities to get a handle on patterns of behavior and communication. Volunteering at local schools or organizations that work with autistic individuals can be invaluable in gaining understanding, perspective, and ability to communicate. For example, locally we have organizations and a specialized school for autistic individuals. They are always eager for volunteers, or even observers. From a personal perspective, it has also been very helpful for me to volunteer and work with individuals with other disabilities, such as Down syndrome, to gain a better and deeper understanding of working with individuals with disabilities, and to broaden and expand my communication skills.

People with autism have a wide range of intellectual abilities and physical behaviors. Intelligence can range from very low to extraordinarily high. Outward manifestations of intellectual abilities can range from being nonverbal to apparent genius level, at least in some areas (for example, the autistic character in the movie *Rain Man*).

The practitioner needs to be aware that the emotions of an autistic individual can change very quickly and that there are other associated behaviors distinctive to each individual person with autism. Often, emotions will have a physical manifestation as a clue. The attorney needs to be very observant and prepared to respond to a range of emotions quickly.

Typically, people with ASD have a narrower scope of understanding and communication; therefore, representing them can be challenging and difficult. The attorney needs to proceed slowly and use communication skills to keep the client on track.

Experience and practice in working with individuals with autism and other disabilities provides the practitioner with a level of comfort that is evident not only to the client but also to all personnel and individuals within the system as the case proceeds. By default, an advantage can be gained thereby, in that court personnel, the prosecutor, and the judge will then view you, the defendant's lawyer, as a reliable expert as the case proceeds.

Educating the Court

A critical aspect in representing an individual with autism spectrum disorder at the bond hearing is educating the prosecution, court personnel, and the judge. It is very likely that the bond hearing, which as previously indicated is many times also the first appearance, may be the first time court personnel have ever interacted with an autistic person.

The prosecutor and judge are likely inexperienced in the mannerisms and actions of the autistic individual. They may harshly require the defendant to speak up, or look them in the eye, when that may not even be possible. Physical behaviors may include rocking, spinning, and flapping or shaking movements. Therefore, it is incumbent upon the attorney to know and understand the client's disabilities and limitations, and to understand the client's perspective of the situation he/she is facing. Accordingly, it is essential that the attorney begin at this early stage to educate the prosecutor and the judge for the benefit of the client, both at the hearing and as the case progresses.

The attorney has an extremely short period of time to assess the client, the charges, and the options for resolving the case. This must usually be done in a particular order so become prepared to proceed. The attorney needs to size up the client and the circumstances quickly. Does the client have a guardian? Does the client understand and is he/she competent? Should the attorney request or secure an expert to evaluate the client?

In some circumstances, it may be that it is in the client's best interest to have him/her declared incompetent. The attorney will need to be aware of guardian ad litem rules, local services, and availability. Having your client declared incompetent and a guardian ad litem appointed may be essential for the best and most productive representation of that individual.

Alternatively, in some jurisdictions there may be some form or fashion of a "friend of the court" option. A friend of the court is a person who is not a party to the case who is requested by the court to assist the court with understanding and making sure there is a proper presentation of difficult issues for a person with a disability. This may be beneficial and helpful for the client, as well as being seen by the judge and prosecutor as a way of assisting their level of understanding.

Further, with experience, the individuals in the court system, including the prosecutor and judge, will see and refer to you, the lawyer, as the highest and most knowledgeable source of information concerning the issues facing a defendant with ASD. This will likely be one of the most important factors in securing the most positive outcome for your client.

Presentation Strategies

The goal during the bond hearing is to obtain favorable and suitable release and pretrial conditions for your autistic client. Special circumstances regarding the needs of the autistic individual must be explained to the court. The likelihood of appearance at court proceedings is what must be pointed out to the court. The practitioner working with autistic individuals needs to take every opportunity to demonstrate, instruct, and point out to the court that anything that seems atypical with the appearance of, demeanor of, or responses from the autistic individual are part of that person's condition and disabilities. The court should be shown how all of these pieces fit together.

Typically, the lawyer is going to be in a position to explain that there is a lower risk of harm to the public from pretrial release than there is risk to the autistic individual if incarcerated or held in detention pending further proceedings. Providing for the pretrial safety and well-being of your client is of prime importance at this stage.

The lawyer will have presentation opportunities and challenges at this first opportunity to be in the courtroom and before a judge. First, the lawyer must be cognizant that this will be a very foreign environment for the client. Although we counselors are used to representing individuals who may be in court for the first time, persons with autism present different challenges, so the lawyer must be aware that they think and process the environment differently than individuals without these disabilities.

Last, having family members or other responsible members of the public present to support your client can be very important. It clearly sends a message to the court regarding the individual's ties to the community, as well as about the quality and character of his/her circle of care. It will give the court confidence to set reasonable and attainable bond, as well as other reasonable conditions of release. Clearly, you want to do everything possible in your presentation to create an atmosphere that supports a finding of favorable pretrial release.

Client Testimony

Putting any client—with or without ASD—on the stand may be fraught with peril. Should your client with ASD testify, even about limited matters such as where he/she will live during the pendency of the case, proceed cautiously because, as the video referenced earlier in this chapter shows, any behavior may be misinterpreted. (*See* Chap. 14, Vulnerabilities of Defendants with ASD and Strategies for Improving Outcomes.) Actual witness testimony, including client testimony, during a bond/first appearance hearing may be unusual, depending on the jurisdiction. Accordingly, it is important for the lawyer to assert that testimony from the client may be valuable and important as a part of the process for full understanding and education of the prosecutor, court personnel, and judge. It is important to convey an awareness and appreciation of your client's autism to the court in order to secure favorable bond and release conditions.

Remember that during every step of the process, the autistic client may view the situation much differently than a typical client would. Simple things like the swearing-in process may be difficult for the autistic client to fully appreciate and understand. Accordingly, the lawyer needs to be prepared and nimble enough to request special procedures as may be appropriate as the hearing progresses. Requesting the court's indulgence for patience and understanding during the process will further help not only your client but ultimately the court.

Questioning an autistic client is very different for the lawyer and for the court. Remember that the questions you ask of your client may elicit odd responses. It is your duty as the client's representative to move this process along in order to obtain favorable release conditions for your client. Due to the unusual nature of this question-and-answer process, the lawyer may have to supply ongoing commentary and explanation rather than just the standard questions and answers.

During the course of the representation, the lawyer has to be cognizant of the differences in communication. The lawyer must understand that all individuals need to respect the personal space of the autistic individual. Autistic individuals tend to respond better if they are made to feel comfortable. Accordingly, being soft-spoken and courteous will go a long way in enabling your client to look cooperative during a court proceeding, and ultimately in securing the client's release.

Patience is essential when communicating with an individual with autism. This patience must be explained fully to the court, and demonstrated to the client. Listening is extremely important in communicating with autistic individuals. Remember that they do not always respond to gestures and facial expressions the way neurotypical people might; accordingly, lawyers need to be specific and careful with our use of words. It is helpful to pay very close attention to your clients to pick up cues about what their behavior is revealing about their comfort and awareness of their situation. When instructing an individual with ASD, you should deliver the instructions one bit of information at a time rather than attempting to explain the entire matter in what might be a monologue. (*See also* Chap. 14, Vulnerabilities of Defendants with ASD and Strategies for Improving Outcomes; and Chap. 15, Perception of Defendants with ASD by Judges and Juries.)

Other Testimony

For purposes of showing how jail can be detrimental to a client with ASD, you may want to call a family member. They can paint a picture for the court of exactly how destructive jail would be for their loved one. Depending on the specific characteristics of that individual, the family member can describe how the person with ASD is sensitive to noise or light, has sleep difficulties, is a picky eater, has difficulty following orders, or engages in behavior that might make him/her susceptible to bullying.

Remember that it is not enough to simply assert that someone is on the autism spectrum. Do not expect that law enforcement, the court, or prosecutors will understand what this truly means. (The response of the arresting officers on the video referenced earlier is a good example of this.) Rather, you must explain, perhaps using a family member or an expert or even (in this particular proceeding) a treatment provider.

Conclusion

Languishing in jail is not in the best interest of the autistic client, and it can be dangerous. Thus, favorable release conditions are certainly in the best interest of the client, and most often of the public as well. Moreover, this will assist you as the lawyer in having access to your client. However, a successful bond hearing is only possible with sensitivity, knowledge of your jurisdiction's pretrial release policies, and—even if you have virtually no time to confer with your client in advance of the hearing—knowledge of the particular challenges faced by people with ASD. At the same time, representation at the bond hearing sets the stage for educating the court about your client.

● ● ●

David Daggett, Esq., is up and running every day at 4:30 a.m.— literally! He's a serious triathlete who has completed more than 195 triathlons, including 29 Ironman competitions (Ironman is a 2.4-mile swim, 112-mile bike, 26.2-mile marathon run).

Mr. Daggett has competed in the Hawaii Ironman World Triathlon Championship eight times. He was presented the Ironman "Everyday Hero" award for his community service work; the national "Trial Lawyers Care" award; and has been featured on ESPN, Universal TV,

Forbes Small Business, Men's Health, 60 Minutes, *North Carolina Lawyer* Magazine, and the cover of *Lawyers Weekly*. He has also been presented a Governor's Volunteer Service Award for his work with the Down syndrome community.

Mr. Daggett has served on numerous boards, including the Board of Governors of the North Carolina Bar Association, as well as serving as president of the Forsyth County Bar and the 21st Judicial District Bar Associations.

Mr. Daggett is the Managing Partner at Daggett, Schuler, Attorneys at Law, in Winston-Salem, N.C. He received his BA from Indiana State University and his JD from Wake Forest University School of Law. In addition to his law practice and numerous community activities, he serves as an Adjunct Clinical Professor at Wake Forest University School of Law. Mr. Daggett can be reached at ddaggett@daggettschulerlaw.com and his website is www.DaggettShulerLaw.com.

7

Working with the Expert: An Attorney's Perspective

Melanie Gavisk

This chapter, "Working with the Expert: An Attorney's Perspective," written by federal public defender Melanie Gavisk, complements the following chapter, "Working with the Expert: An Expert's Perspective," written by Dr. Elliott L. Atkins. An independent mental health expert (not the treatment provider) is a vital component in the representation of a person with ASD. This expert plays a key role in assisting the attorney to communicate with the client, prepare a defense, and help the court understand the unique nature of the defendant's ASD. Without an expert or team of experts, the attorney is going into battle unarmed. Gavisk's chapter details how experts can be selected and how to define their scope of involvement. Dr. Atkins's chapter details how to use the expert for maximum benefit and explores issues relating to how ASD affects the ability to assist counsel and the defense of people with ASD against charges for sexually oriented offenses. Both chapters emphasize that collaboration between the attorney and the expert is crucial in achieving a reasonable resolution of the case.

•   •   •

As in other criminal cases, choosing and working with the right expert for a client with ASD can make or break the case. Although many of the techniques for working with ASD experts are similar to those for working with other experts, this chapter focuses on techniques particular to ASD experts.

This chapter outlines: (1) how to identify and select an expert in ASD; (2) how to develop a clear objective for the expert's assistance; (3) how to ensure that the expert has the necessary materials, including by working with the client, friends, and family; (4) how to leverage the expert's findings; (5) how to prepare the expert for trial or another hearing; and (6) considerations relevant to clients with ASD who may also lack competency. Finally, it provides an outline for a motion for expert assistance in appointed cases (in Chapter Appendix A).

However, this chapter does not set forth rigid rules for working with an ASD expert; every case is different and may require a different approach. Rather, this chapter endeavors to set forth the techniques the author has successfully used in her practice and to draw lessons from court cases involving ASD experts.

Identifying the Right Expert for Your Case

After a lawyer is retained for or appointed to a case (or sometimes before), often one of the first steps he/she takes is to identify potential expert needs. It is critical to identify any expert needs early, for several reasons. First, it may take time to identify the type of expert needed and to locate qualified persons. Second, the expert has to be paid, and it can take time to gather those funds or get court approval for them. Third, experts can be busy. Experts are far more likely to be available to assist you if you can give them plenty of advance notice.

Before the search for an expert begins, it's important to narrow your expert needs. Do you need an expert who can diagnose your client and explain the diagnosis? Do you need an expert who can discuss your client's ASD and how it bears on the client's mental state? Do you need an expert who can educate the court on why your client deserves a lesser sentence in light of the ASD diagnosis? Do you need an expert who can testify about your client's particular medical needs and why a jail or prison cannot meet them? Or do you want someone who can help in all of these areas?

The easiest—and often most efficient—way to find an expert is to ask other attorneys for references. Criminal defense organizations often have email distribution lists for this purpose, and public defender offices may be able to provide references as well. Even at this point, though, it's helpful to identify your particular expert needs before asking for references.

Another way to identify an ASD expert is by reviewing academic and other professional articles about ASD. If someone wrote an article with conclusions that are helpful or relevant to your case, he/she may be a good expert. Even if that professional isn't available, you may end up with some helpful leads.

Another way to identify an ASD expert is by looking for ASD treatment providers. Generally speaking, the person treating your client should not be used as the expert; this would be a conflict of interest for the provider. *What the court needs is an independent forensic opinion that a treatment provider cannot give*. However, the evaluating expert can request information from the treatment provider regarding the client's course of treatment.

Although some treatment providers may not be willing to act as experts, the provider may have leads, insights, and other helpful information.

Once you've identified one or more potential experts, the next step may be to find transcripts of their testimony, court opinions, and other background materials. Many attorneys send emails to criminal defense distribution lists asking for any information—good or bad—about a particular expert. Finally, you'll want to have a conversation with the expert about his/her expertise, fees, availability, and other case-specific considerations.

Developing Clear Objectives for the Expert

After narrowing your expert needs and identifying an expert, it's critical to make sure that you and your expert are on the same page. Obviously, a clear contract helps, but it's probably more important to develop clear referral questions with your expert.

For instance, perhaps you retained your expert because you believe your client has ASD. Your primary referral question could be very simple: What is the client's diagnosis? But you almost certainly will also have secondary questions that are far more important: What impact does ASD have on your client's ability to control his/her behavior? How can the ASD diagnosis explain some bizarre or potentially damaging statements your client made? What are your client's limitations on functioning? What is the relationship between the ASD and the crime charged?

Clearly and specifically discussing the questions you have will ensure that your expert understands the purpose of his/her services. In addition, your expert will often have excellent and helpful suggestions for other areas of inquiry.

It can be helpful to then put the particular referral questions in writing. For example, referral questions in an ASD case may include:

- What is the client's diagnosis?
- Did the client's diagnosis play a causal role in the charged offense?
- Did the client's diagnosis play a contributing role in the charged offense?
- What is the client's probable level of success in psychological treatment and/or probation supervision?

Getting Your Expert the Necessary Materials

An expert's opinion is only as good—and persuasive—as the information he/she used to form it. Some of that information is out of the attorney's control; it depends on the expert's education, experience, and research. Nevertheless, some of that information comes from the attorney through record gathering and other efforts.

The attorney (or an investigator) should gather pertinent records, such as school records, employment records, medical and psychiatric records, and records from any residential treatment placements. The attorney will likely want to consult with the ASD expert to identify other relevant materials and determine whether the expert should interview family or friends as part of the evaluation. Particularly if the client has never been diagnosed with ASD before, obtaining supporting records and information that predate the offense will bolster the reliability of the expert's conclusion. In most cases, the attorney will want to provide the ASD expert with all available evidence about the crime, including police reports and witness interviews.

After the expert has reviewed relevant discovery and records, he/she will almost certainly need to interview at least the client, and perhaps friends and family as well. (If an investigator has already interviewed friends and family, the expert may simply want to review interview summaries.) The client and other interviewees should clearly understand the purpose of the evaluation and the limits of confidentiality. Although the expert will certainly explain this at the time of the interviews, preparing the client beforehand avoids unnecessary confusion. Explaining the importance of the evaluation—and the importance of providing accurate, complete, and detailed information—can ensure that interviewees are candid during their interviews. In addition, preparing the client upfront for the possibility that the report will not be helpful, and clearly explaining that the expert is independent, can minimize anger and disappointment later.

If the expert has not conducted a comprehensive review of relevant materials, he/she may be subject to harmful cross-examination. The expert's failure to review materials can also be grounds for reversal. For example, in federal court in the Western District of North Carolina, an autism expert testified at sentencing about the impact of the defendant's ASD diagnosis on his conviction for possession of child pornography. The court found this testimony persuasive, and gave the defendant a sentence far below that called for by the Federal Sentencing Guidelines. In imposing its sentence, the trial court explained: "The primary driver of this sentence stems from the defendant's neurodevelopmental disorder, namely, Asperger's syndrome." ECF No. 94, transcript of sentencing at 465: 24-26 to 466:1, *United States v. Zuk*, No. 13-cr-0059 (W.D.N.C. Oct. 5, 2016). Relying on the expert testimony it heard, the trial court reasoned, "[d]efendant's condition is lifetime and he will be saddled with it, but it contributed to his deviancy; but on the evidence it can be coped with and overcome with the appropriate treatment, especially at his young age." *Id.* at 470:15-18. The court also observed that "any period of incarceration should be imposed as a last resort for patients like the defendant." *Id.* at 470:5-7.

On appeal, however, the appellate court reversed the low sentence, and in doing so it pointed out some weaknesses in the expert's testimony (as well as pointing to other factors). The defense expert did not know that Mr. Zuk had told an investigator that he knew possessing child pornography was illegal. The court reasoned that the defense expert "acknowledged that he was unaware of certain important aspects of Zuk's offense, including the fact that Zuk had admitted to knowing that his behavior was illegal and wrong." *United States v. Zuk*, 874 F.3d 398, 404 (4th Cir. 2017). The appellate court also reasoned that "no expert testified that Zuk's medical condition caused his criminal conduct" and "Zuk was highly functioning compared to most people with autism." *Id.* at 411. The appellate court remanded the case for resentencing. Notably, the court in *Zuk* pointed to other issues with the trial court's sentence, and the outcome might not have changed even if the expert had reviewed all the relevant materials. Nevertheless, the case highlights the risk of putting on the stand an expert who is not fully informed about the facts of the case.

Similarly, in another case, the court focused on the fact the defense expert had not interviewed any family members:

> [The expert] admitted that according to defendant's medical records, he had never been diagnosed with Autism. She based her decision only on her tests and interview with defendant, and discussions with his lawyers. She never contacted his family.

People v. Quinanola, No. E065316, 2017 WL 3614249, at *4 (Cal. Ct. App. Aug. 23, 2017), *review denied* (Nov. 1, 2017). The court appeared to agree with the prosecution's expert, who "believed that in order to get an accurate diagnosis, a person's work and social history throughout his or her life had to be evaluated." *Id.* at *5.

By contrast, interviews with family members can uncover information that is otherwise incongruent with the expert's conclusions. The expert in one case explained that the C grades the defendant earned were inconsistent with his tested abilities, including an IQ of 73, and "attributed the grades in part to homework help [the defendant] was receiving at home from his mother and sister." In other words, without the added information the court might only see poor testing results and not be able to reconcile them with average grades. The court might believe that the defendant was deliberately doing poorly on a test when he was apparently fully capable of receiving at least C grades. In this case, the family was able to explain that it was only through their help that he earned these grades. *United States v. Rodriguez*, No. 14-20877-CR, 2015 WL 6964671, at *10 n.14 (S.D. Fla. Nov. 10, 2015). Gathering this type of information from family can significantly bolster the expert's credibility and the reliability of his/her conclusions.

Developing the Final Product

After the ASD expert reviews the relevant materials and evaluates a client, the attorney has to decide whether to ask the expert for a report of the findings. I've found that a detailed conversation with the expert, during which he/she can summarize answers to the referral questions, helps with this determination. The expert can also characterize the findings. Generally, I've found that clear and open discussions with the expert *before* the report is prepared are invaluable.

If the expert's findings are not particularly helpful, you may opt against a report, and instead have the expert assist you with developing helpful cross-examination approaches. Alternatively, you may ask the expert to write a short report—for example, one that confirms an ASD diagnosis—without much more elaboration. In many courts, an expert report can be proffered at sentencing without actually calling the witness.

If the expert's conclusions are helpful, the attorney may or may not want him/her to prepare a report. Financial considerations may weigh against report preparation. If the expert prepares a report and you plan to call the expert at trial, the report will likely have to be turned over before trial (e.g., Fed. R. Crim. Proc. 16(b)). The contents of the report—or substance of the expert's testimony—will of course vary depending on the case.

Even if no report is prepared, at least under federal law, the defense still must disclose a summary of the "witness's opinions, the bases and reasons for those opinions, and the witness's qualifications" if the expert will testify at trial. *Id.* Though it's tempting to disclose only a bare-bones summary of the expert's testimony, this approach could backfire if the court strictly limits the expert's testimony to the disclosure.

Preparing Your Expert for Trial or Other Testimony

If you plan to call your expert as a witness, preparation is key—as with all witnesses. In addition to practicing a direct examination, the attorney likely will want a colleague to cross-examine the witness. The attorney should also ensure that the expert remains familiar with the relevant records and evidence; often many months will have gone by since the expert completed the evaluation.

In ASD cases in particular, the attorney will want to tailor the examination to the applicable legal framework. It can be difficult for judges to grasp how someone with ASD—particularly someone who is high functioning—is affected by the disorder. For example, one court explained:

> As to [the defendant's] argument that his autism makes his sentence inappropriate, there are several considerations that bear on the weight, if any, which should be given to mental disorders in sentencing: (1) the extent of the defendant's inability to control his or her behavior due to the disorder or impairment; (2) overall limitations on functioning; (3) the duration of the mental disorder; and (4) the extent of any nexus between the disorder

or impairment and the commission of the crime. We note that autism has not prevented Fulbright from carrying out other basic obligations—he graduated from high school and held a well-paying job for five years. Fulbright himself acknowledges that his autism "does not excuse his criminal conduct." The record indicates that Fulbright was capable of controlling his behavior and he did not have significant limitations on his functioning, and he has not presented evidence of a nexus between his autism and child molesting.

Fulbright v. State, 56 N.E.3d 729 (Ind. Ct. App. 2016) (citations omitted).

An expert's nuanced explanation of a client's ASD and its impact on the client's life or offense can educate the judge and jury and debunk common misconceptions about ASD.

Autism and Competency

Many attorneys hire an ASD expert to assist with competency assessments, particularly if the court-appointed professional conducting the competency evaluation does not have expertise in ASD. Indeed, someone trained to conduct competency evaluations—but without any special training in ASD—may not be the best person to evaluate your client for competency. Unfortunately, court-appointed competency evaluators may overlook deficits unique to ASD.

For example, people with ASD may have outstanding memory abilities. Your client may easily recite the correct answers to typical questions in a competency evaluation about the roles of the judge, jury, prosecutor, and defense attorney. An autism expert will be able to explain that correct answers do not signal comprehension. For instance, an expert in one case explained:

> Individuals with autism spectrum disorder have excellent rote memory but lack insight and the ability to make generalizations. It was [the defense expert's position] that [the defendant] would be able to state back information repeated to him over and over again in a competency restoration group, but without comprehension or understanding [of] such information.

United States v. Rodriguez, No. 14-20877-CR, 2015 WL 6964671, at *11 (S.D. Fla. Nov. 10, 2015). The expert may also be able to provide concrete examples of deficits caused by ASD:

Additionally, when [the expert] interacted with [the defendant]: it was oftentimes difficult to understand what he was saying; he clearly misunderstood questions; he would provide very concrete responses that sometimes were unrelated to the question at hand; he demonstrated a clear lack of knowledge in terms of what was being asked of him; questions would need to be re-asked; he required additional aids, such as providing visual demonstrations, so he could understand the questions.

Id. (*See* Chap. 2, Competency.)

In sum, an expert in ASD may be critical to the effective representation of a client with ASD. An expert without ASD-specific training may overlook or misunderstand the unique characteristics of the disorder.

• • •

Melanie Gavisk, Esq., is an Assistant Federal Public Defender based in Cheyenne, Wyoming. She represents criminal defendants charged with federal crimes in the District of Wyoming. In addition to her law degree, she has a master's degree in psychology.

Gavisk previously worked with the Federal Public Defender in Las Vegas, Nevada, representing criminal defendants, including those sentenced to death; in postconviction proceedings; and at a large international law firm as a civil litigator, where she worked on a wide variety of civil cases and on white-collar criminal defense. She was also a law clerk to the Honorable Lewis Babcock at the United States District Court for the District of Colorado. Gavisk can be reached at mgavisk@gmail.com.

Requests for Funds for Expert Services

The following is a basic outline of an expert request with some relevant federal authority. The request should be tailored to the case and should include any details necessary to show why the expert is needed.

Defendant, Mr. Client, pursuant to 18 U.S.C. §3006A(e)(1), moves this Court for authorization to obtain expert assistance from _____, who has expertise in autism spectrum disorder.

FACTS: [Include a factual description of the case and why you need funding based on these facts.]

Mr. Client is charged with _____. Reports from Mr. Client's parents and siblings, as well as school records, suggest that Mr. Client has autism spectrum disorder (ASD). To confirm this diagnosis and assess its potential impact on Mr. Client's culpability, an expert must evaluate Mr. Client.

AUTHORITY: [Include the relevant authority.]

The Criminal Justice Act, 18 U.S.C. §3006A(e)(1), authorizes payment for expert services that are necessary for the adequate representation of an indigent client. Mr. Client cannot afford to retain an expert himself, and an autism expert is necessary to adequately defend Mr. Client.

SERVICES: [Describe what the expert will do.]

The expert will evaluate Mr. Client by interviewing him, reviewing any relevant records, and interviewing family members if necessary. After conducting the evaluation, the expert will diagnose Mr. Client and opine to what extent any diagnoses affect Mr. Client's culpability. The expert will prepare a report if one is requested and will testify if needed.

EXPERT: [Describe the expert's qualifications, fees, the maximum amount of time needed, and the maximum payment. Include the expert's CV or résumé.]

Chapter

8

Working with the Expert: An Expert's Perspective

Elliot L. Atkins

Once you have selected your expert or the court has appointed one, your work has only begun. Indeed, you may not even realize that your client has ASD. As Dr. Elliot Atkins notes in the following chapter: "It is typical, and most unfortunate, that the behaviors of individuals on the spectrum are often seen by others as willful, stubborn or oppositional. Consequently, these behaviors are very likely to affect the relationship between an attorney and his or her clients, particularly in those cases where the condition remained undiagnosed."

Dr. Atkins's chapter discusses how the unique qualities of an individual's brand of ASD affects his/her competence to proceed and the nexus of his/her ASD to the charged conduct. Furthermore, this chapter will guide the attorney on how best to collaborate with an expert, from the point of the initial evaluation, through the preparation of the report, to the disposition of the case.

•　•　•

In her autobiography on Netflix, "Amy Schumer Growing," the comedienne, spoke of her confusion at some of her husband's peculiar reactions slowly giving way to comprehension upon learning of his being diagnosed as on the autism spectrum:

> Once he was diagnosed, it dawned on me how funny it was because all of the characteristics that make it clear that he's on the spectrum are all of the reasons that I fell madly in love with him. That's the truth. He says

whatever is on his mind. He keeps it so real. He doesn't care about social norms or what you expect him to say or do.

Recent statistics suggest that one in fifty-nine children would meet the criteria to be diagnosed on the autism spectrum. Although autism is a diagnosis that has been in use for many years, more often than not it was applied to children and adults with severe symptoms and extensive intellectual deficits. It was not until the publication of the fourth edition of the American Psychiatric Association's *Diagnostic and Statistical Manual* (*DSM-IV*), at the onset of the new millennium, that a much broader diagnostic framework came into play. Individuals without severe intellectual deficits, and, in fact, even those with very high intelligence levels, were now considered to be part of a more inclusive "autism spectrum." The diagnosis of "Asperger's disorder" came into use and more and more children were given that diagnosis. Since then, our developing understanding of this disorder has led to further refinement. In 2013, the fifth edition of the *DSM* collapsed the diagnosis of Asperger's disorder and the traditional autistic disorder into the diagnosis of autism spectrum disorders (ASD).

ASD is not a mental illness. Rather, it is a developmental disorder: a lifelong condition the challenges of which vary widely across individuals and across life stages and circumstances. ASD individuals have definable neurological deficits that manifest during the developmental process and that contribute to the highly variable outcomes observed in this population. The ASD diagnosis may be applied to accomplished professionals as well as to the homeless. Nevertheless, even those who are doing well occupationally are likely struggling to comprehend their social world, and even those who appear socially typical to the outside world are likely struggling to *appear* normal. In the process of attempting to create a social life for themselves, they are often rejected and targeted by others who view them as different and who do not understand their way of interacting. Language skills may be well developed, but there may be a problem with turn-taking in conversations. Individuals with ASD can easily become anxious or disorganized in overstimulating or unstructured situations, effects that often lead to actions or verbalizations that may be difficult for those around them to understand or tolerate. It is typical, and most unfortunate, that the behavior of individuals on the spectrum are often seen by others as willful, stubborn, or oppositional. Consequently, these behaviors are very likely to affect the relationship between an attorney and the ASD client, particularly in cases where the condition remained undiagnosed—as has been the case with a significant portion of the criminal defendants whom I have diagnosed as being on the autism spectrum.

Awareness of the possibility that a defendant may be on the autism spectrum not only informs the attorney-client relationship but could also potentially yield valuable information regarding the offense behavior. I have frequently found that a defendant's offense behavior reflects the slow processing, inflexible thinking, poor problem solving, and impulsivity associated with ASD. For the majority of individuals with this disorder, this slow processing is a critical element in their very delayed social-emotional interaction skills. Whereas their peers are growing in social understanding as they age, my ASD clients' ability to keep up with, and learn from, social interactions does not develop, creating the differences that result in symptoms such as their poor understanding of nonverbal communication, their limited peer relationships, their inability to understand others' perspectives, their social vulnerability and gullibility, their inflexible thinking, their social passivity, and their black-and-white thinking.

Both the attorney and the forensic mental health professional will be faced with the challenge of carrying out their respective roles within a context that is likely to be insensitive to the role that ASD may have played in the offending behavior. Freckelton and List[1] observed that "traditionally the law has been preoccupied with intellectual, not emotional, intelligence and, in fact, has been problematically unresponsive to the role of emotional impairments in impacting upon volition and decision-making. [ASD] raises this issue starkly."

Despite the charges that they are facing, many of my ASD clients possess a strong moral compass that includes not violating laws and not harming others. However, their underlying social judgment is compromised, making their recognition of complex social communication and occurrences more difficult. The reason they had so often been an easy target for schoolmates is precisely because they were not able to foresee the eventual consequences of their actions.

Next I provide examples of some of the ways that the ASD diagnosis has informed my assessment of criminal defendants in the areas related to competency and sexual offending. (In these examples, the names have been changed.) Following these examples, I provide a sample architecture

---

[1] I. Freckelton & D. List, *Asperger's Disorder, Criminal Responsibility and Criminal Culpability*, 16 Psychiatry, Psychology and Law, no. 1, March 2009, at 16–20.

of a collaborative process that has developed and evolved between me and criminal defense attorneys as we have attempted to fulfill our professional duties toward our mutual clients.

Competency

Alan: an example of the role ASD may have played in affecting his competence to proceed to trial.

In most jurisdictions, the language articulating competency is based upon the U.S. Supreme Court's *Dusky* decision,[2] which requires that the defendant have (a) an intellectual and a rational understanding of trial procedures and the roles of its participants; and (b) the ability to assist counsel in his/her defense. Consequent to a comprehensive forensic psychological assessment, I diagnosed Alan with ASD, a diagnosis that had never before been suggested for him. Alan clearly met the competency requirements for prong a. The requirements for prong b, however, had become an issue. Although he possessed an understanding of the consequences should he be found guilty at trial, Alan was convinced that he had committed no crime and would, therefore, be found not guilty at trial. Consequently, he refused to consider accepting an extremely generous plea offer.

Competency requires the capacity to identify personal options and to logically deliberate among the available options based upon the relative potential risks and benefits. My client's distorted perceptions regarding the evidence against him and the likely outcome of a trial were a direct result of his autistic brain functioning. In this and similar cases, I have observed how these pathologically distorted perceptions eventually served to damage my clients' relationships with their attorneys to the point where communication was no longer feasible. If your client is not able to contemplate a defense that does not incorporate his distorted, possibly delusional, beliefs, he will not be able to assist you in preparing his defense. (*See* Chap. 2, Competency.)

There is no question in my mind that Alan's incompetency was a function of his ASD. To a large extent, his intransigence regarding his belief that he would be acquitted at trial was the product of his remaining convinced that, despite the evidence against him, he did nothing wrong. Neurotypical individuals typically have an understanding of social rules that serves to prevent their crossing the line between legal and illegal behavior. ASD

---

[2] Dusky v. United States, 362 U.S. 402 (1960).

individuals possess much less of a social or legal filter and, consequently, might fail to grasp the extent to which a particular endeavor might be illegal or immoral. They would be less likely to appreciate the consequences of that activity. In addition, they would likely be less capable of fully appreciating the extent to which the other person was being harmed.

As a result of his ASD, it had always been difficult for Alan to appreciate, on an emotional level, how his conduct affected others. His deficits in empathy could theoretically—or in the case at hand, actually—distort his understanding of the nature and consequences of his actions. In my forensic report, I addressed the defense attorney's frustration with his attempts to communicate with Alan:

> What seems obvious to us (e.g., the ethical, moral and legal wrongfulness of Alan's actions) remains obscure to Alan despite your efforts to educate him and despite your admonitions regarding the potential for his intransigence to be both self-destructive and self-defeating. In the early stages of your representation of him—and in the early stages of my evaluation of him—his intransigence was interpreted as his being oppositional, deceitful and/or simply his being in denial. I observed as you reacted to this with frustration, impatience and, at times, with a raised voice.

Although his attorney was better able to understand Alan's intransigence in the aftermath of my ASD diagnosis, he continued to remain hamstrung by his client's unwillingness to consider the plea offer. Alan refused to accept his lawyer's assessment of the likelihood that he would be convicted at trial.

In my experience, I have found that statutory definitions and case-law commentary regarding competency often fail to articulate the specific abilities that would comprise prong b: the client's ability to assist counsel in his/her defense. Some guidance in this regard, however, is provided by McGarry et al.,[3] who broke down the "assistance" construct into several discrete abilities, which have become known as the McGarry Criteria. Relevant to Alan's situation are the following McGarry Criteria:

- The ability to appraise the available legal defenses.
- The ability to plan a legal strategy.
- The ability to appraise the likely outcome.
- Manifestation of self-serving versus self-defeating motivation.

---

[3] A. MCGARRY & W. CURRAN, COMPETENCY TO STAND TRIAL AND MENTAL ILLNESS (Rockville, Md: National Institute of Mental Health, 1973).

Although Alan was somewhat able to appraise available legal defenses and plan a strategy, his ASD compromised his ability to rationally appraise the likely outcome of a trial. As in many other areas of his life, Alan was not able to appreciate the self-defeating and self-destructive nature of his motivation (in this case, to proceed to trial) and was setting the stage for catastrophe.

Sexual Offending: Child Pornography

David: an example of the role ASD may have played in his viewing and collecting of child pornography.

My evaluation revealed that David's almost lifelong constellation of peculiarities and social deficits were the result of a neurological condition—ASD—that had never been diagnosed. The scientific literature is consistent in documenting the extent to which, because of their significant deficits in social, emotional, and psychosexual development, ASD teenagers and young adults typically find refuge in, and become obsessed with, the internet.[4] Misunderstood by others, such individuals tend to withdraw into this cyber world in order to engage in social interaction and to explore their sexuality. Tantam[5] addressed this issue:

> These are intellectually intact people, with good computer skills but extraordinary brain-based naiveté acting in social isolation, compulsively pursuing interests that often unknowingly take them into forbidden territory. The internet provides them with a means of communicating with others that emphasizes this technological know-how and de-emphasizes the subtleties of social interaction, both of which are advantages for people with Asperger's Syndrome.

Nondisordered teenagers may be curious about a wide range of stimuli that they might come across during the time that they spend on the internet. Their awareness of social and legal codes and their common sense, however, will most likely serve to inhibit them from going in the direction of illicit images. An ASD teenager, however, is likely to have much less of a legal or social filter, as he or she peruses the range of images

---

[4] The psychological literature also documents the extent to which Asperger's disorder is underdiagnosed. Not infrequently, such individuals are misdiagnosed with personality disorders primarily because clinicians are more familiar with those constructs.

[5] D. Tantam, *The Challenge of Adolescents and Adults with Asperger's Syndrome*, 12 CHILD AND ADOLESCENT PSYCHIATRY CLINICS OF NORTH AMERICA 143–163 (2003).

available on the internet. In fact, he/she may become obsessed with collecting such inappropriate images. Because ASD individuals interpret the world in such a concrete and literal fashion, it is very likely that such a teenager may not understand the extent to which something so readily available may also be illegal. (*See* Chap. 16, ASD and Sex Offenses: A Son's Perspective.)

Although a typical adolescent may understand the social stigma associated with an erotic attraction to underage children, an individual with ASD would be much less likely to appreciate the social and legal consequences attaching to these pornographic images. It is unlikely that the ASD individual would be capable of appreciating the extent to which the children depicted on the internet are being exploited, or of understanding that they are not capable of giving consent to the activity that is being depicted. Individuals with ASD would likely have difficulty with the concept of consent as a result of their significant deficits in processing and evaluating the cues of others.

Individuals with ASD exhibit an uncommon lack of flexibility in making decisions. They are impaired in their ability to recognize and act on available alternatives. For example, they remained fixated on the object of their interest. It is difficult for those with ASD to appreciate, on an emotional level, how their conduct affects a victim. Deficits in empathy, including the ability to perceive the interpersonal impact of one's behavior, could theoretically distort such an individual's understanding of the nature and consequences of his/her actions.

Sexual Offending: Molestation

George: an example of the role that ASD may have played in inappropriate sexual contact with younger children while a teenager.

As a result of his ASD, George suffered deficits in social functioning and didn't fully appreciate the impact of his behavior on others. Likewise, his self-awareness was severely limited. Stuck in rigid, inflexible patterns of thinking, given to easily formed obsessions, and prone to manifest repetitive behaviors, George's social world had been significantly constrained compared to neurotypical individuals. His neurodevelopmental anomalies caused him to struggle in interfacing with others. As a result of being socially different, George was serially rejected by other children throughout his developmental years.

George's interests as a teenager were eccentric (building with Legos, music, reading, drawing, etc.), and most of his peers didn't share them. George was lonely and was frequently bullied. Outside his narrow window of interests, at which he excelled and which he pursued with great drive, he found little else stimulating and exciting. George's social deficits, awkwardness, and anxiety persisted across childhood and into his late teenage years. George presented a unique combination of neurodevelopmental deficits and functional limitations that contributed to his difficulties in social functioning over the years as well as to the offense. His condition interfered with his ability to fully appreciate his errors of judgment, the deviance of his behavior, or the effect his actions would have on girls. It is difficult for those with ASD to appreciate, on an emotional level, how their conduct affects another individual. Deficits in empathy, including the ability to perceive the interpersonal impact of one's behavior, could theoretically—or in George's case, actually—distort such an individual's understanding of the nature and consequences of his/her actions. Even higher-functioning ASD individuals engage in social behavior that is not as reciprocal as one sees in normally developing people. Consequently, their ability to make and maintain friends remains quite limited.

Beginning when he entered pre-adolescence, George was able to compensate for his loneliness and social isolation through his obsessive and compulsive involvement with the internet, in general, and pornography, in particular. Unfortunately, his immersion in the world of graphic sexual imagery and his compulsive masturbation began at an early age and, as the result of his ASD, it became fixated and obsessive. As stated earlier, nondisordered teenagers may be curious about a wide range of stimuli that they might come across during the time they spend on the internet. Their awareness of social and legal codes and their common sense, however, will most likely serve to inhibit them from acting on these interests and fantasies. An ASD teenager, however, is likely to have much less of a filter as he obsesses about, and becomes preoccupied with, these images and fantasies. Whereas a typical male adolescent may understand the social stigma associated with acting out these fantasies, an individual with undiagnosed and untreated ASD will be much less likely to appreciate the social and legal consequences surrounding such actions. It is unlikely that such an individual will be capable of appreciating the extent to which the object of these actions is being exploited, or the likely inability of the "object" person to give consent to the activity that is being suggested. Individuals with ASD would very likely have difficulty with the concept of consent, as a result of their significant deficits in processing and evaluating the cues of others. It is difficult for them to appreciate, on an emotional level, how their conduct affects the victim. In addition, their lack of flexibility and impaired ability to recognize and act on available alternatives would make it difficult for them to abandon a planned course of action. Moreover, the deficits in empathy associated with this disorder would serve to blind George, and others like him, to the ramifications and consequences associated with their actions.

It is important to note that this deficiency in empathy is different from psychopathy. In ASD, this is considered a neurobiological deficit: there is a genuine unawareness that they have caused harm to someone. This is in comparison to the type of deficient empathy of those with anti-social personality disorder: that is, cold, heartless, and remorseless. The neurological deficits associated with ASD distort an individual's understanding of the nature and consequences of his/her actions. Deviant behaviors are reflective of ignorance of appropriate behavior rather than defiant behavior. (This lends itself to positive rehabilitation implications, as the prognosis for change or improvement in those diagnosed with anti-social personality disorder is grim.) As opposed to acting with malice, an individual with ASD tends to be acting reflexively, but without the capacity to synthesize, interpret, and appropriately respond to the cues of the victim. An individual with anti-social personality disorder, in contrast, is motivated by self-interest, unconstrained by an intrinsic code of morality or a concern for the consequences to the victim. The ASD teenager seeks relationships, although often inappropriately, and functions within a narrowly circumscribed moral framework—a framework that may be inconsistent with prevailing community and legal standards.

Regarding the molestation, George's impaired sense of social judgment permitted him to bypass the naturally occurring obstacles between a teenager and younger children. At the time of his offending, he was functioning socially and emotionally at the level of a pre-adolescent and had common ground with those much younger than himself. Unfortunately, his neurological condition precluded his being able to enact the ordinary constraints that would be second nature to his neurotypical age-mates, and he engaged in the acts that were the predicates for the offenses charged. His insularity and alienation from his peers, as well as his immersion in and obsession with pornography, had also been the product of his previously undiagnosed and untreated ASD.

The Collaborative Process

It is important that criminal defense lawyers become familiar with the indicia of ASD in their clients. A well-informed lawyer may sense, from the first meeting, that a client should be referred for a forensic mental health evaluation. Without knowledge about this condition, the attorney will not be able to properly prepare the case or interact meaningfully with the client, and therefore may not make the best decisions regarding strategy, plea bargaining, trial, and/or sentencing.

The information made available to the attorney as a result of my having made an ASD diagnosis can be invaluable throughout his/her representation of the defendant. Although most cases will not require an interface between the forensic mental health professional and the attorney at each phase of the representation, I will outline the various junctures at which such collaborative efforts might be fruitful. Indeed, many of these points are applicable when working with a mental health expert evaluating a client with any diagnosis.

Pretrial

Consult 1: Though it is most likely that a face-to-face meeting will not be necessary, the two professionals will confer in order for the attorney to:

* Specify the purpose of the evaluation and a proposed timeline.
* Discuss and complete a formal retainer agreement.
* Complete a confidentiality agreement.
* Provide relevant discovery.
* Provide relevant records and documents.
* Provide contact information for collateral interviews.
* Introduce the client to the forensic mental health professional.
* Schedule the initial evaluative session.

(The evaluation process begins.)

Consult 2: When the forensic mental health evaluator has enough information to share his/her preliminary opinion with the attorney, a conference or meeting should be scheduled for the purpose of discussing that opinion as well as the following:

- Whether or not there should be any modifications in the scope and/ or purpose of the evaluation.
- Whether or not a preliminary report should be prepared and/or a meeting be arranged so that they can discuss the preliminary findings with the prosecution for the purpose of plea negotiations and/or the removal of any minimum mandatory sentences.

(The forensic report is finalized.)

The object of the report is to convey the extent to which your client's offense-related behavior was a function of his autism spectrum disorder and, consequently, the extent to which he presents as someone who is significantly distinguishable from those who typically commit such offenses. Although he/she might chronologically be an adult, your client is likely to be a child socially and emotionally—at best, an adolescent. Without an early diagnosis of ASD, neither the client's family, teachers, nor peers would have been aware of the extent to which his/her strange behaviors were a function of this condition or of the extent to which they were typical of the ASD individual's limited awareness of other people's feelings or points of view. It could turn out that this report will be the vehicle through which this invaluable information will be promulgated both for the benefit of the client's legal defense and for the immediate benefit of the client and the client's family.

It is important that the forensic report make it clear that ASD is considered to be the result of a neurological disorder that affects the functioning of the brain and that it is not social pathology. Although the individual often has deficits in empathy, the forensic report must assist the attorney in distinguishing this from the lack of empathy evidenced by those with sociopathy or anti-social personality disorder. ASD is typified by extreme social and emotional immaturity, the inability to respond appropriately in social settings, and the lack of intuitive awareness of social/moral/legal constraints. The report must make it clear that these features interacted in a manner that contributed to behavior that, though offensive to others, had no offensive purpose.

The report should also reference the effects of incarceration. The psychological literature is consistent in underscoring the extraordinary difficulties facing ASD individuals should they be incarcerated. As a result of their social-emotional immaturity, naïveté, and gullibility, they are at great risk of being taken advantage of and victimized. Appropriate treatment will certainly not be available, and their already damaged sense of self will assuredly become further compromised. (*See* Chap. 6, The Bond Hearing; and Chap. 13, Prison Accommodations.)

Consult 3: The report is discussed. The two professionals confer regarding the mental health professional's role, if any, going forward. For example, whether or not there is a trial, the prosecution may have its own expert evaluate the client. If that is so, the defense attorney may want the forensic mental health professional to:

- Be present during that evaluation.
- Take notes and prepare a summary of that evaluation.
- Review and critique the prosecution expert's report of that evaluation.
- Prepare a rebuttal report.

Trial

Consult 4: The two professionals confer regarding the mental health professional's role, if any, should the case go to trial. For example, the mental health professional may be asked to:

- Testify at the trial.
- Assist in the preparation of cross-examination questions for the prosecution's expert.
- Be present in court for the prosecution expert's testimony.
- Assist with cross-examination of the prosecution expert.

(The trial takes place.)

Sentencing

Consult 5: The two professionals confer regarding the mental health professional's role, if any, in the sentencing process. For example, he/she may:

- Assist in the exploration of possible variances and/or departures that might be relevant in view of the ASD diagnosis.
- Assist in the development and implementation of a treatment plan.
- Consult with the treatment provider.
- Prepare a supplemental report for sentencing.
- Meet or consult with the presentence investigator.

- Review the presentence investigation report.
- Testify at the sentencing hearing.

(The sentencing hearing takes place.)
(*See* Chap. 7, Working with the Expert: An Attorney's Perspective; Chap. 11, Creative Mitigation; and Chap. 12, Mitigation Using Community Resources.)

Conclusion

ASD is frequently misdiagnosed. In fact, it is often not diagnosed at all, or confused with conditions such as attention deficit disorder (ADD), conduct disorder, obsessive-compulsive disorder, or bipolar disorder, for example. (*See* Chap. 4, Co-Occurring Disorders.) ASD is one of the less visible disorders. Consequently, those who have it can easily be misdiagnosed as simply "odd," "a loner," or "eccentric," or as suffering from an anxiety or depressive disorder. If the diagnosis had previously been made, the criminal defense attorney's knowledge of ASD will provide a perspective that will enable him/her to work more effectively with, and to better represent, the client. It is more likely, however, that the ASD diagnosis will first come into view during, or subsequent to, the forensic mental health professional's evaluation of the client. The sooner the attorney is armed with this information, the better he/she will be at establishing a working professional relationship with the client and developing the most effective defense. The collaboration between the mental health and legal professionals must be directed toward the objective of distinguishing their client from the typical offender who would commit that offense and from the offender the legislators had in mind when they drafted the relevant sentencing guidelines.

● ● ●

Elliot L. Atkins, EdD, is a clinical, forensic and consulting psychologist who has been in clinical practice since 1977 and has worked in the forensic arena since 1980. Dr. Atkins has been admitted as an expert witness before state and federal courts in both the criminal and civil arenas. He has been called upon by attorneys from across the country to address issues related to professional malpractice, criminal state of mind defenses, sentencing, and the assessment of both perpetrators and victims of sexual abuse. He has provided consultation to defense counsel in multiple high-profile civil and criminal institutional child sexual abuse cases. He has also been retained by both the prosecution and the defense as a trial consultant in sexual abuse cases by the United States Air Force's Judge Advocate General's office. Dr. Atkins co-authored two chapters ("Capacity to Waive *Miranda* Rights" and "Sentencing") in the *Handbook of Forensic Assessment: Psychological and Psychiatric Perspectives* (Wiley, 2011). He has also co-authored a chapter on death penalty mitigation in the textbook titled *Handbook of Forensic Psychology and Forensic Sociology* (Springer, 2013). In 2014, he prepared an amicus brief and testified on the constitutionality of polygraphing paroled sex offenders. He has been an adjunct clinical assistant professor at Widener University and has provided clinical supervision for the doctoral internship programs at both Hahnemann and Drexel Universities. He has been a consultant to municipal, state, and federal agencies and legislative bodies on the issue of substance abuse and rehabilitation. Dr. Atkins has published articles and presented continuing legal education workshops on topics related to the insanity defense, neonaticide, borderline personality disorder, sentencing, and the collaboration of clinicians and attorneys regarding the issue of professional boundary violations. For the past two decades, he has chaired the American College of Forensic Psychology's Forensic Skills panel of attorneys and forensic psychologists as they address professional and ethical issues confronting forensic mental health practitioners. Dr. Atkins can be reached at elliotatkins@msn.com and his website is http://www.elliotatkins.com.

Complete citations are available from the author upon request.

Chapter

9

Testing

Mark A. Stokes and Tony Attwood

When reviewing a forensic evaluation, it is all too tempting for attorneys to gloss over the testing results. After all, testing involves science and math, and some attorneys went to law school precisely so they could avoid these disciplines. Yet, an understanding of testing instruments is vital to representing your client, as well as to maximizing the use of your expert. Additionally, a thorough understanding of the testing instrument and your client's performance will help inoculate you against attacks by the prosecutor and skepticism by the court.

This chapter by Professors Mark Stokes and Tony Attwood provides a guide to the purposes of the tests most frequently administered to people with ASD and describes their strengths and weaknesses.

●　●　●

The current diagnostic criteria for an autism spectrum disorder (ASD) were published by the American Psychiatric Association in 2013 in the fifth edition of the *Diagnostic and Statistical Manual of Mental Disorders* (American Psychiatric Association, 2013). The essential characteristics of ASD are persistent deficits in reciprocal social communication and social interaction; restricted, repetitive patterns of behavior, interests, or activities; and hyper- or hyporeactivity to sensory input.

To provide context, this chapter first briefly discusses the behaviors typically found in people with ASD and how those behaviors may influence interaction with counsel; second, it examines selected testing instruments.

The job of a skilled clinician is to bring together these diverse sources of information and to integrate them into a diagnosis.

Behaviors and Interaction with Counsel

One of the fundamental assumptions regarding autism is that the person with ASD has difficulty interpreting social situations and nonverbal communication. This includes the ability to accurately perceive the thoughts, emotions, and intentions of others and integrate that information into a conversation or other interactions.

There are three adaptations to having a deficit in social interaction abilities. One is to be overwhelmed and insecure in a social situation, being perceived as withdrawn, shy, and an introvert. Another adaptation is to be motivated to be socially engaged, an extrovert, but to have difficulty interpreting all the subtle social signals that regulate and moderate the reciprocity of social engagement. The social behavior of these persons is often perceived as intrusive, intense, and irritating.

Another adaptation, only recently recognized by clinicians and academics, is for the person who has autism to recognize his/her difficulties reading social cues, facial expressions, tone of voice and gestures, but to attempt to discover social rules and conventions by avidly observing and analyzing social interactions over many years. This information is then used to effectively camouflage the person's social difficulties by creating a social "mask," displaying a superficial sociability that is effective but exhausting (Cook, Ogden, & Winstone, 2018; Hull et al., 2017; Lai et al., 2017).

During a consultation with a lawyer, the client who has autism may present as someone who clearly has difficulties engaging in a reciprocal conversation and interaction, is overly withdrawn, or has difficulties encouraging engagement. Conversely, the client who has autism may present the *opposite* behavior, dominating the conversation while the lawyer tries to encourage the person to listen, focus, and not dictate or control the conversation. The third adaptation can be confusing to the lawyer, as the person does engage in a reciprocal conversation and appears to read social cues. The lawyer must realize that this is achieved by intellectual analysis rather than intuition and that the person is "acting," even when the level of performance makes it appear that the person does not have autism.

Recent research has explored the association between autism and *alexithymia*, the inability to recognize or describe one's own thoughts and emotions (Berthoz & Hill, 2005; Bird & Cook 2013; Hill et al., 2004; Milosavljevic et al., 2016, Samson et al., 2012). Thus, during a consultation with a lawyer, the client who has autism will have genuine difficulty converting his/her thoughts and feelings into speech. When asked why they may have done something, or their feelings regarding an event, these clients may simply reply "I don't know." This is not being obtuse or evasive but is an expression of a recognized difficulty with self-reflection and self-disclosure associated with autism.

Various diagnostic aspects of the presentation could affect a lawyer's conversation with someone who has autism. Surprisingly, and unexpectedly, unusual sensory sensitivity to experiences that would not usually be considered aversive may affect the conversation (Tavassoli, Hoekstra, & Baron-Cohen, 2014). There can be auditory sensitivity to the sound of electrical appliances such as an air conditioner, visual sensitivity in terms of perceiving the flickering of a fluorescent light, and feeling nauseated by the aroma of the lawyer's perfume or deodorant. Before starting the consultation, it would be appropriate to ask the person who has autism if any sensory experiences in the immediate environment are causing distress or affecting concentration, and to make appropriate adjustments.

Gender Differences

For many decades we have assumed that the gender ratio for autism was four males for each female. However, recent research and clinical experience has established a ratio of two to one (Rutherford, McKenzie, & Johnstone, 2016). The reason for the revision in the gender ratio is that girls and women who have autism have often successfully camouflaged or compensated for their autistic characteristics, delaying diagnostic assessment. In childhood, girls who have autism have greater social motivation and engagement than their male autistic peers. They ardently observe other girls playing and socializing and may copy or "clone" themselves on other girls, "borrowing" their gestures and phrases to achieve the social abilities needed when playing with peers (Ormond et al., 2018). By the time they are adults, they have a range of personas and social scripts to facilitate social success.

Another adaptation is a preference for playing with boys because they are perceived as engaging in simpler and more logical play and are less likely than fellow girls to be judgmental. An ASD girl may become known as a tomboy, preferring to look androgynous and enjoying sports and physical, rather than conversational, interactions. She may despise feminine characteristics such as an interest in fashion and makeup, boys and dating, preferring to be by herself reading or writing fiction or with the family pet.

Alternatively, she may try to ingratiate herself with her female peers by developing an interest in expressing femininity through clothing and color coordination and becoming knowledgeable about her peers' topics of conversation, such as popular films, music, and social media. She acquires the currency of female friends and a conversational script. However, this social acceptance will have been achieved at some psychological cost. There can be performance anxiety in social situations, as though she has been continually "on stage"; like Cinderella at the ball at midnight, she can maintain the pretense for a while, but then becomes totally drained of mental energy and must return home to recover in solitude. The unrelenting mental exhaustion of processing social information and social expectations can lead to a surface sociability but a lack of social identity, leading to low self-esteem, depression, and self-harm.

Girls and women who have autism may also use compensation strategies such as preferring the company of males, whose social dynamics are relatively simpler, and sometimes identifying with their thinking styles and abilities. Compensation can also be achieved by developing an interest and talent in science and the arts, and becoming an academic, medical specialist, author, artist, musician, singer, or multi-linguist. Social eccentricities in such persons are accepted and accommodated, due to their being valued by peers and society with recognition and admiration for their talent and original thinking. Yet another compensation strategy is to develop an interest in fictional heroes and superheroes, and to have friendships based on shared interests, such as cosplay and comic or science fiction conventions, which provide defined and recognized roles and camouflage via costumes.

Mental Health Issues

Those who have autism appear to be vulnerable to feeling at least mildly anxious for much of each day, and for most of their lives. However, they often experience extreme anxiety in specific situations such as anticipation of changes in routine or expectations, uncertainty regarding what to do, or fear imperfection and making mistakes, as well as crowded and noisy places. Research has confirmed that an anxiety disorder is the most common mental health problem for adults who have autism, with prevalence figures ranging from 11 to 84 percent, compared to the prevalence in the general population of only 5 percent (Mattila et al., 2010; Van Steensel et al., 2011; White et al., 2009). An internet survey of more than 300 adults with autism indicated that more than 98 percent ranked anxiety as the greatest cause of stress in their daily lives: greater than the stress associated with making and keeping friendships and relationships, finding and maintaining employment, and coping with daily living skills (Attwood et al., 2014). Sometimes, the level of anxiety may be perceived as more disabling than the diagnostic characteristics of ASD.

There are many reasons someone who has autism may become depressed (Attwood & Garnett, 2016). These include feelings of social isolation, loneliness, and not being valued or understood by family members and colleagues. Another reason is the exhaustion experienced due to socializing, trying to manage and often suppress emotions (especially anxiety), and coping with sensory sensitivity. The person is constantly alert, trying to endure perpetual anxiety with a deficit in emotional resilience and confidence. The mental effort needed for intellectually analyzing everyday interactions and experiences is draining, and mental energy depletion leads to thoughts and feelings of despair.

An adult with autism may be able to cope mentally during the workday, but by the time he/she returns home, he/she is emotionally drained and pessimistic. There is a heightened sense of self-blame and rumination over a lack of social and career achievement (Sharma, Woolfson, & Hunter, 2014). Whereas typical adults will have several close friends or a partner who can quickly and easily repair their emotions and provide reassurance and evidence that negative self-belief is not true, the isolation of the person with autism not only can be a cause of depression but also may perpetuate those feelings. (*See* Chap. 4, Co-Occurring Disorders.)

Language Profile

There is a "signature" language profile associated with autism. This can include superficially perfect expressive language in terms of semantics, vocabulary, syntax, and technical terms, but impairments in the pragmatic aspects of language or the "art" of conversation. Persons with ASD tend to have formal or pedantic speech, make literal interpretations, and have difficulty understanding double negatives, sarcasm, and inferred meaning.

The person who has autism often has difficulty knowing and following conventional conversational rules regarding how to initiate, maintain, and end a conversation. There can be a tendency to monologue, and frequently such persons do not seek or interpret nonverbal and situational cues that may indicate the conversation partner has something to say, is bored, or the conversation is starting to drift off topic. They may also lack an appreciation of the context, confidentiality, social hierarchy, and social conventions and not know the amount of information needed by the listener.

Another characteristic of autism is a difficulty with conversation repair. This means that people with ASD may hesitate to ask for clarification, as well as take considerable time to reply due to having difficulty processing linguistic and social information. Another language profile characteristic of autism is to interrupt or talk over the speech of others and have difficulty summarizing and getting to the point. Under stress, the person with ASD may also have difficulty organizing and conveying information or thoughts.

Knowledge and accommodation of all these characteristics will be important when a lawyer is discussing legal issues and when preparing a client to give evidence in court. A judge may be able to ensure that when a witness or the accused has autism, modifications are made to the usual procedures and means of giving evidence and cross-examination.

Expert Clinical Opinion

The diversity of autism presentations is considerable. Consequently, there is no one single means to arrive at a diagnosis of autism. One person may manifest the diagnosis in one way, whereas another may demonstrate autism in quite another way (Huerta & Lord, 2001). Some have an intellectual disability that may amplify or mask aspects of their autism; others don't (Volkmar et al., 2014). Some people with autism are nonverbal, whereas others manifest apparently advanced language use. Also, presentation may vary somewhat by age and environment (Risi et al., 2006; Sigman & McGovern, 2005). For example, a child may display some behaviors only in specific environments and not in others (such as school). Hence, it is important that diagnosis consider a person's behavior across a diversity of contexts.

Generally, with children and adolescents, it is considered best to have a multidisciplinary team involved in the assessment process, using medical, psychological, and speech specialists (Gerdts et al., 2018; Huerta & Lord, 2001), although this may not always be possible with adults. Consequently, an individual may be assessed by a number of clinicians, using a host of instruments (other than those considered here) over an array of contexts, and seeking input from other informants, such as parents and other observers of the child, like teachers (Attwood, 2007; Huerta & Lord, 2001; Volkmar et al., 2014). With children, this is not always possible because it may exceed the resources of the parent or guardian or the tolerance of the child. Furthermore, an experienced clinician may not necessarily rely on a particular instrument, or may rely on some aspects and not others.

The essential issue that the clinician needs to address is this: Is there evidence that the individual meets the criteria for a diagnosis of ASD? As previously noted, the skilled clinician will weave together many diverse sources of information and integrate them into a coherent diagnosis. There is no single way to achieve this. (*See* Chap. 8, Working with the Expert: An Expert's Perspective.)

Tests for Autism

In general, there are no particular tests that will diagnose autism; rather, a diagnosis of autism relies on expert clinical opinion. That said, there are a number of tests used to screen for the presence of autism. Each has its strengths and weaknesses. However, there are many dozens of relevant tests that can be used. The variety of approaches is simply too wide to be considered in depth here. Instead, we review a few of the most widely used tests, providing an instance of each major type of approach, including a clinical assessment tool (the Autism Diagnostic Observation Schedule or ADOS), a guided clinical interview (Autism Diagnostic Interview—Revised or ADI-R), a screening instrument (the Autism Quotient or AQ), and a behavioral assessment instrument (the Vineland Adaptive Behavior Scales-III or VABS-III). The reader should be aware that this list is by no means exhaustive.

Conditions for Testing

In every test discussed here, scores are dependent on the respondent having been assessed in ideal conditions. The respondent should be in a quiet environment, free from distractions. Obviously, noise, smells, intrusive visual stimuli such as computer displays and televisions; metabolic distractions such as sleepiness, hunger, or thirst; or other such distractions should be minimized. Individuals with autism often have hyper- or hypo-sensitivity to stimuli in one or more sensory modalities. Respondents should be able to be seated at a table, but should they wish to respond on another surface (e.g., clipboard on knees), this should be made possible. Additionally, the test administrator should be present in some way (for most instruments). This facilitates the respondents' asking of questions to enhance and ensure their understanding of the question(s). Autism is often associated with language issues, so clarification is often needed to obtain a meaningful response. Departures from these conditions will only reduce the reliability of the data obtained.

Evaluating Tests

Each of the tests to be described here, and the plethora of other instruments and approaches, has its problems. Some of the problems are inherent in the approach, and others are failings of the particular instrument.

Before addressing these tests, it is worth establishing what parameters a psychometric instrument requires. Generally, instruments must display stability of measurement, ensuring that what is measured is measured consistently. This is known as *reliability*, which is measured by indices such as Cronbach's alpha (α; Cronbach, 1951) or McDonald's omega (ω; Viladrich, Angulo-Brunet, & Doval, 2017). Both indices range from 0 to 1 if valid. Generally, values greater than 0.5 are required, and usually values greater than 0.7 are sought. When squared, these values show how stable the measure is thought to be. For example, a value of 0.7 when squared gives 0.49, indicating that about half of the variance in the measure is stable. There is also test-retest reliability, which shows whether an instrument gives similar results across a period of time. This is usually shown as a correlation between the measurements. If the scores were to vary considerably, there would be little confidence that the instrument was measuring what it is claimed to measure.

Being reliable is one thing, but it is quite another to show that an instrument measures what it claims to measure. This is one form of *validity*. To be valid, the instrument must first have reliability. There are several types of validity, only a few of which are discussed here. Among those is *construct validity* (Cronbach & Meehl, 1955). *Construct* means an idea or theory. Construct validity requires that the instrument measure what it says it does, and not something else. For example, the ADOS should measure autistic traits, and the obtained score should increase as the number of traits increases. Construct validity is usually assessed by correlation with some other established measure. Scores should range between –1 and 1, with the square of this value indicating the proportion of variance explained. Something that the unwary should be cautious of, which may appear to be construct validity, is *face validity*: where an instrument *appears* to measure what it purports to measure. This is no guarantee that the instrument is useful. Frequently, respondents may be enticed to respond to social characteristics of an instrument, and face validity is believed to make this more likely (Orne, 2009).

A second important form of validity is *criterion validity*, whereby the instrument can be shown to provide results similar to those from other measures of the underlying construct. For instance, the Wechsler Adult Intelligence Scale and the Stanford-Binet Intelligence Scale share criterion validity; they measure similar things. There are multiple other forms of validity, most of which are not pertinent to the current discussion. The interested reader is directed to textbooks on psychometric measurement for further information (e.g., Kaplan & Saccuzzo, 2010).

Other psychometric concepts are also important. An example is the sensitivity and the specificity of instruments, which arise from signal detection theory (Macmillan & Creelman, 2005). A sound psychometric instrument should discriminate that which it is designed to detect; this is known as *sensitivity*. Sensitivity reflects the true positive rate, which is measured as a proportion between 0 and 100%, with scores closer to 100% indicating sensitivity (Macmillan & Creelman, 2005). Similarly, instruments shouldn't capture cases that don't have the property being measured; that is, they should discriminate between those who do and those who don't have the trait. This is *specificity* (Macmillan & Creelman, 2005). Specificity is measured as a proportion and ranges from 0 to 1, with higher scores indicating greater specificity. Thus, the instrument should be sensitive, should be specific to this one condition, and to nothing else. Typically, sensitivity and specificity are presented on receiver operating curves (ROCs), with sensitivity shown on the vertical or *y* axis, and the inverse of specificity (the false alarm rate) shown on the horizontal or x axis (*see* Figure 9.1). ROCs are evaluated by area under the curve (AUC): the higher this is, the better the ROC sensitivity (Macmillan & Creelman, 2005). AUC of 1 represents perfect classification, and 0.5 indicates that the result is essentially random.

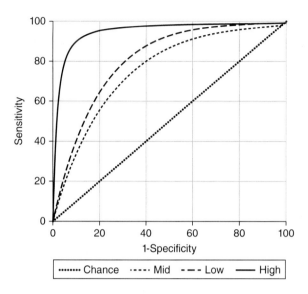

FIGURE 9.1 Schematic of receiver operating curves showing curves for sensitivity and false alarm (1-Specificity) at various levels: Chance, Low, Middle, and High values.

ADOS

The ADOS is generally well regarded and is one of the main instruments used to support a diagnosis of autism. There are in excess of 90,000 citations of this within the literature. It assesses social communication and restrictive and repetitive behaviors (RRB)—the two main autism diagnostic criteria. It has five modules used for different groups: toddlers (toddler module), minimally verbal (module 1), restricted verbal (module 2), verbally fluent youth (module 3), and adults (module 4). Each module assesses both diagnostic criteria. It is believed that the instrument is suitable for use in individuals with mild intellectual disability. Increasing scores are associated with increased presence of autistic traits. Items are scored on a 4-point scale and then summed. To prevent a few items dominating the scale, high scores (2s and 3s) within items are collapsed.

The instrument was developed through an extensive norming process, but these norms were developed with only 22 percent of cases identified as female, and with the mean intelligence scores below the median for the population (Gotham, Pickles, & Lord, 2009). Hence, there have been suggestions that the scale is less sensitive to more intelligent individuals and to females (Frigaux, Evrard, & Lighezzolo-Alnot, 2019).

Nonetheless, the instrument has been demonstrated to show high sensitivity and specificity for module 4 (ROC = 0.89 to 0.71), module 3 (ROC = 0.91 to 0.81), module 2 (ROC = 0.92 to 0.91), and module 1 (ROC = 0.69 to 0.98; Medda, Cholemkery, & Freitag, 2018). For minimally verbal young persons and for older individuals, the instrument has been found to be less discerning. Modules 3 and 4 have good reliability for the social communication domain, varying between α = 0.84 and 0.92, whereas the reliabilities for the RRB domain are lower (α = 0.66 and 0.64 for modules 3 and 4, respectively; Gotham, Risi, Pickles, & Lord, 2007; Hus & Lord, 2014). An item response analysis (Kuhfeld & Sturm, 2018) found that module 3 had high overall reliability (α = 0.91), although for social communication it was high (α = 0.87), and for RRB was only moderate (α = 0.64). These reliabilities cross the range of possible scores. The reliability for module 4 overall was high (α = 0.92) and very stable over the range of scores. For social communication the reliability was high (α = 0.87), but it was weaker for the RRB domain (α = 0.59). ADOS scores have been found to correlate well with other measures associated with the presence of autism, such as receptive and expressive language use (Mazurek, Baker-Ericzén, & Kanne, 2019), thereby displaying criterion validity. Overall, these and many other results indicate that the ADOS is a reliable, well-characterized instrument.

ADI-R

The ADI-R is a structured interview used to assess for the presence of autism or autism spectrum. There are more than 190,000 citations to it in the literature. It is a comprehensive interview-based instrument that covers more than 90 questions. These address RRB, social issues, and communication issues. An interviewer asks a respondent questions and codes the answers as the interview progresses. The respondent is usually a parent or caregiver, although older individuals may act as their own respondent. Respondents provide answers in their own words. The interview takes approximately 90 minutes to administer. Currently, there are a number of ways to score the ADI-R, only two of which are designed to diagnose autism. The interviewer codes a response to each question with a 7-point nonlinear response scheme, in which the last three codes (7, 8, 9) indicate an answer away from the specifics of the question, where the item was not applicable, or was not asked. Greater presence of a trait is indicated by a score of 2 or 3, milder responses are coded as 1, and where the behavior is absent it is coded as 0.

The ROC for data has been established with both specificity and sensitivity indices both exceeding 0.90 (Lord, Rutter, & Le Couteur, 1994). Others have confirmed these results (de Bildt et al., 2004), finding an AUC for the ADI-R of 0.82. Lord et al. (1994) established the reliability by assessing the degree of scoring equivalence between multiple raters observing the same videotaped interviews. Reliability was found to be greater than $\alpha = 0.73$ to $\alpha = 0.78$ for interviewers. The reliability of social items was found to be $\alpha = 0.95$, for communication-related items was $\alpha = 0.84$, and for RRB-related items was $\alpha = 0.69$. Criterion validity has been found to be good, with the ADI-R correlating moderately with the ADOS ($r = 0.52$). Overall, the ADI-R appears reliable, having good sensitivity and specificity and reasonable criterion validity.

AQ

The AQ is generally regarded as a screening instrument. More than 90,000 citations in the literature concern it. It has a number of versions, but there are two principal versions: a brief 10-item version and a fuller 50-item version. Both of these are available for adults, for adolescents, and for children. The adolescent and child versions are usually answered by a parent or caregiver. All versions are questionnaire-type tools. No scoring of the AQ results in a diagnosis of autism. At best, the tool is a screening instrument, where a score above a cut-off indicates that further assessment for autism is warranted.

The AQ-10 is scored by assigning 1 or 0 points to each of the items, depending on the response, and summing. Scores higher than 6 suggest the need for further assessment. There are a number of scoring approaches to the AQ-50. One system scores all items in the autistic direction as 1 and those not in this direction as 0, and then sums these, giving a maximum score of 50. Cut-off scores vary by country and test. For instance, Baron-Cohen and colleagues suggest using a value of 32 for adults (Baron-Cohen, Wheelwright, Skinner, Martin, & Clubley, 2001), while others have suggested alternative cut-off values in other countries (e.g., 29 in Australia; Broadbent, Galic, & Stokes, 2013). For adolescents, the usual cut-off is 30 (Auyeung, Baron-Cohen, Wheelwright, & Allison, 2008). The child version is scored on a 4-point Likert scale. Scores are summed and can range between 0 and 150, with 76 set as the cut-off.

Sensitivity and specificity for the AQ are excellent, with ROC area under the curve for adults being 0.87 (Lundqvist & Lindner, 2017) to 0.99 (Broadbent et al., 2013), reliability being α = 0.70 (Baron-Cohen et al., 2001) to α = 0.84 (Broadbent et al., 2013), and test-retest reliability being shown by a high correlation between the measures two weeks apart being r = 0.70 (Baron-Cohen et al., 2001) to r = 0.95 (Broadbent et al., 2013). An item responses analysis (Lundqvist & Lindner, 2017) suggests that the 50-item scale could be reduced to as few as 12 items without a loss of fidelity. These 12 items formed three unidimensional constructs. Adding more items rendered the test multidimensional. Overall, the AQ is a well-regarded screening instrument with a high degree of diagnostic separation.

VABS-III

The VABS-III is the third edition of the VABS. At present, there are in excess of 56,000 citations to this instrument in the literature. It is used to evaluate performance in several domains of adaptive behavior. It is not a diagnostic instrument per se. However, the particular profile of adaptive failures provides an indication as to whether a person would meet diagnostic criteria. In autism, this would be focused on social-communication dysfunction, as the instrument does not evaluate RRB.

The VABS-III may be administered to individuals of all ages, and it comes in three basic varieties, with variants in each. These are (1) an interview form for a trained professional to administer to parents or caregivers; (2) a parent/caregiver form for a parent or caregiver, or a respondent, to use; and (3) a teacher form for individuals aged 3 to 21 to establish details of a teacher's observations. There are comprehensive and domain-based versions, with five domains: Communication, Daily Living, Socialization, Motor Skills, and Maladaptive Behavior. The instrument results in standardized scores with a mean of 100 and a standard deviation of 15. Raw scores should not be interpreted; these scores must first be converted through a series of complex steps to obtain the standardized scores to account for age.

The VABS-III is a complex instrument to administer because it is designed to get around a number of problems associated with assessment. First, by relying on a semi-structured interview, the instrument avoids the problem of a respondent not cooperating or not understanding the importance of the evaluation, such that a sufficiently well-informed caregiver may respond on his/her behalf. The test has questions for various age bands. Questions are commenced at the appropriate age, with the score to that place being assumed.

The reliability of version 2 of the instrument varies slightly by age group. Results in the group 7 to 12 years old suggest a reliability of $\alpha = .97$ for adaptive behavior assessment, $\alpha = .92$ for communication, and $\alpha = .91$ for daily living (Sparrow, Cichetti, & Balla, 2005). In general, the VABS-III has been reported to have similar levels of reliability: overall reliability of $\alpha = .98$ for adaptive behavior assessment, $\alpha = .95$ for communication, $\alpha = .96$ for adaptive behavior, and $\alpha = .94$ for daily living (Janzen, Delaney, & Shapiro, 2017). Details of validity indicate that the VABS-II correlates between $r = .60$ and $r = .74$ with other measures of adaptive behavior (Sparrow et al., 2005), and the VABS-III is reported to also show moderate correlations ($r = .70$; Janzen et al., 2017). Test-retest reliability has also been found to be reasonable ($r = .73$ to $r = .90$). Issues of specificity and sensitivity are not pertinent in relation to the VABS-III; as detailed earlier, the instrument evaluates behavior, not a particular diagnosis.

Conclusion

The diagnostic criteria for an autism spectrum disorder describe a distinct pattern of abilities and behavior, but clinical experience and research confirm that there are many psychological adaptations to autism that lead to a wide variety of expressions and a vulnerability to having mental health issues. We also know that diagnosing autism is not an exact science; it is based on clinical judgment and the use of one or several standardized instruments. Although there are several well-regarded tests, there are many that are not so well regarded or well characterized. Attorneys should be aware that to be useful tests must show reliability, validity, sensitivity, and specificity—at the very least. It is also clear that the most reliable form of assessment is the opinion of the expert clinician. The criminal justice system must be made aware of the characteristics of autism, the process of achieving a diagnosis, and the means of accommodating those characteristics within that system.

● ● ●

Mark Stokes, PhD, is a registered psychologist. He has been involved in autism research since 1992 and obtained his PhD from La Trobe University in 1996. In 2002 he was appointed to Deakin University, where he developed research programs into autism, sexuality, and relationship development; the female profile of autism; mirror neurons in autism; and the transition to adulthood in autism. He has published more than ninety peer-reviewed publications, eight book chapters, and numerous reports to government; presented at more than 120 conferences; and supervised twenty-five doctoral and PhD completions. He is currently appointed as Associate Professor at Deakin University. He actively supports research into autism through his role as president of the Australasian Society for Autism Research. He has also been active in child injury prevention research and intervention as a board, life member, and former president of Kidsafe, Australia. Professor Stokes can be reached at mark.stokes@deakin.edu.au and his website is https://www.deakin.edu.au/about-deakin/people/mark-stokes.

Tony Attwood, PhD, is a clinical psychologist whose original qualifications were achieved in England, and who now lives in Queensland, Australia. He has specialized in autism spectrum disorders since 1975 and received a PhD from the University of London in 1984. He currently works in private practice and is Adjunct Professor at Griffith University Queensland. His book, *Asperger's Syndrome: A Guide for Parents and Professionals*, published in 1998, became the seminal book on Asperger's syndrome. His subsequent book, *The Complete Guide to Asperger's Syndrome*, published in 2006, has become the primary textbook on Asperger's syndrome. He is the senior consultant at the Minds and Hearts clinic in Brisbane, Australia. His current clinical interests are in developing screening tools and diagnostic procedures for autism and developing and evaluating cognitive behavior therapy programs for children and adults with Asperger's syndrome. He has contributed to more than thirty research publications on autism and is the author or joint author for ten books on autism. He has been invited to be keynote speaker at many international conferences on autism. Professor Attwood can be reached at tony@tonyattwood.com.au and his website is http://www.tonyattwood.com.au.

Complete citations are available from the authors upon request.

10

Risk of Violence for People with ASD

Nancy Kaser-Boyd

No judge wants to learn that a defendant to whom he/she has given a second chance has committed a violent crime. Thus, when designing a plan to keep a client with ASD out of prison, even if the creative criminal defense lawyer has provided for all the supports that client needs (such as housing, transportation, and medical care), the lawyer still must reassure the court that insofar as possible the client will not be a danger to the community. This is a particularly tall order given the myths and misunderstandings surrounding ASD. As this chapter by Dr. Nancy Kaser-Boyd shows, people with ASD are not more prone to violence than neurotypicals, and other factors contribute to violent behavior, such as exposure to violence, preoccupation with violent imagery, and chronic bullying. Although the media emphasize mass shootings and the like, when people with ASD do commit crimes of violence, those crimes are likely to be arson, stalking, and sexual assault.

• • •

Cameron (not his real name) is a handsome, twenty-five-year-old Caucasian man raised in an affluent section of a large city. He was diagnosed with autism spectrum disorder (ASD) in elementary school and received Special Education services through the end of high school. After graduation, he began studies at a community college. Feeling the stigma of being a Special Education student throughout elementary and high school, Cameron declined to identify as such at the community college, thereby depriving himself of the assistance or understanding he could have received. His parents had always been his strong advocates, but because he had turned eighteen, the community college did not permit them to make decisions for him. Cameron could present well to adults, due primarily to very good socialization by his doting parents. His disorder could therefore go unnoticed by teachers or professors who did not spend much time with him.

Cameron's problems began with his community college English professor. He was assigned to write a story about a character and that character's emotions. With his first attempt, the professor spent a few minutes giving him feedback and asked him to resubmit the assignment. He worked on this diligently and resubmitted it. The professor returned it with redlining on almost the entire assignment. Sadly, she did not know about Cameron's disability. Because the assignment was a large part of the final grade, Cameron failed the class. As a young person who had always been given a lot of support and encouragement from teachers and his parents, Cameron was devastated. He felt humiliated. He also felt angry. He stewed about this throughout Christmas vacation. As he was preparing to start the next quarter, his anger rose again. Cameron decided to compose a message to the professor to express his anger. At the end of the message, he impulsively added a veiled threat, indicating that he would be returning to campus for classes, and he would be armed. Cameron was therefore referred for an evaluation of his violence risk.

Autism spectrum disorder by itself does not predispose an individual toward violence, according to the largest, most comprehensive study to date examining the relationship between ASD and convictions for violent crime. In this population-based study, comprising more than 295,000 individuals followed between fifteen and twenty-seven years of age, individuals with ASD appear to be more prone to violent offenses (Heerman et al., 2017). However, much of the risk of violent offending in individuals with ASD is attributable to concurrent attention-deficit/hyperactivity disorder or conduct disorder, and individuals with ASD who do not have these concurrent disorders have a markedly lower risk of offending than individuals with ASD who have either of these concurrent disorders. Individuals with ASD who commit violent crimes tend to be male, have a concurrent psychotic disorder, have a concurrent substance-use disorder, have parental criminal and psychiatric history, do not have an intellectual disability, and/or come from poor socioeconomic backgrounds. Thus, ASD alone is unlikely to engender violence, and violence perpetrated by individuals with ASD is driven by extenuating factors that also influence violent criminal behavior in individuals without ASD. A significant number of those with ASD who become involved with the criminal justice system have a history of Adverse Childhood Events (ACEs) (Hoover & Kaufman, 2018). These include bullying, neighborhood violence, parental divorce, and income insufficiency (which delays diagnosis and initiation of treatment). One of the core issues for those with ASD is their difficulty in reading nonverbal social cues such as facial expressions, gestures, and voice inflection. These deficits can often result in misinterpretation of social situations. In addition, ASD individuals have a literal interpretation of language that makes it difficult to decipher sarcasm, joking around, and other socially nuanced speech. They often view the world in concrete terms and engage in black and white thinking. Social behavior is complex and often situation specific, which is beyond the scope of their awareness. These individuals have social anxiety that causes them great discomfort in social settings. They often react to stress with fight or flight behavior (Barney, 2004).

In addition to factors that influence violent criminal behavior more generally, specific social cognitive deficits inherent to ASD may influence violent criminal behavior, including limitations in theory of mind, emotion regulation, and moral reasoning. Individuals with ASD may demonstrate substantial impairments in theory of mind; that is, they may lack the ability to infer the thoughts, emotions, and behaviors of other individuals. Thus, defendants with ASD may have difficulty expressing empathy for others or remorse for how their actions may have caused harm to others. This lack of insight may be misperceived as callousness. Individuals with ASD also demonstrate difficulties with emotional regulation, the ability to appropriately modulate emotional responses and control emotional impulses. A defendant with ASD may show generally flattened emotional responses, which may appear overcontrolled, and heightened emotional reactions to certain challenges, which may appear threatening. Finally, individuals with ASD often demonstrate difficulties with moral reasoning, the ability to make logical inferences about the personal responsibility of individuals to behave morally. A defendant with ASD may therefore rigidly apply similar judgments about an individual's actions across different contexts without adequate consideration of mitigating factors, which may be misperceived as intentional errors in judgment. Predictably, social cognitive errors in ASD may have strong, negative consequences in certain contexts.

In considering factors that may provoke violent criminal behavior in individuals with ASD, it is also critical to look beyond the intrinsic social and cognitive deficits in ASD and consider the influences of situational context on aggression and violence.

Autism and Extreme Violence

There is no support in published research for a greater risk of extreme violence from individuals on the spectrum of autistic disorders, although the Sandy Hook mass killing of children by Adam Lanza, who was reported to have ASD (but had many other psychiatric disorders as well that may have contributed to his violent preoccupations and behavior), caused many to fear that those on the spectrum of autistic disorders, with impaired social communication and empathy, were at higher risk of committing interpersonal violence. To understand violence risk, particularly the risk of homicide, this chapter first reviews two research studies that focused on the descriptive features and warning signs of two groups of individuals who have killed others: mass murderers and school shooters. The research on autism and violence risk is then reviewed, ending with a checklist of points to consider in evaluating violence risk in individuals with ASD.

The Dynamics of Homicide

Both violence risk assessment and threat assessment focus on events that are relatively rare; they are "low-base-rate" events and thus difficult to predict. What follows is a summary of known background dynamics of different types of low-base-rate homicide. The empirical knowledge base on these types of extreme violence is less extensive than it is for high-base-rate phenomena, such as interpartner violence.

Mass Murder

Mass murder is defined as the killing of multiple people—usually at least four—in a rampage, in a short period of time. It is distinguished from serial murder, in which killings are carried out over a period of time and often have a sexual motive. The number of cases of mass murder seems high due to the quick reporting of such cases in the worldwide media. Statistics appear to clearly indicate that this phenomenon is much more frequent in the United States where access to guns is easy. Nevertheless, as in the case of Anders Breivik, the man who shot many individuals at a summer camp in Norway, such horrible events do occur in Europe as well, although some countries have few mass murders. A review of all mass murder cases (sample size of eighteen) that occurred in Europe during the period 2000–2009 (DeRuiter, 2011) found that Finland and Germany were overrepresented. Between 1976 and 2010, the United States experienced 645 mass murder events in which at least four victims were killed; this is about twenty U.S. cases per year. Because the number of cases is not large in an absolute sense, and a proportion of the perpetrators kill themselves (or are killed) after the attack, it is difficult to conduct formal research on this population.

A review of psychiatric, psychological, and criminological databases from the United States and Canada; reviewing scientific articles, books, videotapes, audiotapes, newspapers; and interviews with law enforcement officers, victims, and acquaintances of perpetrators (Hemple, Melov, & Richards, 1999) identified thirty mass murderers who had committed their crimes between 1949 and 1998. This is the only large-scale study of this type of crime and provides important demographic and clinical information about these perpetrators, although none were clearly identified as being within the diagnosis of autism spectrum disorders.

- All of the mass murderers were male and the majority was Caucasian. Their mean age was 38.3.
- Sixty-seven percent of the group were divorced or never married. Ninety-four percent could be described as "loners," defined as spending most of their time alone.
- Sixty-three percent were unemployed at the time of the murders. Half had been employed in blue-collar jobs, and 30 percent had professional occupations.
- Forty-seven percent had served in the military—an important variable because of their acquired familiarity with weapons.
- Fifty percent had a documented psychiatric history, defined as at least one psychiatric hospitalization or one visit with a mental health professional before the mass murder. Thirty percent had no psychiatric history. The most common Axis I diagnoses were paranoid schizophrenia, delusional disorder, and major depression. Forty percent evidenced psychotic symptoms at the time of the mass murder, usually paranoid and/or persecutory delusions. An additional 27 percent exhibited behavior suggestive of psychosis.

- Forty-three percent had a history of violence, defined as at least one violent act against a person or animal prior to the mass murder.
- On Axis II, Cluster A and B traits and disorders predominated. Fifty percent exhibited anti-social traits, 37 percent paranoid traits, 40 percent narcissistic traits, 17 percent schizoid traits, 10 percent depressive traits, and 7 percent schizotypal traits. Obviously, some individuals were categorized as having more than one of these personality traits.
- Alcohol was consumed by only 10 percent of the perpetrators prior to the killings; there was no information on their use of drugs.
- The most common precipitating event was job-related (50 percent) and involved termination, envy of another's promotion, confrontation by an employer, denial of a job reinstatement, bankruptcy, denial of tenure, and anger at employers for employment disability leave. The second most common precipitant was related to a close relationship (23 percent) and involved actual or perceived abandonment, jealousy, erotomanic beliefs, or child custody or support issues.
- Fifty-three percent committed suicide after the murders; 33 percent were captured; 10 percent were killed.

The authors report additional findings that are particularly important for threat assessment. Thirty-three percent of the murderers had previously made a specific threat against others. These were made either verbally or in writing and clearly described the future mass murder location, victims, and/or time. Twenty-three percent made a generalized threat, defined as lacking a specific location or victim pool. These included statements such as "I am going hunting" and "Society had their chance." Thirty-three percent made no threats before carrying out their acts.

Mass murderers had often been stockpiling weapons, ammunition, and battle gear. The authors write:

> The number of weapons brought to the mass murder ranged from one to 11, with a mean of 3.1. Weapons and other paraphernalia included semi-automatic pistols, semi-automatic rifles, revolvers, bolt-action rifles, hunting knives, a samurai sword, shotguns, nylon cord, shooting glasses, ear plugs, hand grenades, materials to manufacture homemade bombs, black talon bullets, machine guns, silencers, flammable liquids, karate throwing stars, gas masks, bullet-proof vests, binoculars, machetes, charcoal lighter fluid, rope, hatchets, and matches.

Also, the authors found that 63 percent of the men were preoccupied with weapons or war regalia, defined as spending a significant amount of time in matters centered on themes of war and violence. They write:

> Behaviors included ownership of a large number of weapons such as guns and knives; ownership of large numbers of audio, visual, and reading materials with war, terrorism, or weapons as the main theme; ownership and frequent wearing of military uniforms and combat fatigues; frequent trips to a gun range; practicing martial arts at inappropriate times and places; prophetically violent bumper stickers such as "You'll get my gun when you pry it from my cold, dead fingers"; excessive verbiage focusing on themes of weaponry and violence; evidence of grandiose fantasies centering on war and weaponry; infatuation with Nazi regalia; idealizing famous fictional and nonfictional violent characters; and setting up a gun range inside one's home.

The preoccupation with themes of violence and the collection of weapons and battle gear are important and observable features that can be used in threat assessment, as can the individual's interpersonal stance and world view. The authors note, "The interpersonal histories of mass murderers suggest a paranoid-schizoid position toward others and the world: a perception of others as persecutory and malevolent objects along with the absence of a desire, and perhaps a capacity, to form affectional bonds." These individuals, they note, have a particular tendency to externalize blame. The study authors state that this "predicts the accumulation and incubation of insults over time, magnified through the lens of hypervigilance, and washed in feelings of anger and resentment."

A second study (Fox & Levin, 2012) reviewed cases reported in printed media in the United States from a sociological perspective and had similar findings about mass murderers. Fox and Levin report that 95 percent of mass killings are committed by men. The mass murderers tended to be loners and to feel alienated from others. They often have histories of being rejected and feeling humiliated and worthless. Over time, they develop resentment, and they externalize their anger onto others—sometimes onto specific individuals such as co-workers, but sometimes in a more global way in the form of anger at "the world." They have impaired empathy for others and often feel contemptuous of others. They may be set off by an event that seems to them like a catastrophic failure. Their homicidal ideation involves fantasies of killing. They may stockpile ammunition and engage in planning and dress rehearsals. Often, they are in complete control of their emotions and know exactly what they want to do. They rarely hear voices, although they may have delusions. They are often nihilistic and don't expect to live after their rampage. They will shoot until shot down, or kill themselves as police are closing in. In the eyes of the perpetrator, the shooting may bring immortality and the rampage is his crowning achievement.

A lack of explicit threats of violence is common in workplace violence and in the targeted killing of political and celebrity victims. Researchers (Meloy et al., 2011) analyzed public records of 282 lethal workplace attacks and found that just 27 percent of the perpetrators had previously threatened violence. Researchers at the Secret Service (Vessekuil & Fein, 1995) who have studied mass shootings note, "The assumption of many writers is that those who make threats pose threats. While some threateners may pose threats, sometimes those who pose threats do not make threats." In their research on assassins of political figures, they found that fewer than one-tenth of the assassins and near-lethal attackers they studied had communicated a direct threat to the target or a law enforcement agency. Although there may be an absence of direct or implicit threats in targeted violence (Meloy, Hoffman, & Guldimann, 2012), researchers note that there are often behaviors that "warn" of increasing threat. They define *warning behaviors* as factors that constitute change and are evidence of increasing or accelerating risk. Emphasizing that their typology of warning behaviors is rationally derived and requires further empirical research, they include:

- Pathway warning behavior—behavior that involves research, planning, or preparation for an attack.
- Fixation warning behavior—behavior that indicates a pathological preoccupation with a person or a cause. This is often accompanied by social or occupational deterioration.
- Identification warning behavior—behavior that indicates a desire to be a "pseudo-commando," identify with previous attackers or assassins, or identify oneself as an agent to advance a particular cause or belief system.
- Novel aggression warning behavior—behavior that is new for the person but may be used to test the ability to commit a violent act.
- Energy burst warning behavior—an acceleration of goal-directed behavior involving the target.

- Leakage warning behavior—communication to a third party of an intent to commit harm to a target.
- Last resort warning behavior—increasing desperation or distress, feeling that there is no alternative other than the act, and that the consequences are justified.
- Directly communicated threat warning behavior—written or oral threat that implicitly or explicitly states a wish or intent to harm the target.

School Shooters

Well before targeted school shootings became an epidemic in the United States, the Secret Service began a study of school shooters (Vossekuil, Fein, Reddy, Borum, & Mordzeleski, 2002). Their study reviewed thirty-seven incidents of school shooting. Two or more reviewers reviewed data about (1) motives and plans, (2) mental state, (3) life circumstances, and (4) other relevant factors. The age range of the subjects was from eleven to twenty-one. No single profile or set of characteristics described all or even most of the attackers. Academic failure was not a regular part of the picture. Most (81 percent) acted alone. Many were described as loners or part of a fringe group that was disliked by mainstream students. Almost three-quarters had been bullied and felt persecuted and mistreated. Several were clearly identified by classmates as someone who was chronically teased or bullied. Eighty percent held some sort of grievance against someone. Sixty percent of the attacks appeared to be motivated by revenge. Additional but less common motives of attackers were trying to solve a problem (34 percent), suicide or desperation (27 percent), and attempts to get attention or recognition (24 percent). All but one of the attackers had experienced or perceived a major loss prior to the attack. These included a perceived sense of failure or loss of status, or a loss of a romantic relationship. Most of the attackers had a history of suicidal attempts or thoughts prior to the attack and had a documented history of serious depression. However, less than a third had received a mental health evaluation.

Although these youths were not available for the type of mental health triaging this chapter recommends, they gave indications of their high risk for violence that teachers or parents could have noticed. Most demonstrated a preoccupation with fantasy violence through movies, books, or video games. More than one-third wrote about violence in poems, essays, or journals. Many shared their violent fantasies with friends or on the internet. Many gave subtle or overt warnings of their impending acts that were ignored. In more than 80 percent of the cases, at least one person—typically a friend—knew that the student was thinking about or planning to attack others at school. Dylan Klebold and Eric Harris, the youths who carried out the Columbine High School shooting (one of the best-known and earliest cases of school shooting), had made threats for at least a year about shooting people and setting off bombs. They posted angry, threatening messages on the internet. One of them wrote in gruesome detail about torturing and killing a bully who had teased him. They made repeated references to committing acts of violence in videos and plays. In some of the cases reported in the Secret Service study, friends assisted the attacker in obtaining weapons or in some other ways. There was typically no direct threat to intended victims that would have initiated a *Tarasoff* warning.

The attacks were not impulsive and almost always were carefully planned events. In some cases, they had been planned for almost one year. Supporting the finding that school shooters were depressed and nihilistic, the researchers found that 13 percent of the attackers killed themselves. A study of the subset of school shooters who committed suicide after their attack found that, although the school shooters were younger, all four groups struggled with similar personal problems, including social marginalization, personal crises, or issues at home, school, or work.

Studies have suggested (*see* Bonanno & Levenson, 2014) that school shooters pass through five stages before the final violent act: (1) chronic strain, (2) uncontrolled strain, (3) acute strain, (4) planning the attack, and (5) the school shooting. The youth experiences an environment that is chronically stressful, as in repetitive bullying at school, and has chronic depression. He then experiences an acute event, such as failing a grade or losing a friend. The youth, already vulnerable, feels he has nothing else to lose and begins to plan the attack. Chronic strain appears to be a factor for school shooters; one should note that most school shooters felt bullied and threatened by others. The identification of chronic problems at home seems to be supported by the fact that some shooters kill their parents or other members of their family prior to the school shooting.

Synthesizing elements from the available literature, the following risk factors emerge:

- Exposure to violence, either in the home or the community.
- Preoccupation with violent imagery.

- Lack of success with the normal tasks of childhood/adolescence.
- Social rejection, especially chronic bullying.
- Poor social support.
- Psychological conditions such as intense anxiety, depression, and/or anger.
- Inability to express or resolve feelings in adaptive ways.
- Impulsivity.
- Lack of empathy.
- Externalized defenses.

Autism Spectrum Disorders and Violence

This chapter focuses on the risk of homicide, although the offenses linked to autism are more likely to be arson, stalking, or sexual assault, due to the fixations that are seen in ASD (Barry-Walsh & Mullen, 2004). It should be noted that they are more likely to be victims of violence than perpetrators. Individuals with ASD may have a greater risk of criminal behavior due to features of functioning that are unique to ASD. These are:

- An inability to understand the mental state of others, interpret social intentions, and understand social nuances. Persons with ASD have difficulty understanding the emotional impact of their actions on others.
- Poor emotional regulation. This can include impulsivity and difficulty controlling strong emotions or urges.
- Difficulty with moral reasoning. Moral reasoning requires a degree of abstract thinking, and those with ASD tend to be concrete in their reasoning.
- Intense restricted interests (i.e., fixation).

Researchers on violence risk (Meloy & Mohandie, 2001) note that a fixation on aggression and violence is a warning sign; "aggression immersion" is commonly observed among violent offenders who commit mass homicide.

Are individuals with ASD more likely to commit violence or extreme violence? One study (Im, 2016a) reviewed seventy-three mass shootings from published and online sources covering the years 1982 to 2015. I'm found strong evidence of ASD in 8 percent of the cases and some indication of ASD in 21 percent of the total sample, but he noted that the ASD individuals often had other risk factors such as physical or sexual abuse, making them different from the typical ASD individual. This is frequently noted by other researchers. Im (2016b) also explored the role of trauma as a contributor to violence in ASD. He describes the neurobiological deficits in ASD and the neurobiological effects of trauma as affecting the same areas, suggesting that this makes the individual with ASD particularly vulnerable to the effects of trauma and thereby increases the risk for violent behavior. The person with ASD who experiences trauma may experience a "network overload" in which already impaired prefrontal and cortical abilities to modulate limbic output are further compromised, resulting in violent behavior.

Bullying is an especially relevant experience in ASD. Children in Special Education or with developmental disorders (e.g., autism spectrum disorders) are more susceptible to bullying than their mainstream peers (Whitney, Smith, & Thompson, 1994). Through social media, bullying can carry over from the school environment and make the adolescent feel that the whole world knows of his/her humiliation. Bullying has been found to have long-term social, emotional, and psychological effects. Bullying is related to sleeplessness, difficulty concentrating on academic work, and even physical illness. Researchers (Penning, Bhagwanjee, & Govender, 2010) conducted a formal study on a sample of 486 students, employing a measure of bullying (the Olweus Bully/Victimization Scale (OBVS)) and the Trauma Symptom Inventory for Children (TSCC-A). They found that depression demonstrated the highest correlation with bullying, followed by posttraumatic stress disorder (PTSD). The relationship was affected by the frequency and severity of bullying. The authors likened repetitive trauma to other repetitive traumas (such as child abuse) that can result in complex PTSD. Interestingly, the anger scale had the lowest mean score for victims of bullying.

Violence Risk Assessment for Those with ASD

White, Meloy, Mohandie, and Kienlen (2017) outline areas to review in violence risk assessment for individuals with ASD. These include:

- Developmental history that includes problems relating to peers, early ritualized intense interests, and environmental stressors (e.g., child neglect or abuse, bullying).

- Social communication deficits.
- Marked naïveté.
- Problematic intense interests (e.g., fixation on weapons or violence).
- Poor tolerance for frustration.
- Stressors and provocative contexts (e.g., history of bullying, current loss/humiliation).
- Comorbid major mental disorders (e.g., mood disorders, paranoia, PTSD).
- Comorbid psychopathy.
- Pathway to violence planning (i.e., evidence of warning behaviors and preparatory actions).

As with any other individual being triaged for violence risk, the individual with ASD should be screened for recent stressors, grievances, suicidal/homicidal ideation, access to weapons or lethal materials, and evidence of planning. (*See also* Chap. 3, Criminal Responsibility.)

* * *

Nancy Kaser-Boyd, PhD, ABAP, is a Clinical Professor of Psychiatry and Biobehavioral Sciences at the David Geffen School of Medicine at UCLA, where she teaches Advanced Psychodiagnostic Assessment and Violence Risk Assessment, and is a consultant to the USC Gould School of Law on the effects of trauma and adolescent brain functioning. She serves as a forensic psychological consultant to the Superior Courts of Los Angeles County in child abuse and neglect, delinquency, and criminal cases, conducting forensic psychological evaluations and testifying as an expert witness. She is co-author of *Forensic Psychological Assessment in Practice* (Routledge, 2015) and numerous book chapters and articles. Dr. Kaser-Boyd can be reached at nkbforensics@gmail.com and her website is http://www.nancykaser-boyd.com.

Complete citations are available from the author upon request.

11

Creative Mitigation

Allison Jackson Mathis

The legal standard for competency is extremely low, whereas the standard for insanity is extremely high. Thus, the vast majority of cases involving defendants with ASD will be disposed of through plea bargains, and mitigation will be used. (Or, following a guilty verdict, mitigation may be used as well.) The two following chapters, the first by public defender Allison Mathis and the second by attorney Jessica Oppenheim and Dr. Jeffrey Allen, provide creative ways to craft a probation plan that accommodates the defendant with ASD while assuaging the court's likely concerns about recidivism and community safety.

In particular, Mathis's chapter provides suggestions about recognizing clients with ASD and dealing professionally yet compassionately with them. She also provides strategies for how a lawyer can advocate for a client when funds for an expert are limited or unavailable.

• • •

Mitigation, especially for people who are as misunderstood as people with autism spectrum disorders (ASD), can be daunting and frustrating—but it doesn't have to be. This chapter provides practitioners with a tool box of mitigation techniques to help demystify the process and "eff," so to speak, the ineffable.

One of the major issues lawyers who represent indigent clients face is lack of funding—whether you are a private practitioner begging the court to give you money for experts or a public defender working within the confines of limited office resources. If you are able to secure resources for a mitigation expert, wonderful; this chapter is not really for you. But if you, like many attorneys, are faced with having to develop mitigation on your own, read on.

There is certainly great value in sentencing mitigation practice, but this chapter focuses predominantly on what I call pretrial mitigation practice: that is, steps the lawyer should take during the pendency of a case. Indeed, many of the procedures outlined in this chapter will also be extremely beneficial in preparing for sentencing hearings.

When a client I'll call Dino and his mom came into my office for the first time, I did everything wrong. Dino was accused of a moderately serious assault against a convenience store owner, and he already had a significant juvenile record of which I was aware. The new offense was captured on video, and there were not really any legal issues to wrangle. This was his first adult offense. Sheepishly, his mother pushed him into my office nearly an hour late for our first appointment. "He was sleeping," she said, quietly. "I didn't want to wake him up." I looked over at the clock on my desk. It was 1:45 p.m.

I was irritated and showed it. I like my clients to take at least some interest in their own cases, and I disliked that his mother was so tentative that she "didn't want to wake him up" for an appointment in the mid-afternoon. "Sleeping? Isn't this case the most important thing in your life right now? More than that, aren't you supposed to be in school?" I asked. Silence. Dino didn't look up at me. His mom squirmed after a few seconds of me trying to make eye contact with him. "He . . . dropped out two years ago," she said. "Oh," I said, a little pointedly, "then do you have a job?" More silence. Dino drummed on the side of his chair with his fingers and looked out the window. "No, he's . . . not working right now." "Oh? What do you do? What do you want to do?" Silence. More drumming.

"Hmmm . . ." I said, "Well, this isn't great. What are we going to tell the prosecutor and the judge? What are we going to tell them about you that makes them not want to send you to jail?" Silence. More drumming.

At no point in the conversation did Dino or his mother tell me that he had been diagnosed with ASD. What I was reading as "bored, disrespectful, flippant teenager" was actually ASD. I only found out after I watched him struggle to write his name on a form, and it finally dawned on me to ask if he had been diagnosed with any learning disabilities in school. His mother, unsure of the right terms, told me that he had and managed to show up to our next meeting with a handful of paperwork from the high school's diagnostician showing an ASD diagnosis from several years ago.

It seemed odd to me that a mother wouldn't know what the diagnosis was or that it was important to discuss it with an attorney representing her child in a criminal case, but in the years of practice I've had since then, I've realized that this is actually extremely common. Furthermore, many times clients who have struggled with poverty and an overburdened school system have never been diagnosed at all.

It may sound obvious, but the first step in being able to provide quality mitigation for clients with ASD is to identify that they have ASD. I think this is worth asking when we do an initial intake meeting with any client. The diagnosis of autism spectrum disorders has increased significantly in the past several years, and the Centers for Disease Control is now estimating that by the age of eight about one in fifty-nine children has been diagnosed with ASD.[1] There are many reasons to believe that the percentage of criminal defendants with ASD is even higher than the national average, considering, for example, the difficulties some people with ASD have in speaking with police officers and the misinterpretation of socially awkward "stimming" behaviors. (*See* Chap. 14, Vulnerabilities of Defendants with ASD and Strategies for Improving Outcomes.)

PRACTICE TIP: Be careful when communicating with clients who have suspected ASD. A common symptom of ASD-related disorders is *echolalia*, in which the person repeats a word or phrase even if he doesn't understand it. This can lead an attorney to believe that the client is actively listening when in fact he is merely repeating what the attorney just said.

A friend of mine who teaches Special Education classes recounted that one of her students, a teenage boy with ASD, compulsively masturbated as a method of coping with stress. It was a benchmark of her career when she was able to help him stop, but as a lawyer, when she was telling me the story, all I could think about were the myriad legal issues and misunderstandings that might come with compulsive masturbation. Fortunately, my friend's student had a teacher who cared about him, in a school district that fully funded Special Education, and engaged parents who were

---

[1] This number varies significantly based on location, with an increase in diagnosis in places where school systems are better funded, it seems. *See* Jon Baio et al., *Prevalence of Autism Spectrum Disorder Among Children Aged 8 Years—Autism and Developmental Disabilities Monitoring Network, 11 Sites, United States, 2014,* MMWR Surveillance Summary 67 (No. SS-6), 1–23 (2018). DOI: http://dx.doi.org/10.15585/mmwr.ss6706a1.

willing to do anything to help their son. Many of my clients do not have such advantages.

We can also assume that, in addition to our younger clients who are lacking diagnoses because their school systems failed them, our adult clients did not benefit from the surge in ASD awareness and improved diagnostic techniques that has taken place over the past several years, and that a significant percentage of them remain undiagnosed. This is why it is so vital that we be able to identify some of the signs of ASD in our clients, even if they don't disclose a diagnosis to us. (*See* Chap. 5, Adults with ASD.)

In Dino's case, during the introductory meeting I was provided with more than enough information to initiate further investigation of possible ASD. I should have identified that he was failing to make normal eye contact with me, and that he struggled with school, as evidenced by the fact that he had dropped out, that he was sleeping in the middle of the day (often autism is comorbid with sleep disorders), and that he was exhibiting stimming behavior by repetitively drumming on the chair. Of course, all of this could have been nothing more than a disengaged teen, but the point that we should all take away with us is that ASD is often disguised in these ways, and we need to be paying attention.

If your client or his/her family does report a diagnosis to you, the next step is to get the records from the diagnostician, whether that be from the school, a doctor, or both. If you don't have a diagnosis but have reason to suspect ASD, you need to start requesting school records and doing whatever your jurisdiction requires to get an evaluation by an expert. Part of a diagnostician's evaluation should include review of whatever school records are available, so your obtaining those records will be beneficial in getting a quicker result.

PRACTICE TIP: If your jurisdiction is one in which you must move the court for expert funds, file the motion to request expert funds *ex parte* and under seal. Include with the motion an affidavit stating all the reasons you believe that your client may have ASD and that an evaluation is material to your ability to provide mitigating facts (and possibly even to mount a defense, depending on your fact pattern). If you are able to provide educational or medical records showing suspected ASD, include those as an exhibit. If the motion is denied, specifically request that the court seal the records and send them along with the file for potential appellate review.

After the preliminary diagnostic steps, what next? What if you can't get the funds for an evaluation? What if you get an evaluation and the diagnostician says that the client does not have ASD? I think the answer in such situations is that you can and should move forward with gathering mitigation evidence in a way substantially similar to the way we would proceed if your client did have a diagnosis of ASD. We have to remember that ASD is, at heart, a spectrum disorder, meaning that people at the far ends of the spectrum may evade diagnosis but still suffer. Furthermore, even if the client does not have ASD but still has a considerable number of the symptoms that you are recognizing such as social discomfort, anxiety, or learning disabilities, this method of collecting mitigation material will be helpful.

The first thing I do in any mitigation case is task the client and his/her family with assisting me. As attorneys, the court process is familiar to us, but it is not to our clients. Anxiety comes from a lack of control over the situation, and the criminal process is designed to remove as much control from the individual charged as possible. Most of my clients have a poor understanding of the legal system in general, and they are forced to trust me to be their interpreter and guide for some of the most important decisions they will ever make. Giving assignments to our clients and their families gives them a sense that they have some level of control over and input into the outcome of their case, and in my experience they have been glad to be able to play a role in their own defense.

This could even start when you are trying to request educational and medical records. It is generally much easier for an individual or his/her guardian to obtain copies of records rather than for the lawyer to have to go through the tedious and often frustrating exercise of getting records on behalf of someone else. The exception to this is if you happen to have incredible support staff who are excellent at getting records and are more efficient at the process than your client would be. I have worked in four different indigent defense offices in four different jurisdictions in addition to private practice, and I have found exactly one investigator who was superlative at gathering records. (Incidentally, she is not an investigator anymore. If you have any of these people in your life, never let them go.)

The focus in mitigation should be on developing a picture of the client as a person outside of a criminal offense. Initially, we want to provide the prosecution with a thick packet of important-looking papers that will justify them giving your client a good deal, both because the content is so powerful and because it is thick enough to look substantial when said prosecutors are explaining to their supervisors why they dismissed or pled down the case. This has the additional effect of suggesting to the prosecutor that you are the kind of attorney who is going to work your cases a lot, and that you have more time to draft things than the invariably overworked prosecutor. The truth of the matter may be that you are also terribly overworked, but by using templates it is not horribly time-consuming to put together a mitigation packet that looks polished and impressive. At the end of this chapter I have provided several templates for use in your own cases. Please make them your own and use them freely.

I like to have a specific mitigation meeting with my clients. When I meet them at the beginning of representation, I tell them that we are going to be talking about mitigation. I briefly explain what mitigation is and ask them to start thinking about things that will help us tell their story. I generally give them a copy of the handout (Appendix A to this chapter) and tell them that these are some things I want them to start thinking about before our next meeting.

PRACTICE TIP: With clients who have ASD, it's important to ask how comfortable they feel with different types of communication. Some people with ASD are gifted writers; others can write well on a keyboard but would be stymied trying to hand-write something; and some feel very uncomfortable with written expression at all. You also need to know how they best retain information. For one client, I convinced my office to pay for a cheap audio recorder that allowed me to record instructions that my client could play back later (I wouldn't put anything privileged on these recordings, but did record basic instructions such as what is in the handouts at the end of this chapter). Many of my clients like having written handouts to remind themselves of what I want from them or to ensure that their families understand what it is I'm asking for.

At the mitigation meeting itself, I ask the client to talk to me about his/her life. I might say to a client: "OK, so let's talk about you. Tell me what it was like for you growing up: Who did you live with? Where did you go to school?"

A neurotypical client would likely understand that I was asking for a narrative answer. "Oh, I had a pretty normal childhood," the client might say, "I lived with my grandparents because my mom was very young when she got pregnant and still lived at home. She's more like my sister than my mom. But yeah, we lived in Oakland for most of my childhood, and then we moved to Dallas when I was fourteen. I went to high school there."

A client with ASD might answer the questions I asked like this: "My grandparents. Oakland Elementary School. Dallas High School."

Clients with ASD are often very forthright, but it can be difficult to get them to elaborate without prodding. Neurotypical people are often able to catch on to social cues that encourage them to continue talking, but people with ASD have trouble picking up on that kind of nuance. Be careful not to confuse the ASD client's direct answers with a disinclination to continue talking.

The goal of the meeting is to gather the information you think you need to tell this person's story from your perspective. When the client is someone with ASD, you may feel like this is akin to pulling teeth, but the key is to continue asking singular, direct questions and not to overwhelm clients by peppering them with too many questions at once. It should be as casual a conversation as you can muster while still gathering information. It is OK to give the client examples you feel comfortable sharing from your own life that might serve to illustrate what kind of answers you are looking for. "I went to school in Houston at Memorial High School, but I didn't like it much. My favorite teacher was my debate coach because he was funny and smart and cool, but I always hated math and was bad at it."

If you notice the client doing any kind of stimming or repetitive coping behavior, ask if he/she would like a break for a few minutes or decide if you've gathered enough information to end the meeting.

I like to have these meetings without family members present, but then I pull the family in at the end to ask them to help with writing letters of support. (Examples appear in Appendix B of this chapter).

Letters of support will add bulk to your mitigation packet. I explain to the family members what I am asking them to do. I task them with enlisting other friends, family, and community members with writing letters as well, and I ask them to return the letters to me. I specify that I will be reading the letters before I submit them to the prosecutor, and if there are any that I think are unhelpful, I will not include them, so these letters can only help.

I also emphasize when I need the letters back and call this a *firm* deadline. I need to review the letters and put them together in the mitigation packet, and to avoid wasted court appearances, I want to get it to the prosecutors in time for them to review it prior to court. I usually set the deadline a week before I actually have to have the letters. I have found that two weeks is a good amount of time to give people to get the letters done: it is not so long that they forget about it or put it off, but it still allows some time for thoughtful reflection.

The first page of the support letter handout is basic instructions, including what I am asking them to do, the charges my client is facing, and how to return the completed letters to me. Initially, I didn't mention anything about the pending charges in the template, but I quickly realized that I need the prosecutor to know that the person writing the letter is aware of the charges. If the person writing the letter is not aware of the charges, the prosecutor might think either that the writer is not very well acquainted with the accused or that his/her opinion of the accused might be different if he/she knew about a pending criminal case.

If the person writing the letter argues that the charges are untrue, what we are doing is no longer mitigation. Many people think they are helping their loved one by saying the charges couldn't possibly be true. You (as the lawyer) and the prosecutor both know the case better than most of the family members who will write support letters. You know what the evidence is and whether or not the charge is defensible. If you are at the point where you are ready to mitigate, it will not do your client any good to have family members say that they "know" the client is innocent when the client has pled guilty. It will just look like the family is willing to say anything to defend the client.

The second page is a sample of what the letter should look like. I generally modify the sample letter to be similar to what I am expecting the client's family members to write, but not exactly the same. When I have modified the sample letter to be too similar to the facts of my client's case, some family members end up adopting too much of the sample and not using their own words. This is especially a problem if you practice in a smaller jurisdiction. You don't want your mitigation packets to lose their effectiveness because all of your support letters for all of your clients sound the same.

PRACTICE TIP: You almost certainly have much more reliable access to a printer than your clients do. Whenever possible, give clients a hard copy of handouts, templates, and the like. I generally give clients/family members five copies of the support letter template handout so they can enlist more family members to fill it out without having to photocopy or print it out on their own. If the client's family member is unable to come to your office, send that person an email copy and a postal mail copy. I also include a self-addressed stamped envelope so the client can return the letter when I send the template via postal mail.

I tell my clients and their families that I am looking for quality over quantity, and if we can get three to five well-written letters, I will be thrilled. I also emphasize that we are still at the beginning of this process, and that they should not request letters from anyone that they don't want to know about the charges. Although it is good to have letters from family members, everyone knows that your mom loves you. Letters from other people—teachers, employers, church members, counselors, or family friends—are very meaningful.

Many of these things may sound intuitive to you, but they are not. The quality of support letters I have received has increased drastically since I started handing out simple, straightforward instructions and samples like this. A bonus is that this gives family members something to do other than call you every twenty minutes.

Once you get the support letters, review them for anything glaring that you do not want included. I request that support letters be typed whenever possible, but most of them are handwritten. That's fine, except when I get three letters that are all in the same handwriting and sound alike. What's worse than no letters of support? Letters of support that are obviously forged. I've also had letters that supply information that contradicts other letters. In those cases, use your discretion to determine whether the contradiction is something that is important. (Did they just misstate something? Is it something that reasonable people could disagree on? Is it fairly material, making it sound like the letter writer doesn't actually know the client?) Does the rest of the letter make up for the mistake (it tells a great story about the client, for example).

PRACTICE TIP: You can follow a substantially similar procedure to move for a bail reduction. In those cases, change the support letter template to have the letter writer specifically *not* mention the offense, but *do* specifically mention the impact it would have on the family if the client had to stay in jail pending trial. The letters can then be filed along with the motion for bail review.

If your client has an ASD diagnosis, the mitigation packet should include information about that diagnosis. This should include evaluations from the school and the diagnostician. If you can't find documents that show any kind of evaluative process, but only show the literal diagnosis, try to obtain another evaluation.

If you are unable to get another evaluation, include whatever documentation of the diagnosis you can, as well as printouts of information about ASD. These printouts do not have to be serious medical literature—and most of the time should not be. They should be from reasonably reliable lay medical resources or publications (the Mayo Clinic, National Institute of Mental Health, and even WebMD are some examples of such resources). You don't want the prosecutor to have to pretend to be a doctor, and you don't want the prosecution to think you are pretending to be a doctor by giving them a ream of convoluted medical journal articles. The information should be well-established and common sense.

The purpose of this is to show the prosecutor that the client's ASD diagnosis is *related* to the offense in some way. Go through and highlight specific parts of the literature or the evaluation that you want the prosecutor to notice.

In Dino's assault case, for example, we might have highlighted sections of literature that talk about inflexible adherence to routines or rituals. Every day after school, Dino went to the same convenience store and purchased a bottle of soda. On the day of the assault, the soda was out of stock. This had never happened before, and Dino's routine was interrupted in a way that he did not know how to handle. He got frustrated and angry, didn't know how to communicate his emotions in a productive way, and assaulted the clerk in a split-second moment of pique. This is not the same as a neurotypical teenager who planned out the assault, or did it to bully or harass the clerk.

Once you have the support letters and the evaluation or literature in hand, your work begins. The front page of the mitigation packet should be a formal memorandum-style letter from you to the prosecutor. Even if you know the prosecutor very well, the letter should be formal enough to sound like you've never met this person before.

Your cover letter should include the facts of the offense presented in a candid way that doesn't make it sound like you are skewing it too much in favor of your client. The purpose of this is to orient the prosecutor, who likely hasn't even had a chance to review the case file yet, and orient him/her to your version of events. If you include slanted language that appears biased toward your client, it is going to make the prosecutor look through the offense report with a fine-toothed comb, trying to bust you in a lie or misrepresentation. If the prosecutor reads through your version of the facts and says, "Yeah, that sounds about right, I don't need to spend a bunch of time agonizing over the offense report," that's most likely a great thing for you and your client.

After you address the facts of the offense, you will turn to mitigating circumstances. You might address the client's childhood, lack of education, struggles in school, failure by the system to diagnose, failure by Special Education to help the client adequately prepare for life on his/her own, and any other abuses or harms he/she has suffered that you think reasonably relate to the offense. What you want to avoid here is making it sound like you are throwing everything but the kitchen sink into your mitigation letter in an effort to play on the prosecutor's emotions. You want the prosecutor to realize that any of your client's history that you include in the letter is there because it is relevant as something that explains the client's actions rather than a tawdry attempt to tug at the prosecutor's heartstrings. The history may in fact tug at the prosecutor's heartstrings, but you don't want him/her to think you're intentionally making an emotional play.

Although the letter is formal, I generally include my personal reflections on the client as well. "When Dino first came into my office, I thought he was just like a lot of other young, male defendants. He seemed unconcerned about his case and wouldn't meet my eyes. After I learned that he had been diagnosed at the age of nine with autism, it became clear that I was totally wrong—that those were symptoms of his disorder and not reflective of his feelings at all. Dino is a really interesting, multifaceted young man, and he has a passion for horses. He can tell you every horse that has ever won the Kentucky Derby and will be glad to chat with you all day about proper care for animals."

Another thing that is different about mitigation is that you are admitting that your client did something wrong. Because of this, you need to include something for the prosecutor to rest his/her hat on that this will not happen again. Sometimes that is a rather shallow couple of sentences, but I think it makes the packet complete. Is your client going to Alcoholics Anonymous now? Has she started taking/changed medication? Is he seeking counseling or life skills classes? Many of these are resources you can encourage your client to take advantage of prior to handing over your letter. Remember, you want everything in the letter to be unimpeachably *true*.

If there are any legal issues I don't mind disclosing to the prosecutor ahead of time, I also include those in the mitigation letter. My rule of thumb is that if the issue is something the prosecutor can't fix, I don't mind disclosing it, but if it's something the prosecutor can fix if given notice, I let it be a nasty little surprise if we go to trial. Your calculation in any individual case may be different, so trust your judgment here. However, I have had good success with including some personal mitigation and then suggesting to the prosecutor that I have a pretty good suppression issue (or the like) and citing some case law.

Finally, I end the mitigation letter with a "requested disposition." I ask the prosecutor to consider dismissing my client's case or making the offer I want. If I am going to ask for anything other than a dismissal, I do not give the prosecution a mitigation letter until they have given me an offer. I am still a firm believer that the first rule of negotiation is not to talk first.

I hope these templates serve you well in your practice. One of the things I believe most strongly as a criminal defense attorney is that our clients deserve to have their stories told. We can all identify with the pressures of overwork and compassion fatigue, but we are duty-bound to do what we can where we can, and mitigation falls into that bucket. Clients with ASD and other social and communication disorders especially need our advocacy in a system that will judge them harshly and incorrectly without our intervention.

Agenda for Client Mitigation Meeting

LAW OFFICES OF DREADFUL AND NIGHTSHADE

P.Q. Dreadful, Esq.

1313 Mockingbird Lane, Ste. 42

La Conner, WA 98257

(360) 555-5555

pqd@dreadfulnightshade.com

Things I would like you to think about before our next appointment on FRIDAY, June 11, 2020, at 4:00 p.m.:

> When were you diagnosed with ASD? Do you remember it? How did you feel about it?
>
> How has having ASD affected your life?
>
> What things do you think you're really good at?
>
> What things are you really interested in?
>
> What are some things you have accomplished that you are proud of? Or that your mom/dad/family is proud of?
>
> What do you want your life to be like in five years? Ten years?
>
> What things have changed since you were arrested/charged with this offense?

Mitigation Letter
to Prosecutor

LAW OFFICES OF DREADFUL AND NIGHTSHADE
P.Q. Dreadful, Esq.
1313 Mockingbird Lane, Ste. 42
La Conner, WA 98257
(360) 555-5555
pqd@dreadfulnightshade.com

To: Firstname Lastname, Prosecutor
From: Penny Q. Dreadful
Re: Sylvester Serpentine, Case No. 12345
March 02, 2020

Dear Ms. Lastname,

I write you this letter as an offer of proof in mitigation for my client's case. Please understand that I consider this letter to be in furtherance of plea negotiations and therefore inadmissible should this case proceed to trial on the merits.

FACTS OF THE CASE:
[Plain-language brief description of the events that led up to your client's arrest. Include all pertinent information, such as names of officers involved, dates, and anything that happened that indicated or should have tipped off police officers that your client has ASD or a mental health issue. This description should be forthright and should present things in a factual, inarguable way.]

MEDICAL AND SOCIAL HISTORY:
[Information you think is pertinent about the client's family history, medical diagnosis, educational history, etc., and how it relates to the client's actions during the incident, or how it relates to appropriate disposition of the case. Information about a client's

medication, such as being noncompliant during the offense and being compliant currently, or a medication change, should also go here, as well as information about current therapeutic treatment.]

FAMILY HISTORY AND SUPPORT SYSTEM:
[Information about the client's family, including who wrote letters of support, what they are willing to do to help the client avoid conflict with the law in the future, where the client will live, etc.]

OTHER MITIGATING CIRCUMSTANCES:
[Anything else you think is important to let the prosecutor know about the client's situation.]

REQUESTED DISPOSITION:
In light of the foregoing information, I am respectfully asking you to consider (counteroffer/request for dismissal) of my client's case. Please do not hesitate to contact me if you have any questions or concerns.

Yours,

P.Q. Dreadful, Esq.
Partner
Law Offices of Dreadful and Nightshade

● ● ●

Allison Jackson Mathis, Esq. is an assistant public defender in Harris County, Texas, where she lives with her husband, Mike, and her daughter, Julia, who is named after Julius Caesar. She was previously a Tribal Advocate for the Swinomish Indian Tribal Community in LaConner, Washington; a public defender in Aztec, New Mexico, where she lived in a yurt; and the chief public defender of the Republic of Palau. She writes a regular column for the American Bar Association's *Criminal Justice Magazine* titled "Ask Allison." Before she became a lawyer, she was a superlative late-night diner waitress. You can reach her at tallisonmathis@gmail.com.

12

Mitigation Using Community Resources

Jessica S. Oppenheim and Jeffrey Allen

The ABA Mental Health Standards of 2016 provide that "attorneys should be familiar with local providers and programs that offer mental health and related services to which clients might be referred in lieu of incarceration, in the interest of reducing the likelihood of further involvement with the criminal justice system" (Standard 7-1.4, Roles of the attorney representing a defendant with a mental disorder). This chapter, by Jessica Oppenheim of The Criminal Justice Advocacy Program of The Arc of New Jersey and Dr. Jeffrey Allen, illustrates the importance of being knowledgeable about and accessing community resources, among other issues. As the authors point out, knowing what kind of resources your client with ASD needs can only be gained by a thorough understanding of your client: his/her history, tendencies, vulnerabilities, and current supports (or lack thereof) within the community. Only then can a criminal defense lawyer present to the court a proposal that will provide the defendant the resources he/she needs, prevent him/her from re-offending, and keep the community safe. Much of the information provided by these authors is helpful when designing a plan for people with ASD who are convicted of sexually oriented offenses.

● ● ●

The Criminal Justice Advocacy Program of The Arc of New Jersey is unique. Its website (https://www.arcnj.org/programs/criminal-justice-advocacy-program/) provides a host of sample motions and other helpful materials. If criminal defense lawyers are not familiar with the criminal justice resources for those with intellectual and developmental disabilities in their own area, they might begin by contacting their local or state Arc.

Identification

Although we do not know specific numbers of offenders with developmental disabilities involved in the criminal justice system, we do know that the most commonly presented statistics state that at least two in ten prisoners and three in ten jail inmates report having a cognitive disability (*Disabilities Among Prison and Jail Inmates, 2011-12*, Department of Justice, Bureau of Justice Statistics (Dec. 14, 2015), NCJ 249151). Thus, statistically, there is a good chance that a client may have a developmental disability, and in particular, be on the autism spectrum.

Defense attorneys are trained to seek the least restrictive resolution of a criminal matter. This includes pretrial motions related to the waiver of rights and suppression of statements based on the individual's cognitive limitations; competency to stand trial; sanity at the time of the act; any accommodations needed during trial; and finally, alternatives to incarceration that would limit a client's exposure to jail or prison. As we'll discuss in detail in this chapter, a defense attorney should educate himself/herself about a client's specific diagnoses, as well as about resources and options available in that jurisdiction. It is also invaluable to develop relationships with agencies, clinicians, evaluators, and programs that provide services, and then use this knowledge to develop a plan outlining needs and services. Developing subject matter expertise on both the characteristics of autism spectrum disorder (ASD) that might affect your client and also the services available in your community is the key to effective planning. An effective plan can hold clients accountable for their actions while at the same time addressing the needs of the individual client, thus reducing recidivism, increasing public safety in the long term, and benefiting the client.

In New Jersey, with the assistance of the New Jersey Division of Developmental Disabilities and support of The Arc of New Jersey, we have been able to develop a unique program to assist attorneys. The Criminal Justice Advocacy Program, created in the mid-1980s, provides case management and alternatives to incarceration for people with developmental disabilities in the criminal justice system. At a statewide level, case managers can identify services, assist clients with eligibility issues, create a written plan, and support clients through probation or parole periods. Without this kind of independent program, defense attorneys themselves will need to take on the role of planning in order to create alternatives to incarceration.

Defense attorneys may shy away from what seems to be "social work" activities, believing that the job of counsel is to handle the criminal matter before them and obtain the most advantageous outcome possible for the client. In fact, planning is an invaluable part of presenting a defense. By taking the time to educate prosecutors and the court about the client's cognitive differences and humanizing the client and his/her cognitive disability, you open the door to understanding why a plan with support services can be effective. In addition, taking every opportunity to educate yourself about what effective evaluations of cognition can provide, what supported services actually exist in the community and how to access them allows you to control the narrative and have a direct impact on crafting an appropriate outcome. Providing good planning to the court identifies ways in which a client's risk can be reduced and recidivism can be lowered; in turn, prosecutors and courts, as well as victims of this defendant, can feel more comfortable reducing charges and limiting prison exposure.

The first obstacle can be identification. For the most part, the profile of offenders with ASD looks similar to the profile of offenders with no disability: young men from economically disadvantaged backgrounds with poor academic and employment histories. You may see school records and prior evaluations that cite a wide range of diagnoses, such as personality disorders and mental health issues, that fail to accurately assess the client's ability to understand the world around him/her. These kinds of diagnoses reinforce an idea that this individual is simply oppositional or difficult and thus not a good candidate for traditional alternative dispositions. Consequently, without education and training, lawyers often fail to realize that such a client is unable to process the information being given to him/her and is unable to effectively communicate with teachers, other students, community members, or counsel. In light of that cognitive difference, other paths may have to be taken (*see* Chap. 11, Creative Mitigation).

Many people with ASD are arrested and processed without identification; have never been diagnosed at any point in their lives; are misdiagnosed by professionals with no expertise in working with people with developmental disabilities; are not part of the service system; go unnoticed by counsel, prosecutors, and the court; may have a co-occurring diagnosis that complicates identification; and may present in a way that leads an uninitiated professional to think that this person has a mental illness rather than ASD. Moreover, offenders with ASD, like offenders who have no developmental disability, may enter the system for many different reasons: there may be an addiction or self-medication; there may be sexual issues that result in sex offending; there may be a lack of socialization so that offenders with ASD spend time with people too young for them, or with people who engage in criminal behavior. This only further obfuscates the disability, making it harder to identify.

If you are working with a client and have reason to believe that this is a person who has a disability, you will need to document proof of the disability. Learning the system of service provision in your state is the first step to locating proof of a disability. Knowing the language used in your state before you talk to your client will assist you in knowing whether he/she is receiving or has received services. Individuals who are receiving Special Education services in school will be familiar with a child study team and an Individualized Education Plan (IEP). You may, for example, ask whether they were in Special Education class, or in a classroom that was separate from other students; the answer will tell you that you want to contact the school district for the client's records. This is only one possibility. School records may have been destroyed by the district if their records retention policy permits or if they simply fail to follow a records retention policy. Families may have retained these records, but many do not. Many clients who become involved in the criminal justice system lack a supportive family circle and are essentially on their own, so record retention of any kind is poor.

The next step is to know the names of the state agencies that provide services to people with disabilities. Familiarize yourself with the specifics of your state's table of organization; try to identify professionals and staff who can assist you and understand what population each of the agencies serves. Often, knowing which "door" to walk through to access records is an important aspect of this process.[1]

---

[1] For example, in New Jersey, individuals with ASD are served by the Department of Children and Families, Children's System of Care until they reach age twenty-one. After age twenty-one, services are provided through the Department of Human Services, Division of Developmental Disabilities. Knowing the agencies and the population each serves will speed up the processes of locating records and identifying services, as discussed later in this chapter.

Once you know the agencies, improve your familiarity with the language used by the social service system in your state and locality. Understanding the specialized language, acronyms, and phrases that agencies use will improve your ability to communicate with staff from those agencies and speed up the process. Often, being able to ask clients if they have a case manager or support coordinator can open up information about who they have received services from in the past. This will provide a path for contacting the state agency, community providers, and direct support providers who will have access to institutional records.

Consider federal agencies as well, such as the Social Security Administration regional office for your area, which will have records if your client receives SSI and Medicaid. If your client has a prior juvenile or criminal record, then your juvenile justice agency, county jail, or state prison will have records that might include information about disabilities or mental health issues. Any and all doctors that the client can remember can be contacted for records. Medical records may reveal difficulties in understanding, possible older or prior diagnoses and other medical conditions, or incidents such as a traumatic brain injury that can help illuminate your client's cognitive ability.

The most common diagnoses you will encounter are a mild to moderate intellectual disability or autism spectrum disorder. These developmental disabilities are good examples of "hidden disabilities," in that they are difficult to recognize or identify simply by looking at an individual or by conducting a brief, introductory conversation. Particularly for individuals who have suffered previous trauma, survival instincts take control. This can manifest by such persons showing the world a "tough shell," using language they may not understand, or by hiding important information such as their illiteracy. There may, however, be shared characteristics that affect criminal justice involvement: impaired language; memory problems; limited attention span; impulsivity; denial of the disability; suggestibility; lack of social skills or inappropriate social skills; poor executive functioning that includes difficulty predicting consequences, organizing time, and understanding directions; poor planning; immaturity; and various kinds of communication difficulties. Identification of a disability in a client is challenging because each individual manifests his/her disability differently.

Having considered your client's demeanor during the course of working with the person, you may suspect that he/she has a developmental disability that has never been identified and diagnosed. Many people are not identified in the public school system, for many different reasons. They may be compliant students, so that even if they fail to meet academic goalposts, they present no discipline problems and so are passed from grade to grade. They may, in contrast, present serious discipline problems that are misidentified and misinterpreted. Many students with developmental disabilities and learning disabilities (such as dyslexia) are identified simply as oppositional and are subjected to suspensions and other punishments instead of diagnoses and treatment. There is no one way to identify a client with a disability, and no one way that this individual will move through the system. It becomes important to have a grasp on all possible characteristics and presentations and be flexible in determining the best path for a particular client.

If your client has never been identified or diagnosed, but you suspect a disability that affects his/her cognition and ability to understand either the nature of the offense or the criminal justice process, then you will need to begin to document proof of the existence of a disability. Again, obtaining any available records from doctors, schools, jails and prisons, and any type of program in which your client may have participated (such as drug treatment, therapy, or anger management) may provide a clue to diagnosis. Any records that can be provided to an evaluator will assist in accurate diagnosis.

Retaining or having the court appoint a good evaluator for your client is the next step. In the case of an individual who is charged with a sex offense, it is most effective to work with a clinician who has a background in sex offender specific treatment and also is familiar with working with people who have developmental disabilities. If your client is charged with a non-sex offense, the best option is a clinician with knowledge of people with developmental disabilities. Try to ensure that the clinician is well versed in IQ testing. Clinicians with a specific background in working with people with developmental disabilities can be difficult to locate. Often, a clinician with this background will have been a professional in special education, a teacher, a guidance counselor, or a child study team member who has now obtained additional training to become a clinician. (*See* Chap. 7, Working with the Expert: An Attorney's Perspective; and Chap. 8, Working with the Expert: An Expert's Perspective.)

An additional issue to keep in mind is the age of your client, particularly if the offense is a sex offense including child pornography charges. There is a large body of research about the differences between the juvenile and adult mind, and this can be an important issue in many of the questions raised in the criminal justice process, including planning.

In selecting a qualified evaluator, both education and experience are important. If you determine that the client's IQ is a relevant factor in the case, then a licensed practicing psychologist will be required. In most states, licensed psychologists alone are qualified to administer and interpret tests of cognitive functioning (IQ). The relevant degrees for psychologists are the PhD, the EdD, and/or the PsyD. You should also be aware that the definition of "intellectual disability" has recently changed. According to the latest edition of the *Diagnostic and Statistical Manual of the American Psychiatric Association* (*DSM-5*), the primary emphasis is now on the client's level of *adaptive functioning*, and secondarily on the client's level of cognitive functioning. A variety of measures of adaptive functioning are available now. The psychologist you select should be familiar with these issues and experienced in interpreting measures of both adaptive functioning and cognitive functioning to determine the client's overall intellectual disability.

For other diagnostic issues, you can select an evaluator from other disciplines, if the professional also has experience with evaluation of ASD. These disciplines include clinical social work (MSW, DSW), counseling (MA, MS), and nursing (NP, APN-c). Like psychologists, evaluators from these disciplines can be qualified to administer and interpret tests of autism and various other mental disorders.

When hiring an evaluator, you are in the best position if you have a general understanding of the components of a quality evaluation. The first component is the referral question(s) that you want the evaluation report to address. As noted earlier, these questions may include: (1) the formal diagnosis of ASD; (2) the relevant ASD symptoms that are associated with the behaviors in the criminal case; (3) the obstacles related to the disability that block successful life in the community; (4) recommended management, placement, and treatment strategies; (5) the cognitive and social limitations to be managed; and (6) evidence of competencies such as competency to understand the offense, to plead, or to stand trial.

The second component is an analysis of the information contained in the referral documents you provide the evaluator, as well as information from collateral records and sources. This analysis should highlight aspects of the client's history that support answers to your referral questions. Examples are past diagnosis of ASD, intellectual disability, substance-use disorders, sexual disorders, or other major mental health disorders; also important are descriptions of current symptoms and their impact on the client's current functioning. There should be a discussion of past treatments, such as hospitalizations, outpatient counseling, and medication, as well as a discussion of the client's response to past treatments.

Then there is a diagnostic interview—the third component. This includes the mental status examination. It also includes elements such as the client's account of the offense behavior, or problematic behavior if not charged; the client's evaluation of the efficacy of any prior treatments; and the client's insight and understanding of his/her disability. Clients with ASD vary widely in their understanding and acceptance of their condition. Clients with a poor understanding and/or acceptance of their ASD can be difficult to counsel and may also have difficulty accepting your legal defense plan if it is built on their disability.

The fourth component is the interpretation and application of any testing results. These results should be linked to diagnosis of the client and to possible management and treatment strategies. The testing results can be used to confirm or disconfirm the evaluator's impressions from the formal interview. (*See* Chap. 9, Testing.)

The fifth and last component is the summary and recommendations, which should be focused on your referral questions. The answers should be evidence-based as much as possible. Where it is warranted, the evaluator will of course address the questions in the client's favor, but evaluators must also note any significant limitations to the findings of their evaluations.

Once you have accumulated all needed materials and obtained a reliable evaluation, the next steps will depend on whether your client is now receiving services from a developmental disability service system. Additionally, even though a client has a developmental disability, he/she may have a co-occurring condition (such as drug addiction or a mental illness) that has been identified and for which the client has received treatment. The key will be to bring all of this information to bear in a planning document that can encompass all the client's needs and supports. (*See* Chap. 4, Co-Occurring Disorders.)

A technical advance in the evaluation of offenders that you may wish to take advantage of is called *risk assessment*. This is a structured method of determining the likelihood that an offender who has committed a crime at least once will do so again in the reasonably foreseeable future.

Risk assessment is a fairly new technology in the legal field. At present, there are three classes of behaviors that have been studied and for which there are risk assessment tools: (1) violent behavior, (2) setting fires, and (3) sex-offending behaviors.

Two varieties of structured risk assessment tools are available for these three classes of behavior. The first is called Structured Clinical Judgment, which means analyzing the offender's case and comparing it to a list of risk factors that are known to be associated with the class of behaviors. The evaluator rates each risk factor as present, possibly present, or absent. Then the evaluator uses clinical judgment to arrive at an overall opinion of the offender's risk of re-offense. The second variety is called Actuarial Assessment. This entails first identifying a list of risk factors that have been found to have at least a moderately strong association with re-offending. These risk factors are then rated as applied to the particular case and assigned a numerical value. After all risk factors are rated, then the point values are summed across all the factors and a total score is calculated. This total score then is related statistically to a rate of re-offense (0 percent to 100 percent).

Risk assessment tools can be useful if they are applicable to people with developmental disabilities. To be applicable, they must have been developed on groups of offenders that included at least some persons with developmental disabilities. Very recently, researchers have begun to develop sexual risk assessment tools that are specifically for persons with developmental/intellectual disabilities. An example is the ARMIDILO-S (Assessment of Risk and Manageability of Individuals with Developmental and Intellectual Limitations Who Offend), a risk-review and community-management instrument that has been normed for this population.

Risk assessment can be useful at any of several steps in the legal process. You can use the results of a (low) risk assessment to argue for bail. You can also use the results in the plea bargain process or in arguing for a probation sentence rather than incarceration. (*See* Chap. 10, Risk of Violence for People with ASD.)

ADA and Accommodation Issues

As you begin to use all the data you have acquired regarding your client's cognitive and functional capability, the next concern is securing appropriate accommodations for the client in the courtroom and in the jail. If your client is in a jail, he/she is entitled to reasonable accommodations, and you should consider what is needed to ensure that this person is safe, secure, and able to engage in activities of daily living. A client's disability and need to be in the community may be a basis for a bail motion or (in states such as New Jersey, which have implemented criminal justice reforms to replace bail) a basis for a response to a prosecutor's detention motion. (*See* Chap. 6, The Bond Hearing.)

Consider what services, supports, or accommodations your client may need when appearing in court. If the client is sensitive to noise or activity, you should request that the matter be held at the end of the day or that the matter be heard first. This can avoid unnecessary emotional upheaval for a client and improve his/her behavior in the courtroom. Your client may need more time to understand what is being said, so the court and prosecutor may have to wait while you repeat directions and information, possibly more than once and in different ways. Discuss with any available family members, friends, or advocates what technical assistance or reasonable changes to procedures can be made to ensure that your client is able to comprehend the proceeding. Determine whether your court has an ADA coordinator and use that person's services to ensure that the necessary and appropriate accommodations are made.

Planning

Many of the principles concerning recidivism that apply to a person with ASD are the same as for those who have no developmental disability. Research informs us that individuals are less likely to commit new offenses if they feel that they have some level of supervision and if they have some meaningful work. Similarly, people with intellectual and developmental disabilities can conform more effectively to societal norms if they have a structure to comply with and if they have activities—whether this is a job, volunteer work, or a day program—to occupy their time.

We know that offenders with developmental disabilities statistically are more likely to plead guilty and are more likely to plead guilty to the original charges than their nondisabled cohorts. We know, too, that the profiles of offenders with developmental disabilities look very much like those of their nondisabled cohorts in terms of external characteristics: for example, they tend to be males between the ages of twenty and forty; are often economically disadvantaged and have little employment history; and commit a wide variety of offenses. This mirrors the general offender populations. Added to these disadvantages, they are often aware of their disability and yet try to hide it. Survival instincts can be strong, and the desire not to appear weak can result in persons with ASD developing some effective strategies to hide their disability, such as parroting "street" language that is not understood, avoiding situations in which they would need to read or write, and developing an aggressive personality that keeps people at arm's length. They may be part of a criminal group, committing crimes in concert with others and then being the first co-defendant to be caught. Because they frequently fail to understand their civil rights and believe what law enforcement may promise, they often provide a confession, which may or may not be true.

Probation, drug court, and other diversionary programs may not be used as frequently for offenders with ASD because they may not be considered good prospects for success. An inability to read, to write, and/or to understand the consequences of failing to comply with the conditions imposed for these programs can make them appear to be poor candidates for alternative dispositions. In particular, programs such as drug court require a great deal of "homework": completing workbooks, listening to lectures, completing high school equivalency and other education and job training programs. It can seem to a prosecutor or the court that persons with ASD will inevitably fail to meet these conditions, placing them in the same position as when they started. Probation also brings with it many conditions that must be met, from simple reporting requirements to obtaining advanced degrees or meeting job training requirements. For individuals who are functionally illiterate, many of the materials to be read and completed are simply beyond their cognitive capacity. For an individual who has an IQ in the average or above-average range, meeting conditions may be limited not by literacy but by a comprehensive lack of executive functioning or social skills, both of which are needed to successfully maneuver through a program. When limitations in executive functioning and social skills are caused by ASD, a client may lack the ability to follow directions, may fail to attend and participate in required counseling, may find reporting to an office and conducting regular face-to-face meetings overwhelming, and thus may in the end violate conditions of probation as a direct consequence of the disability.

Finally, statistically, offenders with disabilities often spend more time incarcerated than their nondisabled counterparts and are unable to participate in programming that jails and prisons may have to assist re-entry.

Against this backdrop, it becomes even more important to identify any and all services and supports that can improve the likelihood that the court and prosecutor will agree to a lower charge and/or an alternative disposition.

For clients who receive Social Security and Medicaid, a period of incarceration longer than thirty days will result in suspension of benefits, and incarceration for more than a year will result in termination. Not only will this affect available financial assistance to help pay for housing and food, it can also result in the suspension of services from the disability or mental health service system. Such clients will then re-enter the community with no services available to them. Often individuals with ASD would be eligible for housing vouchers for independent or supported housing. However, many public housing authorities will reject individuals with criminal histories. For example, HUD has a lifetime ban on HUD housing vouchers for individuals who are lifetime registration sex offenders.

Furthermore, we know that many offenders with developmental disabilities engage in sexually inappropriate behaviors that result in prosecution and conviction. The reasons for this are myriad. It can be the lack of social skills, coupled with a lack of appropriate healthy sexuality, that lays the groundwork for a person with ASD to commit acts that result in criminal charges. In some instances, offenders may have received sex education in schools or worked with a program or behaviorist who teaches healthy sexuality. However, many people with ASD are not able to "generalize" a rule learned in one setting and then apply that rule to a new setting. This characteristic inability to apply a previously learned rule to a new situation can cause difficulties in many areas of a person's personal and professional life. They may not understand that what is appropriate in one context may not be appropriate in another context (for example, word choice and actions such as hugging and kissing). At worst, the result can be criminal conduct, despite the best attempt to teach healthy sexuality. Other solutions, some long term, may be needed to avoid such scenarios.

Conviction or adjudication of delinquency for a sex offense brings with it another host of collateral consequences, including registration requirements, community notification, supervision by a parole officer for life, and commitment as a sexually violent predator. These consequences raise another set of issues that an attorney should try to address in the context of planning. (*See* Chap. 16, ASD and Sex Offenses: A Son's Perspective; and Chap. 17, ASD and Sex Offenses: A Parent's Perspective.)

Once the problems have been identified, we then look to solutions. Understanding the problems is an important precursor to identifying solutions. These include prevention strategies, education and training, supports in the community following arrest, and services that can address behavior and reduce potential recidivism. One way to address the problems is to coordinate all the identified diagnostic information and all of the services into one document that can be presented to the court.

What Does a Plan Look Like?

Once you have identified your client's disability, located and collated all documentation, reached out to agencies that can provide services and understood what services they can give, and determined what your client needs to live in the community, then you can coordinate the creation of a plan to provide to the prosecutor and the court. In addition to identifying all appropriate services for this client, it is important to consider the input of all involved parties, including the client and family members.

The client must be involved in the planning process and "buy in" to meeting any conditions included in the plan. Obtain the client's agreement to conform to the goals and expectations that will be set forth in the plan. One method for helping to ensure compliance is to create a contract for signature by the client that lists all the obligations and conditions of each aspect of the plan. The contract must be written simply; also, if you are working with an individual whose reading ability is limited, you will need to read it aloud and be very careful to obtain an affirmative indication of comprehension. Although such a contract has no legal force or effect, it can be effective in helping a client understand the nature of the conditions, the need to comply, and what compliance will look like. This is also a good opportunity to gauge the ability of family members or other individuals who help support the client to aid in compliance. The act of signing a document can feel formal and as a result convey the gravity of the plan, increasing the likelihood that there will be compliance.

Any plan should begin with an introduction, diagnosis, and prior history. It should include an explanation of the individual's disability, outlining as much as possible not only the diagnosis but also what the diagnosis means in terms of the client's daily living (referred to as *activities of daily living*). Provide research and background information about the client. What is the diagnosis and what are the characteristics that result in this diagnosis? How does that diagnosis manifest in this individual? There are many possible characteristics of ASD, and not all of these characteristics are present in each person. Take this opportunity to make clear what this client's communication obstacles are. He/she may find it difficult to listen and process, may be overwhelmed by sound or light, may have an aversion to being touched or near people, may find it unbearable to make eye contact, and/or may engage in self-stimulating (stimming) behavior such as flapping or jumping. A client may demonstrate none of these characteristics, some of them, or one or more of many others. It is important to be clear to the prosecutor and the court that each person with ASD may present differently; to this end, present the research that informs us that, once diagnosed, ASD will affect communication and comprehension. Describe this person and his/her obstacles based on his/her specific characteristics.

Formats for such planning can be accessed from The Arc of New Jersey's Criminal Justice Advocacy Program or the National Center for Criminal Justice and Disability at The Arc of the United States. The presentation of a plan can be in letter form or a more formal document. The plan should address multiple areas of need and should be tailored to meet the needs of the particular client. No two plans will be the same.

Available services may include disability service providers such as residential programs (e.g., group homes or supervised apartments); supported employment services; respite care; recreational or day programs; and partial hospitalization programs that assist with medication monitoring. You should identify any psychologists, psychiatrists, social workers, or other professionals who address issues particular to your client, such as sexual offending behavior, drug and alcohol addiction, anger management, or other negative behavioral issues.

The plan should address the following issues:

- **Residential** options—Where will the client be living and with whom? How will this be accomplished (e.g., which agencies are linked to the client, what mechanism is being implemented to locate and place the person in appropriate housing)?
- **Activity** options—Where will the client be spending the day and how?
- **Therapeutic** options—What, if any, therapy does this client require? How will it be provided? By whom and how often?
- **Medical** options—Does this client have any medical needs that should be addressed by medication or in some other fashion?

- **Transportation** options—Does this client have a vehicle and a valid driver's license? If not, has he/she been connected to your jurisdiction's transportation choices, such as public transportation and a subsidized ticket or Access Link?

- **School or employment** options—Is this person able to seek additional schooling, training, or certification to improve job options? If so, how is this being implemented? Is this person connected to your state's vocational rehabilitation services and/or supported employment options, or (if not job-ready), then to the appropriate day program setting to work on that issue?

- **Financial** options—Is this person on SSI and Medicaid? If needed, has a representative payee been identified?

- **Other services**—Does this person need 24/7 supervision or what may be called "line of sight" supervision? Even if the person is not in need of 24/7 supervision, must there be available overnight staffing? If so, what agency is going to be responsible for this, and how will it be accomplished? Does this person need assistance with activities of daily living (such as grocery shopping, cleaning, hygiene, etc.), and if so, by what means will this be accomplished? If this person engages in inappropriate or illegal sexual behavior, what can be provided in terms of safety planning?

- **Other conditions**—Is this person connected to his/her probation or parole officers? Does the person know how to report to probation or parole? Does he/she know when to report? If this person will be registering as a sex offender, do both the person and any caregivers or direct support providers understand how to ensure that the person is properly registered and when? If fines, penalties, or restitution have been ordered, has it been determined whether a payment plan is in place and by what means payment will be made?

Conclusion

In the end, a coordinated plan of services and support must meet the needs of the client and the needs of the court. Accountability and responsibility remain with a competent defendant. The goal of the plan is to improve the likelihood that the services provided will address inappropriate or criminal behavior, as well as allow the client to live in the community and lead a law-abiding life. A review of the considerations discussed in this chapter should make clear that not all of these issues and conditions will arise in each case. Many of them require lengthy and strong advocacy with state agencies and service agencies. Simply identifying a need is not sufficient; locating and securing the elements needed for an individual can be a complex process. Keeping the court informed of your progress and what obstacles have been faced can help educate prosecutors and the court about the system and may aid in enlisting their assistance in securing needed evaluations and services. *Knowledge is the key.* Successful advocacy on behalf of defendants with ASD depends on knowledge and understanding of both the criminal justice system and the social services system, and the ability to communicate with both.

●　●　●

Jessica S. Oppenheim, Esq., is the Director of the Criminal Justice Advocacy Program of The Arc of New Jersey, a statewide program that provides advocacy for people with developmental disabilities who become involved in the criminal justice system. Prior to joining The Arc in 2010, she was an assistant prosecutor in the Middlesex County prosecutor's office and a deputy attorney general in the Division of Criminal Justice, Department of Law and Public Safety, from 1985 until 2010. In that capacity, she was bureau chief of the prosecutor's Supervision and Coordination Bureau, the unit that oversaw the twenty-one county prosecutor's offices and 600 law enforcement agencies on behalf of the attorney general. She represented the state in the appellate division and supreme courts on criminal matters and Megan's Law matters. She also drafted and implemented the attorney general's Megan's Law guidelines; prosecuted Megan's Law and domestic violence cases; and provided training, policies, and protocols for law enforcement agencies and prosecutors throughout the state on domestic violence, sexual assault and child abuse, internal affairs policies, Megan's Law, and dealing with diverse populations. She represented the attorney general on the Domestic Violence Fatality Review Board, and the governor's Child Abuse and Neglect Task Force, as well as other task forces and worked with SANE/SART nurses, multidisciplinary teams, and county victim-witness offices. She has taught as an adjunct professor for the Paralegal Studies Program at Fairleigh Dickinson University. She is a board member of the New Jersey Association for the Treatment of Sexual

Abusers, the Middlesex County Bar Foundation, and Women Aware, the domestic violence survivor agency for Middlesex County. Ms. Oppenheim can be reached at joppenheim@arcnj.org and her website is http://www .cjapnj.org.

Jeffrey Allen, PhD, is a forensic psychologist who has been in private practice for approximately thirty years. Before that, he worked as a prison psychologist in New York and then New Jersey; as director of psychology at the correctional sex offender treatment program in New Jersey; as developer and first psychologist of a juvenile sex offender treatment program for the New Jersey Department of Children and Families; and as developer and clinician at three private community residential programs for developmentally disabled persons with sexually abusive behaviors. He currently consults on treatment programming and staff training with state and private agencies that serve the developmentally disabled. Dr. Allen has authored several articles, including "Forewarned Is Forearmed: What Staff and Caretakers Need to Know About Sexual Behavior Problems," *NADD Bulletin* 15(6), Nov./Dec. 2012; and "Psychosexual Evaluations in Intellectually Disabled Clients," *Sex Offender Law Review* 11(6), 2010. Dr. Allen can be reached at psychealthassociates@gmail.com and his website is http://www.psychealthassociates.com.

Chapter

13

Prison Accommodations

Jack T. Donson

The sad reality is that sometimes people with ASD are sentenced to prison. If you as a lawyer have reason to believe that a prison sentence is likely (for example, because of the nature of the offense, your client's record, or mandatory penalties), the task of seeking an appropriate facility or of securing the appropriate accommodations within a given facility begins long before the sentencing hearing.

This chapter, by Jack T. Donson, a federal prison consultant, helps the criminal defense lawyer navigate both the state and federal systems. The chapter also explores issues that should be explained to the client with ASD, and his/her family, in advance of remand to a facility. Those issues include the importance of counts, getting along with other inmates, following the chain of command, and handling disciplinary issues.

● ● ●

When representing people with autism spectrum disorder (ASD), it is important to understand what our country's correctional systems do and do not offer. Although my focus will be relative to my experiences at the federal level, much of the information in this chapter will also apply to local and state jails and prisons.

Justice Anthony Kennedy summed it up best before the House Appropriations Committee in 2011 when he stated:

> I think, Mr. Chairman, that the corrections system is one of the most over-looked, misunderstood institutions we have in our entire government. In law school, I never heard about corrections. Lawyers are fascinated with

the guilt/innocence adjudication process. Once the adjudication process is over, we have no interest in corrections. Doctors know more about the corrections system and psychiatrists than we do. Nobody looks at it.

This observation is important to view from a wider perspective: If justice professionals and practitioners are disconnected from the basic understanding of general correctional practices, what kinds of misconceptions and outright ignorance exist regarding treatment modalities for specialized populations like those diagnosed with ASD?

I have been interacting with attorneys, probation officers, and judges on classification and correctional program issues for more than thirty years. In my view, there is no better understanding of correctional treatment today than there was in 1986 when I began my career at the state level. The deficit of cohesiveness, communication, and synergies among the courts, agencies, and correctional administrators adversely affects correctional treatment, re-entry, and public safety.

Pretrial Considerations

Remand

The first consideration focuses on clients who are remanded at any point during the pretrial stage. The abrupt removal from family and any community support network is traumatic and unpredictable for clients with ASD. Immediate communication to transport officers and facility administrators regarding a diagnosis of ASD is crucial. This establishes a record and documentation so any behavioral issues are considered in context and not misinterpreted. This communication also allows treatment professionals to identify, document, and provide follow-up services, medication, or other counseling after intake (as limited as those services may be). Depending on where clients fall along the spectrum, behaviors within a correctional setting can lead to incident reports and cause removal from the general population to a more restrictive housing unit setting, such as solitary confinement. (*See* Chap. 6, The Bond Hearing.)

Clients may display manic episodes caused by environmental factors inherent in a secure correctional setting. For instance, sudden loud noises such as a PA system or radio alarms, or bright lights, may trigger behavior problematic to a correctional environment from a security standpoint. These controlled environments will range from isolated cell living to large open and unruly dormitories, any or all of which may be in drastic contrast and unfamiliar to the day-to-day environments clients experienced in the community. Constant noises, close proximity to others, and the absence of total darkness may also impair sleep.

Clients may also be exposed to predatory behavior because of their naïveté and inability to discern motives. Extortion and sexual predation are not unusual in these environments. Diligence must be exercised, not only in making correctional administrators aware of the diagnosis but also in facilitating regular communication with the client while attempting to establish a professional relationship with treatment providers such as facility counselors and mental health professionals.

It is also important to familiarize oneself with specific facility characteristics such as educational, counseling, and recreational programs. Most facilities have inmate handbooks to identify any services conducive to your client's needs and previous community program activities. These handbooks are provided at or shortly after intake screening, and sometimes they can be accessed on the internet.

Special attention should be given to a client's medication regimen. It is not uncommon for medication to be discontinued or substituted depending on what the facility has to offer by way of its formulary. At the federal level, the Federal Bureau of Prisons (BOP) publishes a formulary of approved drugs dispensed by the institution's pharmacist. Two common FDA-approved medications prescribed for ASD, risperidone and aripiprazole, are included in the BOP formulary. When a person is remanded and is taking a nonformulary medication, an appropriate substitute may be provided. Prison officials may not be aware of the individual's medical profile and thus not make the proper determination regarding the efficacy of the substitute. Although there is a process for requesting nonformulary medication, requests are often denied based on the limited historical medical data.

I once had a client who had been denied gabapentin upon arrival and given a substitute. The client's community doctor had previously prescribed this substitute, but it had proved ineffective and caused migraines. It took several weeks to finally get nonformulary medication approval because we first had to obtain the medical records with proof of the adverse side effects. Each case and medication regimen is unique, and the policy and process are usually established to proactively manage these situations.

There are various pretrial detention operations throughout the country, including local, state, federal, and even private prison companies. One should be aware of and attempt to review any memorandum of understanding (MOU), statement of work, and/or specific contract agreements authorities have with the holding facility regarding medical treatment and services. Remember that the holding facility has certain obligations to the entity on behalf of the prisoner it is holding. These obligations will be clearly defined in writing, especially when the U.S. Marshals are involved; however, be aware that private prison providers are often cited for deficiencies by audit authorities, particularly when it comes to the delivery of medical treatment.

Clients should be encouraged to participate in as many pretrial work and educational programs as possible. They should obtain progress reports and/or collect certificates of program completion, which can be used in sentencing mitigation. Although protocols vary among organizations, I have obtained powerful letters of recommendation from facility staff regarding positive aspects of an individual's work and programming efforts that were used for sentencing mitigation.

Bond

Clients on bond do not face the challenges just described and can start to proactively prepare for the eventuality of a term of incarceration should one be likely. It is a time to begin "planting seeds" to slowly and incrementally prepare clients for the experience. From a mitigation standpoint, it is important to help facilitate, continue, or improve on a multifaceted community treatment plan so you can measure any progress made since arrest, while arguing that there is no equivalent treatment plan in a controlled prison setting. Although prison bureaucrats will never concede that their facilities provide inadequate treatment, there is a plethora of hard data from authorities such as the Government Accountability Office (GAO) and the Department of Justice Inspector General (IG) about inadequate medical treatment, overcrowding, and understaffing. (*See* Chap. 12, Mitigation Using Community Resources.)

The court must be reminded that any treatment progress made during bond will be quickly erased, and possibly reversed, upon imprisonment. It could take months for a new arrival to begin a correctional treatment program regimen, given the classification process, resources, and program waiting lists. Throughout my career in case management, I saw that judicial recommendations for individual mental health treatment were ignored by mental health professionals because they simply did not have the capacity for individual counseling aside from "crisis intervention."

18 U.S.C. §3552(b) and (c), Presentence Study and Psychological or Psychiatric Examination, allow the court to order the defendant to undergo a psychological or psychiatric examination. This evaluation may be completed by a community consultant unless the judge finds there is a compelling reason for the study to be done by the Bureau of Prisons. The statute allows sixty days for the completion of the study, with an extension not to exceed sixty additional days. The format of the study report should generally follow the format used in the other statutes, specifically addressing the court's concerns.

18 U.S.C. §4244, Hospitalization of a convicted person suffering from a mental disease or defect, provides that if a defendant is found guilty of an offense, but a question is raised as to his/her mental condition prior to sentencing, the court may order a hearing and a mental examination to determine whether the defendant is suffering from a mental disease or defect such that commitment to a suitable facility for care or treatment, in lieu of imprisonment, is appropriate.

Sentencing

At the federal level, the court considers the "history and characteristics of the defendant" under 18 U.S.C. §3553(a). It is important for mitigation efforts to accentuate the unique and inherent challenges and hardships for someone diagnosed with ASD. It is important to point out how the potential victimization, lack of specialized treatment, and overall prison environment will be far more punitive for someone on the autism spectrum.

It is also important to be as comprehensive as possible in a sentencing memorandum and to include as much information as possible in any presentence report. For example, the BOP does not have access to the sentencing memorandum when processing the initial designation because this document is not typically uploaded into the E-DES system, which is the centralized database for designations processing that relies heavily on the presentence report (PSR). I recommend that counsel ask probation officials and/or the court to upload or otherwise include any additional relevant data, to make it part of the record to be considered when processing a designation.

Finally, it is important to provide a specific list of medications, dosage units, and the diagnosis relative to each medication for inclusion in a presentence report. Several BOP clinical directors have informed me that knowing the diagnosis connected with each medication assists them when making the decision to continue it upon incarceration and/or consider supporting a nonformulary medication request. Some federal district courts allow psychological reports and other pertinent information to be uploaded to the E-DES database.

At the end of this chapter, in Appendix A, is a redacted excerpt from an actual declaration I submitted as a consultant for a client with ASD.

Designation, Classification, and Programs

There is no specific federal program targeted to ASD. Moreover, there is no "one size fits all" when it comes to a designation at a facility. For instance, should the classification likely be minimum security (camp), paramount to designation may be proximity to the family, as federal prison camps are fairly benign environments with minimal exploitation. However, small satellite camps have minimal staffing, and thus programs and activities may not be a good fit for some clients.

It is crucial to conduct facility research in advance of sentencing, regardless of whether the court accommodates recommendations. According to the U.S. Sentencing Commission, the BOP accommodates 75 percent of judicial recommendations at sentencing. In my experience, recommendations are not followed when the recommended facility is not commensurate with the individual's classification and/or program needs.

If the circumstances of the case require a higher classification due to the severity of the instant offense, violence, criminal history, or other criminogenic factor, one should seriously consider a specialized program, if applicable, to avoid predation. As referenced in the sample report included in this chapter (*See* Chapter Appendix B), the focus was on the SKILLS program, which is explained later in this chapter. However, federal and state program offerings are fluid, especially in light of the First Step Act. It is prudent to access state and federal correctional websites to determine what is available. The BOP periodically publishes a *Directory of National Programs*, which references the SKILLS program. This can be found on page 13 at https://www.bop.gov/inmates/custody_and_care/docs/20170913_Directory_of_National_Programs.pdf.

In many states, inmates are initially transferred to prisons designated as classification centers or reception centers for an indeterminate amount of time. During this period, they receive a risk assessment and are evaluated for programs, and then are transferred to a permanent facility. It is important for the correctional administrators to have all pertinent information during this initial evaluation. Never assume that a bureaucracy will have all the records relative to a client's diagnosis.

One action I cannot emphasize enough is to pick up the telephone and reach out to correctional administrators. When I am reminded of the unresponsiveness encountered when calling most agencies, my comeback is "you need to at least try." It is sometimes a frustrating experience, but being persistent and reaching a responsive person along the chain of command can move mountains.

When my business partner and I train federal defenders, I ask everyone in the room to raise their hand if they ever tried to call a prison. About half of those in the room raise their hands. I then ask them to keep their hands in the air if no one answered the phone, and just about all of those hands remain in the air. I also attended a BOP presentation at a United States Sentencing Commission annual seminar and watched the General Counsel from the Designation and Sentence Computation Center (DSCC) hand out an entire box of business cards and encourage phone calls to the center.

When it comes to unique circumstances like a client's ASD, sometimes the most productive tactic is learning how to navigate the bureaucracy via the chain of command. Calling facilities directly can sometimes be a dead end, so it is more important to cultivate regional contacts and resources at the federal level and the department of corrections headquarters at the state level.

I emphasize this point because of its importance. My experience indicates that attorneys are apprehensive about even trying and/or not knowing who to call in a particular bureaucracy. I have obtained great results in helping clients just by understanding the nuances of who to contact, and then cultivating relationships when a responsive person is found.

At the end of this chapter is a version of an actual redacted letter I drafted for counsel to the DSCC for a client diagnosed with ASD (*See* Chapter Appendix A). The client was a good fit for the Life Connections Program, which was in close proximity to his family and offered faith-based resources. I find these letters effective in the federal system, more often than not, especially for cases with unusual circumstances. A variation could also be effective in a state system.

When I first began writing this chapter, I submitted emails to the general information contact on the Department of Corrections websites for New York, Pennsylvania, Texas, California, and Florida. I asked for the following:

> I work with populations who are going to prison but are diagnosed with Autism Spectrum Disorder (ASD).
>
> I was wondering if you had any specialized programs, literature, or a contact person at the DOC I can speak with regarding programs and classification issues?
>
> Any information will be greatly appreciated.

I received one reply from California, which was as follows:

> Hello,
>
> For more information visit the links below:
>
> https://www.cdcr.ca.gov/rehabilitation/
>
> Thank you

There was some general information on treatment and programs at that link, but no specific references to ASD. It is clear that more efforts will be needed in identifying programs and services for clients within any specific jurisdiction. Although the lack of targeted programs in any jurisdiction may be problematic, the absence of such programs may prove to be a positive in mitigation efforts.

Daily Prison Life Issues and Preparation

There are various prison settings throughout the country, ranging from secure, controlled environments where individuals are locked in cells up to twenty-three hours daily; to open, campus-type settings devoid of walls, fences, or other barriers. Classification factors such as risk will dictate the specific environment where a person will eventually serve a sentence. However, pretrial "jail" environments are ordinarily restrictive and unpredictable and run the gamut of facilities from small-town county jails to large urban city jails, regional jail complexes, and private contract facilities.

Most practitioners will know about one or two facilities close to them, but it is always practical to do as much research as possible on all potential pretrial settings in an area in order to help clients navigate the system and participate in treatment programs. At the same time, attorneys should attempt to establish a line of communication with correctional treatment professionals and/or case management staff. For instance, the U.S.

Marshals might have more than one contract for pretrial confinement that may be more conducive to a client with an ASD diagnosis. County governments and/or local sheriffs might have written or verbal agreements with neighboring jurisdictions for special circumstances.

Upon arrival at any facility, clients should be encouraged to review the inmate facility handbook and seek out the various bulletin boards with specific memoranda to the population from management to inform them of institutional procedures and the expectations of the administration. Prison life cannot be successfully navigated without understanding the inmate subculture, as well as the blind eye staff often turn to conduct that deviates from the written expectations. In layman's terms, "*Just because you see things going on all around you, don't assume they are authorized unless you read it for yourself.*" These nuances and subcultural cues are even more difficult to navigate for those in the ASD population.

I often use the following analogy: BOP disciplinary code #328 prohibits giving anything of value to another inmate. It is customary within the subculture, and often ignored by staff, for newly arriving inmates to be given shower shoes and toiletries by other inmates as a welcoming gesture. I have witnessed new inmates receive incident reports for accepting these items. Aside from that, prison is predatory, so there may be personal interests and ulterior motives associated with such acts of "kindness." Although counsel must understand that there is a fine line to walk to avoid raising your clients' anxiety about the experience they are about to face, look at it as simply making them aware of the environment, and reinforce the concept that it is better to play it safe and act in accordance with the written rules rather than what they observe around them.

The following are examples of high-priority issues viewed as extremely important by correctional officials in most local, state, and federal correctional environments. It is important to understand how clients might function within these environments so they can be prepared to handle the challenges. It is important to cover prison preparation challenges with all clients and their family members when possible, especially when preparing people with ASD.

Counts

The most fundamental priority in a prison is security and control, so it is important to emphasize that there is zero tolerance when inmates do not appear or otherwise cooperate with the count. All facilities count the population numerous times in a twenty-four-hour period. For instance, the BOP conducts five official counts (two stand-up) plus two daily census counts and unannounced random special census counts. Inmates often receive incident reports for being in unauthorized areas, sitting during "stand-up" counts, and attempting to distract officers during the count procedures. Clients should be notified to take count procedures seriously, and always to be in the area they are supposed to be. Count-related incident reports often result in special housing placement.

PRACTICE TIP: Clients with ASD who are sensitive to light and noise may cover their eyes and ears and thus be unaware that a stand-up count is in progress, which may interfere with count procedures.

Work

Aside from pretrial environments, most facilities require inmates to work. Job placement should be discussed with clients regarding the most practical jobs given appropriate to their diagnosis and prior job experience. It is common for newly arriving inmates to be assigned to the kitchen for dishwashing and sanitation-related responsibilities. This may sound like a harmless occupation, but food service workers are often pressured by other inmates to steal food for the housing units. Stealing is a "high severity" incident in the BOP, of severity equal to fighting and minor assault, and will result in the loss of good conduct time. Although it is difficult for new arrivals to obtain the more desirable facility work assignments, consideration should be given to jobs that place more vulnerable offenders in close proximity to treatment staff, in positions such as orderlies for religious services or psychology services. Teaching jobs should be avoided because of the social skills required and the ability to understand the subcultural aspects inherent in a diverse population.

PRACTICE TIP: Clients with ASD may be assigned to a detail in the kitchen where they can be pressured or tricked into stealing food, which is commonplace to the food service work environment.

Correctional Staff

As with life in general, there are professional correctional workers who take pride in what they do, and there are unprofessional workers who are just collecting a paycheck. Unfortunately, my experience is that there is an inordinate amount of the latter in the correctional environment. It would take a separate book to get into the reasons and dynamics of organizational culture, but the fundamental concept is that correctional staff too often view inmates as "the bad guys" and are desensitized to the more abhorrent behavior they have experienced on a daily basis. Clients should be advised to treat all staff with the utmost respect and minimize regular contact with correctional officers so they are not labeled as informants. Simply put, do not make friends with correctional officers! Some correctional officers like to engage inmates in philosophical discussions out of boredom and/or a desire to cultivate informants, but no good comes from those situations. A correctional officer may view someone with ASD as a potential source of information, which can be dangerous in a prison setting.

PRACTICE TIP: Correction officers might view clients with ASD as a source of information and attempt to cultivate them as informants.

Treatment Staff

One would think treatment staff would approach the staff/inmate relationship differently, but for the most part, counselors and case managers are sometimes former correctional officers who carry over the same mindset within the correctional agency culture. However, clinicians such as medical doctors and psychologists may not be as tainted, and they are more likely to be direct hires from the community rather than climbing the ladder via a correctional office path. It is important to understand who clients are interacting with as far as their specific position responsibilities.

PRACTICE TIP: Have one or more consent forms signed and on file prior to contacting prison administration officials and/or treatment staff. Consent forms can be executed prior to incarceration, during a legal visit or by institution staff at your request.

Chain of Command

Correctional agencies are quasi-militaristic organizations with a rank structure including captains, lieutenants, and so on. Administrators respect the chain of command. Clients as well as counsel should always begin at the bottom and move up the chain but must avoid upsetting someone along the way who might have been able to help on a given issue. One of the first questions a seasoned warden will have for a person complaining is regarding with whom they have spoken previously. In the federal prison system, staff participate in what is referred to as "mainline," where department heads and the executive staff stand in the center of the dining hall during the meals and thus are accessible to the population. In some correctional systems, inmates can email staff with specific concerns and requests.

Intake

All prisons have a formal intake screening process, which begins with the collection of documentation, including any available classification materials such as the presentence report and sentencing orders. It is important to ensure that relevant medical information, such as the diagnosis and medication regimen, is included in those materials. In addition, any advance directives and consent forms should be hand-carried when possible and given to the officials conducting the intake screening. Most BOP facilities allow inmates to surrender with some "legal materials." All materials should be copied and mailed to the facility if they are not accepted upon arrival.

PRACTICE TIP: A specific list of each medication, dosage unit, and specific diagnosis for that particular medication should be provided to prison officials to avoid interruption of the medication regimen.

Classification and Programs

Subsequent to intake and aside from pretrial operations, all facilities will have a formalized classification system, treatment programs, and re-entry services. Case management staff are required to recommend programs and track program progress at regular intervals. In state facilities, case management staff may be in a separate area of the facility. The federal government practices a unit management concept with classification staff stationed within each housing unit.

Clients should be encouraged to take the initiative and go beyond the programs that are formally recommended. Some state and federal facilities have vocational training programs and prison industries that may be appropriate, depending on your client's aptitude and ability to adhere to a more structured work-related program. It is also practical to determine if a facility has a viable community volunteer program and to encourage clients to take advantage of any such programs. It should be noted that, if the client is of a particular religious faith, local clergy can be contacted and may be able to be placed on the visiting list as a "Minister of Record." Most facilities also allow educational correspondence programs, which is why it is important to research what can be accomplished to supplement the recommended correctional treatment plan available at the facility. Regardless of religious belief and practices, clients with ASD will find a more supportive environment in the religious services area when it comes to work assignments and programs.

Incident Report Issues and Mitigation

Clients should be encouraged to communicate with counsel when they are charged with any disciplinary infractions. Staff sometimes downplay dispositions of the more minor behaviors. However, even minor infractions can negatively affect classification, parole guidelines, and program eligibility. By law, correctional systems have to adhere to formal disciplinary protocols, but these are sometimes haphazardly applied and overturned on appeal. Although it is unwise to get into an adversarial situation with prison authorities on most issues, the disciplinary appeal process is routinely exercised. Consideration should be given to how the diagnosis and inherent behavior related to ASD contributed to the infraction, in the event the report can be expunged.

Re-Entry and Community Resources

Re-entry preparation begins on day one regardless of the length of the sentence. Every person should have short-term and long-term program goals with a focus on the eventual release plan. For instance, a short-term goal might be to obtain a GED, which leads to qualification for an electrical apprenticeship program and earns a Department of Labor certification. Obtaining identification, developing a résumé, reinstating disability benefits, and determining a viable release plan are examples of re-entry programming. Probation and parole officials like to see release plans that include family support and potential employment opportunities in the immediate vicinity rather than a release plan to an area devoid of such support. Careful consideration should also be given to release to a halfway house because that shift may interrupt the familiar routine of prison life. Moreover, many transitional halfway house environments are chaotic.

All of this may be destructive for the client with ASD. Probation and parole officials have case information, so it is practical for counsel or the family to reach out to the assigned officer prior to release to ensure a smooth transition. Probation and parole officers are sometimes assigned by geographic location when the office has other specialized officers who were trained for caseloads with mental health issues.

There is a comprehensive resource, titled "Community Release Planning Guidelines for Social Workers and Treatment Professionals" (2014), which is applicable to federal, state, and local jurisdictions. It can be found at https://www.bop.gov/resources/pdfs/community_rel_planning_guidelines_for_social_work.pdf.

Conclusion

It is imperative that the prison experience be proactively managed. It will be labor-intensive for the more vulnerable populations like those diagnosed with ASD. It is vital to document the diagnosis, medications, and the unique characteristics of your client in court filings, namely, the pre-sentence report. This can provide mitigation while "planting seeds" with prison officials so the diagnosis can be addressed in the event of a custodial term. It is also vital to review the available specific internet agency resources and protocols, as well as to make efforts to establish formal and informal communication with treatment professionals at specific institutions and even the Department of Corrections headquarters. Although attorneys sometimes disengage with clients after sentencing, periodic follow-up is necessary to ensure that clients, especially those with ASD, are supported throughout the prison experience up to the point of re-entry.

Letter to BOP for Defendant with ASD

Mary Doe, Attorney at Law
1234 Main Street
Anytown, Anystate 54321

January 24, 20__
Designation and Sentence Computation Center
346 Marine Forces Drive
Grand Prairie, Texas 75051
Attn: Hotel Team Operations Manager
Re: _____
Docket No.: xx-xxxx

Dear Ms. X:

Please find attached the Judgment for the above-referenced individual who was recently sentenced in the District of Maryland. It is my understanding that the order was recently uploaded into the E-DES system and is awaiting your review and action. Although I am sure you receive a significant amount of correspondence, I respectfully request you consider the below information relative to Judge Y's recommendation for placement in FCI Petersburg (Low), VA.

Specifically, Mr. Z is diagnosed as having "Autism Spectrum Disorder" (*DSM-V*). He is extremely passive and introverted with no social support system aside from his family. We are concerned that a designation outside of Petersburg will inhibit the family's travel and thus remove his only support system. The Bureau of Prisons is aware of the positive impact social visiting has on adjustment and re-entry. Mr. Z's diagnosis may make his adjustment difficult should he be housed away from the family unit. In addition, Petersburg has the "Life Connections" program, which may eventually assist Mr. Z during incarceration.

While I realize that judicial recommendations are not binding on the Bureau of Prisons, I am also aware that your agency is responsive to judges and attempts to comply when possible. In addition, enclosed is the disposition from the State of Maryland that indicates the pending state case has been resolved with a concurrent sentence that completely expires within the federal term.

I respectfully request that the above information be considered when processing the designation to allow my client to be in close proximity for visiting given the unique circumstances of his diagnosis.

Your cooperation and responsiveness will be greatly appreciated. Please do not hesitate to contact me at your convenience if you require any additional information from Judge Y.

Sincerely,

Mary Doe
Cc: Judge Y
Cc: GRA-DSC/chief@BOP.gov

B

Declaration Submitted by Consultant to the Court for a Person with ASD

General Observations

In general, the most profound autism characteristic in the prison environment is regarding communication. Autistic individuals ordinarily may not possess the communication skills necessary for a prison environment. For instance, the failure to maintain eye contact can be misinterpreted as evasiveness, deception, and even disrespect. This is not only a deficit for staff-to-inmate interactions but is also extremely problematic for inmate-to-inmate interaction.

Autistic individuals may also have other sensory issues, such as sensitivity to loud noises, bright lights, and strong smells, and many do not like being touched. Secure federal prison living environments are often bright, noisy, and odorous given the need for security, ability to cook with microwaves within the unit, and the crowded conditions. Male and female correctional officers frequently pat-search inmates throughout the facility on a daily basis given the security protocol. A recent report by the Inspector General indicates that the BOP is nearly 35% over capacity, so the agency has converted TV rooms and other program areas to dormitories where the aforementioned sensory conditions are exacerbated.

Autistic individuals commonly have processing delays and may need extra time to respond to questions or instructions. They take things very literally and may not fully understand instructions unless those directions are concise. The failure to immediately get on the ground or respond to a staff command in an institutional emergency situation can result in being physically taken down and/or make the individual subject to the disciplinary system for failure to comply.

Autistic individuals may not understand the unwritten social rules in the secure prison environment, such as maintaining proper body spacing, which may be interpreted as rude or disrespectful by both staff and inmates. Disrespect in a secure prison environment can be detrimental regarding inmate peer relationships and can even result in assault by inmates and the issuance of incident reports by staff.

BOP Specific Issues

There are no specific programs designed for autistic individuals within the BOP. The BOP classifies inmates with psychological and medical conditions according to what is referred to as "Care Levels." There is a medical care level and a separate psychological care level. It is a four-level system, with 1 being totally healthy and 4 either being terminal from a physical perspective or acute mental illness from a psychological perspective. Ordinarily, care-level 3 and 4 inmates require medical center placement. Based on Dr. X's report, the behaviors of autism do not rise to the level of need for a medical center placement and will most likely fall within the care level 2 range for a mainstream secure facility placement.

From a BOP Program and Correctional Treatment perspective, there is only one BOP program remotely appropriate for Mr. X, in my professional opinion. The "SKILLS" program at the Federal Correctional Institution (FCI) in Danbury, CT (secure) is a unit-based residential treatment program for offenders who have intellectual and social deficiencies. Although some of the criteria suggest that Mr. X may be an appropriate candidate, in my experience, a significant percentage of the SKILLS population have low IQs and neurological deficits such as from fetal alcohol syndrome. In addition, Danbury is far from his family, which is problematic when it comes to institutional adjustment.

It is more likely that Mr. X will be designated to a secure, mainstream facility (FCI) where Psychology Services staffing levels do not provide for the regular, weekly treatment sessions referenced in Dr. X's report. In fact, at any given FCI of more than 1,000 inmates, there are only two or three psychologists, who are thus unable to conduct regular, individual counseling. They are more focused on crisis intervention and group programming. BOP facilities are not staffed in accordance with the current policy PS # 5310.12, *Psychology Services Manual*, Chapter 1, Attachment B.

In fact, aside from direct inmate services, the psychology services personnel are responsible for staff training, custodial duties, and the Employee Assistance Program. Mr. X will not be able to receive the continuity of care he has been receiving in the community referenced by Dr. X.

Individual Circumstances and Characteristics

Classification Issues: Based on the available information, I have determined that Mr. X will be classified as a 13-point "low" security offender. However, it should be noted that a more specific scoring cannot be determined without the presentence report. In addition, the scoring estimate is 2 points short of medium security. It also assumes that Mr. X will eventually be allowed to voluntarily surrender. If he were remanded upon sentencing, he would actually score out as medium security (16 points), which would be extremely problematic given the population composition of a medium-level facility where inmate characteristics include more of a propensity for gang affiliations, violence, and victimizing sex offenders and younger, passive offenders who are more subject to manipulation.

An additional consideration is that even if Mr. X is determined to be a 13-point, low-security offender, he could quickly be reclassified to medium if he incurs an incident report given any of the concerns expressed earlier in this report.

The Federal Bureau of Prisons classifies inmates as minimum (camp), low, medium (FCIs), and high security (USP). Mr. X is ineligible for camp placement based not only on the classification score but also on the assignment of the "Sex Offender" public safety factor (PSF). The BOP classification manual does not differentiate between types of sex offenders, so inmates who are predatory rapists are assigned the same public safety factor as someone in possession of child pornography.

Equally troubling for Mr. X is the fact that new inmates arriving at secure facilities are confronted by other inmates to "show their papers." This is a way for inmates to identify cooperators and sex offenders and has the potential for harm depending on how Mr. X reacts to such pressure. It is very common for "sex offenders" to request or be placed in the Special Housing Unit at the perception of staff when they feel the sex offender's safety is in jeopardy. Special housing unit placement, often referred to as "Solitary," can sometimes last for months pending a threat assessment and/or transfer to a new facility if the inmate cannot return to the population. I have witnessed countless sex offenders repeat, over and over again, a vicious cycle of protective custody and then transfer.

According to Dr. X's report, Mr. X's only pastime coping activities are watching game shows, re-enacting movies, and magic. These outlets will be nonexistent in a federal facility. It is difficult to say what behaviors will manifest as coping mechanisms; however, the absence of these outlets in combination with the termination of his biweekly therapy will make serving the sentence extremely difficult. I have had inmates on my caseload with autism remark that it was like serving double the amount of time given the obstacles inherent with their condition.

Conclusion: Consideration should be given to the above factors. Any custodial term will be extremely problematic given Mr. X's autism spectrum disorder diagnosis. Although we are too far from the actual designation process, it is clear that any custodial term imposed will be served in a secure facility, with more predatory offenders, far from the family unit without the benefit of regular, individual treatment. The lack of the necessary social skills and coping mechanisms raises the potential for repeated victimization and perpetual solitary confinement, which will negatively impact correctional treatment goals for successful re-entry.

●　●　●

Jack T. Donson is a consultant and advocate with a passion for federal prison reform. He retired from the Federal Bureau of Prisons and has more than thirty-two years of experience working in case management capacities. During his career, he held positions within the Correctional Programs Division in diverse prison environments, including pretrial and witness security unit operations. He held assignments in the Philadelphia Regional office and New York Community corrections office.

From an administrative perspective, he participated in national policy writing workgroups, drafted policy, monitored programs, and trained facility staff. In addition, he was used as resource staff by the DC Central Office program review division and participated in auditing facilities throughout the northeastern United States. During his career, he received three national awards and more than thirty other meritorious performance awards.

Prior to his federal government service, he was a probation and parole officer in the Commonwealth of Pennsylvania. He received an honorable discharge from the U.S. Army, where he served as a military policeman.

Mr. Donson serves on several nonprofit boards, including Out4Good, FedCURE, and Choosing Integrity. He is a member of the National Association of Criminal Defense Lawyers and American Bar Association Corrections committees. He has testified on federal prison issues throughout the United States and the United Kingdom. He provides training to federal defenders, judges, and CJA panel members through the company Prisonology, which he co-founded with Walt Pavlo, a writer with *Forbes*. He has taught criminal justice courses, such as "The American Prison" and "Community Corrections," at Marywood University.

Mr. Donson has been quoted in the national media, including *Forbes*, *The New York Times*, *Sports Illustrated*, and *Bloomberg News*. He has appeared on CNN, FOX 5 New York, and in documentaries on CNBC and for the Center for Public Integrity.

Mr. Donson can be reached at jack@mfpcllc.com and his website is http://www.mfpcllc.com.

Complete citations are available from the author upon request.

14

Vulnerabilities of Defendants with ASD and Strategies for Improving Outcomes

Laurie Sperry, Clare Hughes, and Michael J. Forsee

ASD is often called "the hidden disability" because the disability is often not obvious, and when it is, it is mistaken for something else. As this chapter by Dr. Laurie Speery, Clare Hughes, and former FBI Agent Michael J. Forsee points out, people with ASD are uniquely vulnerable at each stage of the criminal case, from arrest and interrogation through sentencing to release from prison. In addition, this chapter discusses strategies that people with ASD can use to empower themselves, as well as measures attorneys and law enforcement can take to ensure that the criminal justice system is fair.

Public Perception: Why Are the Police Called?

Autism spectrum disorder (ASD) is and always has been an impairment involving social deficits (Kanner, 1943). The fact that the impairments are not immediately obvious to the casual observer may place the person with ASD at greater risk for having the police called than if the person had a more obvious disability. Many times, the police have been called in because the person with ASD has been misunderstood or has acted inappropriately in a situation. The general public, including most police officers, doesn't know what to expect when dealing with a person on the spectrum. The person's behavior is not necessarily dictated by social context, and given their challenges, they likely will not consider how the public is perceiving their behavior. This is compounded by potential inherent biases leading the public to assume that the person is dangerous. The fact is that people on the spectrum are much more likely to be victims of a crime than perpetrators. (*See* Chap. 10, Risk of Violence for People with ASD.)

Improving Outcomes

People on the spectrum have the right to be included in their communities. Increasing presence in their neighborhoods will result in opportunities for positive contact and raised awareness. If the person lives independently, it would be helpful if he/she frequented local businesses and participated in community events. If a person on the spectrum lives with family or has a care provider, the carer should ensure that the person participates within the community as much as possible. Anecdotal reports suggest that this strategy has been successful in reducing the likelihood of neighbors calling the police because of behaviors that are misinterpreted as dangerous or bizarre.

First Contact with the Police

The initial encounter with the police will affect everything else that follows. ASD has been referred to as "the hidden disability" because it is not immediately obvious to anyone—including a responding police officer— that the person with ASD has a disability. They do not use wheelchairs, they don't have any obvious physical characteristics. However, they may not respond to police in a manner that most other people would. Due to deficits in receptive (what they can understand) and expressive (what they can produce) language capabilities, they may not understand police directions or be able to respond to police questions. Some people with ASD will feel so intimidated upon being approached by a person in a uniform that they may be overly suggestible and agreeable, thus unwittingly compromising their own rights.

A responding officer will approach the person and immediately determine if he/she is a danger to the officer or others nearby. The officer wants to see both hands at all times. Officers have been trained in rapid-response decision making and will initially try to determine the identity of the person to whom they are speaking. In many cases, the officer does not know what is going on at the scene of a call or when approached by a complainant. The officers themselves may escalate the situation. Their training requires them to immediately assess and take charge of a scene. If someone is acting in an unexpected or atypical manner when police arrive, this trained response will likely escalate the situation. In an emergency situation, it is very likely that the person on the spectrum will be in a heightened state of arousal and thus be least likely to be able to access the language ability he/she does have. Unfortunately, the officers' training may require them to subdue and gain control of the person by any force necessary. The likelihood that the situation will deteriorate precipitously at this point is very high.

Most of the time, after asking for the person's name, the officer will also request to see some type of identification (ID). In most states, it is the law that a person has to produce an ID when requested when stopped by an officer who has cause to approach. That is all that is required by law. A person does not have to answer any questions other than providing his/her name. Some officers may view this as lack of cooperation, thus escalating the situation further. In all states, a driver must submit to a field sobriety test or breathalyzer test if so requested. Failing to do so will cause the person to be arrested immediately and possibly an automatic forfeiture of the person's driver's license. Persons on the spectrum must be educated to know that if they are driving and are stopped by an officer they should make sure their hands are in sight of the officer at all times and make no sudden movements. They may have co-occurring disabilities or coordination challenges that make it difficult for them to pass a field sobriety test. If the driver can make the officer aware of this beforehand, the officer can suggest a different test of sobriety.

Improving Outcomes

Cooperating with police is paramount. However, persons on the spectrum can cooperate without giving up their rights, because from the point of first contact onward, they are at the mercy of the officer. The officer may arrest a person or issue a summons, but if that person has been taught to remain quiet, he/she will not complicate a potential court case by making statements that are self-incriminating.

I Have Autism:

I have been medically diagnosed with autism spectrum disorder. My medical condition impairs my ability to communicate with others. As a result I may have difficulty understanding your directions, and I may not be able to respond to your questions. I may also become physically agitated if you touch me or move too close to me.

Please do not interpret my behavior as refusal to cooperate. I am not intentionally defying your instructions.

(Please see reverse side for additional information) ━━━▶

FIGURE 14.1 Alabama ID card.

A person on the spectrum may want to carry a card or affix a sticker to his/her identification card that identifies him/her as an individual with ASD. It may include verbiage such as "I have Autism Spectrum Disorder, I do not want to answer any questions without my parents, guardian, or an attorney present." For example, the Alabama Department of Public Safety provides such cards to people on the spectrum: https://themighty .com/2015/02/these-cards-are-trying-to-make-life-easier-for-drivers-with-autism/ (*see* Figure 14.1).

New York State has enacted a statewide program to ensure that police and first responders are appropriately trained to recognize and respond to people with ASD. New York State has also passed legislation to create state autism ID cards, available to people with ASD and their families as a communication support in times of emergency when they are interacting with first responders.

The Asperger/Autism Network provides a card (https://www.aane .org/resources/wallet-card) that explains some of the behavior a person on the spectrum may engage in, as well as providing emergency phone numbers for the officer so the person on the spectrum can have his/her identified contacts called (*see* Figure 14.2).

Regardless of what card they carry, it is essential that persons with ASD be taught not to reach for such a card unless they are instructed to do so by the responding officer, because the officer might misinterpret this movement.

On-scene response cards (https://www.debbaudtlegacy.com/autism-scene-response-cards/) are also available for first responders. The front of the card describes the communication and behavioral challenges the person

To: A Law Enforcement Officer or other First Responder

**I have a diagnosis of *Asperger Syndrome*
a social/communication disability related to autism.**

My Name: _____

Home phone: _____ D.O.B. ____/____/____

In case of emergency, or to assist both you and me in communicating
and in resolving this situation, please contact one of the following people:

1. Name _____ Phone: _____

2. Name _____ Phone: _____

Asperger/Autism Network

617-393-3824   w w w . a a n e . o r g

**I have a diagnosis of *Asperger Syndrome (Autism Spectrum)*
a social/communication disability related to autism.**

Because of my Asperger's Syndrome, I may

- Panic if yelled at, and lash out if touched or physically restrained.
- Misinterpret things you tell me or ask me to do.
- Not be able to answer your questions.
- Appear not to be listening or paying attention.
- Tend to interpret statements literally.
- Appear rude or say things that sound tactless, especially when anxious or confused.
- Have difficulty making eye contact.
- Speak too loud, too soft, or with unusual intonation.

I would like to cooperate. To help me cooperate, PLEASE:

- Clearly identify yourself as a law enforcement officer/first responder.
- **Call one of my emergency contacts.** (Please see **reverse** side of this card.)
- Do **not** assume that my Asperger's traits constitute suspicious behavior.
- Avoid touching me or restraining me.
- Speak to me in normal, calm, non-confrontational tones.
- Tell me exactly what I need to do politely, clearly, simply, literally, and step by step.

FIGURE 14.2 Asperger/Autism Network ID card.

on the spectrum may exhibit; the back provides tips on how to respond. The tips include giving space, speaking slowly, using simple language, using concrete literal language, and allowing the person extra time to respond. It is important to remember that a delay in responding is just that, a processing delay, not lack of compliance. It's also essential that the responding officers seek input from care providers on the scene, if there are any.

Some states have developed a voluntary registry that allows families to let dispatchers and first responders know that there is a person at their home who is on the autism spectrum. This has been demonstrated to allow first responders to reflect back on any autism-specific training they may have had and prepare themselves when responding to the situation (*see* https://www.maine.gov/dhhs/reports/ASD_SurveillanceOptions.pdf).

Education is a key component both for the person on the spectrum and the first responder. How can an officer recognize that the person he/she is approaching is under the influence of drugs or alcohol, a deranged killer, or someone with special needs? Nobody would question the use of force if a person moves toward the officer aggressively or does not respond to verbal demands to show their hands. Expecting the person with special needs to always remain calm and listen to instructions is unrealistic. Special efforts must be made to educate and stress to the person on the spectrum that he/she must always follow instructions. Educating officers to be patient and not rush to act is likewise imperative in avoiding an escalation.

As a lawyer, it is essential that you have the client's rights protected and ensure that they have some way to make their challenges known to first responders.

Charges Filed/Taken to Police Station

If a decision is made to take persons with ASD to the police station, they will be handcuffed and placed in the back of the police car, for their own safety and that of the officer. The act of being handcuffed will likely cause them to respond adversely, especially those who have a history of being restrained or have a strong aversion to being touched. Depending on particular procedures, sometimes the arresting officers will photograph and fingerprint the detainee themselves, or the jail personnel may do this. The act of being fingerprinted may also cause upset. Being touched and having their fingers pressed into the ink pad may result in a negative sensory reaction by persons with ASD.

Improving Outcomes

Unfortunately, the aforementioned procedures are almost never flexible. Priming persons with ASD, as part of a comprehensive education plan, should include familiarizing them with first responders, including walking through the process of being processed in the event they are ever arrested. For example, a police department in rural Indiana routinely hosts an annual safety program for its community. Officers go to schools, pass out stickers, and fingerprint the students. These fingerprint cards are given to the parents to keep in the event something happens to their child. Sometimes police departments will use fingerprints to assist in identifying people who cannot identify themselves because they are incapacitated. Providing persons with ASD an opportunity to go through this process in a relaxed atmosphere will likely help them in managing this event more successfully in an actual arrest situation.

Custodial Interview

Due to their receptive and expressive language deficits, people on the spectrum are particularly vulnerable to having their rights compromised during the custodial interview. This concept of vulnerability may be met with skepticism by prosecutors not familiar with ASD, who often argue that the person does not *appear* to have an intellectual disability. In a study by Charman et al. (2011), more than half (55 percent) of the children with a diagnosis of ASD scored in the intellectually disabled range, whereas approximately 45 percent *did not* have an intellectual disability. However, *all* of the participants in this study, regardless of their IQ, had significant impaired adaptive functioning. In other words, the way in which they were able to navigate their world was negatively affected by their ASD, regardless of their intellectual functioning.

In order to understand the substantial communication deficits associated with ASD, it is essential to understand the difference between speech and language. *Speech* is the verbal output of language. *Language* encompasses much more: it is the entire process of giving and receiving information, which includes verbal and nonverbal exchanges (body language, facial expressions, tone of voice, nonliteral language) as well as written forms of communication (https://www.asha.org/public/speech/development/language_speech.htm). Most people with ASD understand language in a very concrete and literal manner, meaning they take the words they hear at face value rather than understanding the way the meaning of words is affected by facial expression, tone, body language, and context. It can be difficult for people not familiar with ASD to appreciate just how much of the meaning of communication people on the spectrum may miss during a custodial interview. This is because the person with ASD only understands the specific words that come out of a person's mouth rather than the broader meaning of the communication.

As a result, the most disturbing and incriminating evidence against a person on the spectrum is often gathered during the police interview. There is a concern that when a defendant with ASD is read the *Miranda* rights and asked if he/she understood those rights, he/she may respond "yes." A person with a disability that includes receptive language deficits (affecting what he/she can understand) should, at the very least, be asked to repeat back, *in his/her own words*, what he/she thinks the *Miranda* rights mean (Salseda et al., 2011). In a worst-case scenario, defendants on the spectrum may waive their right to counsel. Many people have shared with these authors that when they asked for a lawyer and one didn't materialize they did not self-advocate or refuse to answer further questions. Moreover, they did not understand the nuanced differences between "I think I need a lawyer" and "I need a lawyer."

People with ASD may be overly suggestible and agreeable, in part because they believe it will truncate an odious social interaction. They may fail to read the social intent of the investigating officer. Given the common ASD concrete and literal understanding of language, if an officer were to say they were "just having a little chat," the person with ASD might not realize that this "chat" served as a confession.

Due to their agreeableness, social naïveté, and inability to determine the intentions of others, a person with ASD may continue to talk, without benefit of counsel. Those responses may constitute a confession, which will likely be used against the person at trial.

Improving Outcomes

The United Kingdom has successfully developed a program that entitles vulnerable people, including people with ASD, to an "appropriate adult" (advocate) as soon as they contact the criminal justice system.

Easy-to-read versions of the *Miranda* warnings for people on the spectrum could be developed as a visual support (*see* Figure 14.3). Responding officers would still be required to read the official caution, but they could supplement this with the easy-read version to be shown to persons on the spectrum, so they have a better understanding of their rights.

Defendants should be asked to repeat back, *in their own words*, what they thought their *Miranda* rights meant.

It would be helpful if, as a matter of course, interviews were recorded. If there is no recording, the officer's recollection is what will be written down in the report of the interview. In some cases, there will be more than one officer, so that there is another witness to what was said. Nevertheless, bizarre or tangential comments and excessive candor may be interpreted as admissions of guilt by people unfamiliar with ASD. In the absence of a recording, the comments of the person on the spectrum are subject to interpretation that is unlikely to be in his/her favor.

Nothing good can ever come from agreeing to be interviewed without a lawyer present. People on the spectrum must be educated not to speak or agree to be interviewed without a lawyer present. Clear guidelines should be established with persons on the spectrum. They should be taught to say "I want a lawyer" and told not to say anything until a lawyer arrives. If a lawyer does not arrive, they should be taught to continue to say "I want a lawyer" until one does arrive, as well as to continue to keep silent otherwise. This is how concrete the information should be for a person on the spectrum. They need to be told that "spontaneous utterances" can be used against them. They need to be told that this means what they say at the scene of the incident or what they say in the back of the police car can be held against them. Again, they should be instructed to say nothing until a lawyer arrives.

If a lawyer was not present during the interview and the accused has a pre- or postcustodial diagnosis of ASD, you as the lawyer may want to explore suppressing the statement.

FIGURE 14.3 *Miranda* warnings card.

Holding Cell

It would be extremely difficult to adequately prepare a person with ASD for the sensory assault of a holding cell. When they arrive at the station, they may or may not be interviewed; depending on the charges, they may go straight to a jail cell. The cell could contain one person or fifty, depending on the jurisdiction. Given their sensory challenges, a jail cell will be untenable for a person with ASD, due to the loud sounds, bright lights, and smells prevalent in the cells. For many people, when the cell door closes, they become either the predator or the victim. For people on the spectrum, their social challenges make them especially vulnerable to being exploited and/or the target of aggression from other detainees. They may be in the cell for one night or several, depending the day of the week, the court schedule, and whether bail has been set or other arrangements have been made. Once this phase of the legal journey begins, a person may sit in jail awaiting trial for a prolonged period of time.

Improving Outcomes

It is incumbent upon everyone in the criminal justice system to intervene and protect the rights of the person on the spectrum. Do not assume that courts have personnel who are trained to identify people with ASD; remember that such disorders are often not immediately obvious to the untrained eye, and the person may be viewed as combative and/or nonresponsive. If the person with ASD is identified as being such, or discloses that he/she is on the spectrum, the court should be advised immediately that the person is in custody. Arrangements must be made to place the person in a safe holding cell and do whatever is necessary to mitigate the sensory assault and reduce the risk of exploitation.

As with all other clients, it is essential to tell the person with ASD not to "confide" in other detainees. This information has been used by fellow inmates to the benefit of themselves and the detriment of the person on the spectrum. If persons with ASD need someone to speak to, they should be encouraged to speak to their attorney or a trusted friend or family member. (*See* Chap. 6, The Bond Hearing.)

Trial

It is essential that the judge and jury be informed that the defendant has a diagnosis of ASD. In the absence of this information, the jury does not have the opportunity to consider key factors in the trial as they relate to ASD. There is a risk that a defendant with ASD who has a flat affect (neutral facial expressions) may be perceived to be "cold-blooded," "remorseless," or psychopathic. Affective control theory suggests, in part, that defendants who are perceived negatively by the individuals in charge of sentencing are given harsher sentences than those who are perceived positively (Tsoudis, 2000). The perceptions of judges and juries are affected by displays of emotion. It has been repeatedly documented that people on the autism spectrum may maintain a flat expression or an expression that does not match their internal state. For example, defendants may smile to mask anxiety. They may engage in bizarre or completely absent demonstrations of remorse. A neutral, negative, or ambiguous display of affect could put the person with ASD at a disadvantage during the penalty phase. (*See* Chap. 15, Perception of Defendants with ASD by Judges and Juries.)

Improving Outcomes

From the beginning of the process, the arrestee should be walked through the process by his or her lawyer. The lawyer has the obligation to make sure the defendant understands all the charges. This serves two purposes. First, it primes persons with ASD so they can better prepare themselves for the events to come. Second, it more adequately enables the defendants to assist in their own defense. If they cannot offer any assistance in their defense, the court may ask for a competency hearing to determine the defendant's ability. It is essential that the person conducting the competency evaluation be familiar with ASD.

The family and/or care provider responsible for the person with ASD must make sure their lawyer is acting in the best interest of the defendant. The defendant has the right to request another lawyer, preferably one with disabilities experience, if deemed appropriate.

Testifying

Due to the manner in which people with ASD react to affective displays of emotion and the way in which juries or judges interpret these bizarre or absent demonstrations of remorse, our nonlegal opinion is that it is almost *never* advisable to put the person with ASD on the stand to testify. When we authors are in a position to advise the legal teams of people with ASD, we advise against their clients testifying. It is essential that the defense team be aware of the diagnosis of ASD, so they can make a more informed decision about whether to put their client on the stand. If put on the stand, typically the defendant with ASD may be able to successfully answer questions from his/her own attorney on direct examination; however, the responses may be reflective of an overly simplistic understanding of social relationships and may demonstrate the client's impoverished emotional vocabulary, difficulty attributing mental states to self or others, and an inability to understand other people's intentions.

The excessive candor and dispassionate description of the incident may lead prosecutors, jurors, and judges to assume that the client has psychopathic tendencies, or at the very least a complete lack of empathy. When people with ASD are under stress, their ability to access language drops immediately and precipitously. Faced with the prosecution's questions, which often included multilayered questions, nonliteral language, and sarcasm, the person on the spectrum is at a distinct disadvantage to competently participate in his/her own defense. Due to their common difficulty in ascribing mental states to others and determining the intent of others, and the potential difficulty of following long, narrative-type questions, persons on the spectrum are vulnerable to self-incrimination on the witness stand. (*See* Chap. 15, Perception of Defendants with ASD by Judges and Juries.)

Although the decision to testify should be left up to the attorney and the defendant, in our opinion, there are very few cases in which it is advisable for persons with ASD to testify in their own defense.

Improving Outcomes

Preparation is tedious and demanding for anyone planning on testifying, whether a witness or a defendant. If the decision is made for the person with ASD to testify, preparation should be broken up into small segments of time to help the person maintain focus.

When being prepared to testify, the defendant might respond best to questions in writing. If this is so, the lawyer could request that the court allow the lawyer to continue that practice at trial. If the defendant had a hearing impairment or a visual impairment, reasonable accommodation would be made. Likewise, presenting information visually is a reasonable accommodation for many people with ASD.

The person with ASD should be asked questions one at a time, on both direct and cross-examination. Multilayered questions may result in the person answering only one of the questions, and there is a risk that this answer will be extrapolated and applied to all of the questions.

Defendants should be educated by the lawyer to understand that the act of taking the oath to tell the truth means they must respond to all questions, and that the jury will be judging them on everything they say.

Defendants also need to be aware that what they say sitting at the defense table can be heard by others in the court. They are not to object, overrule, or engage in any other utterances (regardless of what they may have seen on television).

Finally, the defendant with ASD must be prepared to realize that the trial could end with him/her being taken to prison. Social stories are helpful in describing what happens during the sentencing phase. Specifically, the following steps should be outlined in writing or pictures to the person with ASD: the judge will read the sentence; the person will have to leave with officers of the court. He/she will not be allowed to hug or touch the family. He/she can turn around and say goodbye. He/she should leave with the officers of the court quietly and peacefully.

Prison

From a behavior analytic perspective, prison is a very ineffective consequence for offending behaviors committed by people with ASD (Apel & Diller, 2017). *Punishment* is a consequence that occurs after a problem behavior occurs, with the intent of reducing the likelihood that the problem behavior will occur again in the future. If we agree that the offending behavior results in large part due to the social deficits inherent in an ASD diagnosis, compounded by the lack of prosocial experiences, then it is clear that incarceration is a misguided and actually counterproductive consequence for offending behaviors. Within the neurotypical prison population, there are high rates of recidivism within five years of release from prison. People with ASD who are incarcerated are exposed to what has been referred to as a "criminal apprenticeship," which may make them more criminally savvy (Durose, Cooper, & Snyder, 2014). Moreover, people with ASD are vulnerable to developing cognitive distortions that in the absence of appropriate peer models could serve to justify their offending behavior. Paradoxically, prison culture may increase the likelihood of re-offending because of the social acceptance of offending behavior within prisons (Megens & Weerman, 2012).

As for the actual prison experience, consider that once defendants have been convicted or entered a plea requiring prison, they will be taken from the court or ordered by the court to report on a specific day. Upon arrival at the prison, prisoners will be taken to the receiving area where they will surrender all their belongings, clothes, valuables, and shoes. Many people with ASD have items that they use to self-regulate, such as headphones, a journal, or a visual support. At a time when the person most needs these self-regulatory accommodations, they are taken away. The prisoner will then be subjected to a full body cavity search. For people with ASD who have sensitivity to touch, this experience would likely be torturous. Prisoners will be fingerprinted and photographed and provided with a prison uniform. Many people with ASD cannot tolerate the feel of certain fabrics or tags, so in this way they are being subjected to an extremely aversive experience. The prison cell could be private, a double, or even a ward housing many other prisoners.

Persons without autism who enter prison usually quickly affiliate themselves with people who share similar characteristics and beliefs. In other words, they seek and join a group that offers belonging and protection. In contrast, persons with ASD who have profound social deficits do not know to do this, nor do they likely have the skill set to join a group. Thus, in most cases, people with ASD become "unaffiliated prisoners." As such they are vulnerable to becoming the target of verbal, physical, and sexual assault by all groups.

Finally, what is the person learning in prison that will decrease the likelihood that he/she will engage in the behavior that resulted in the conviction? When we analyze behavior, we must consider behavioral excesses and deficits. It is essential to teach replacement behaviors that are as effective and as immediate as the problem behavior. Prison does not teach any appropriate replacement behaviors that the person on the spectrum will need to function successfully once his/her sentence is completed. (*See* Chap. 13, Prison Accommodations.)

Improving Outcomes

Depending on the seriousness of the crime, courts should consider diversion programs that avoid prison altogether. The person with ASD could be connected with social services through the prison's developmental disabilities resource center; a plan should be developed to increase the person's skill set, as well as providing formal and informal supports and services within the community.

Prison personnel should be made aware of and receive special training on how to support people on the spectrum, including the use of visual supports, how persons with ASD may respond differently to directions than other prisoners, and how to de-escalate a crisis safely.

Long-Term Impact of Criminal Record

Overcoming the stigma of a criminal record is an arduous task for most people. Incarceration of people with ASD has long-lasting, damaging effects on their lives. High rates of unemployment and underemployment and a lack of housing options, combined with a criminal record, further limit their already limited options. Most good jobs are not available to people with a criminal record, and the jobs that are available are low-pay, service-type jobs with no benefits. If a person with ASD is convicted of a sex crime, he/she can expect to be put on a registry that will affect where he/she can live and work. Specifically, these people most likely cannot live at home if they have a minor sibling who also lives in the home. They cannot live in most group homes; they cannot live within a certain distance from a school or daycare center.

Moreover, steep legal fees place a financial burden on their families (Vallas, 2016). This stress is heightened by societal judgments, as if the families were complicit in the commission of the crime (Schwartz-Soicher, Geller, & Garfinkel, 2011). Compounding this problem is that many services set up to support people with developmental disabilities will not work with people who have a criminal record due to the presumed risk. As a result, persons with ASD who have served their time are further punished through isolation, lack of structure, unemployment, a paucity of housing options, and an absence of meaningful activities and social contact with others. (*See* Chap. 12, Mitigation Using Community Resources.)

Improving Outcomes

Vocational training or education while in prison could improve a person's chances for employment outside of prison. The United Kingdom has developed successful catering and coding programs with links to outside employment to prepare prisoners for work after incarceration.

After release from prison, the person will need to be connected with prosocial peers to separate him/her from the influences and habits that may have shaped the previous criminal behavior.

People with ASD who have untreated depression or anxiety may have self-medicated with drugs and alcohol. It is essential that they have a treating psychiatrist, one familiar with ASD, who can address their mental health needs and addiction problems.

Conclusion

A person with ASD, if given the proper supports, such as rules, meaningful employment, inclusive opportunities within the community, and a structured schedule, can do very well and lead a productive life. People with ASD have not been found by studies to be more dangerous than the general population. Indeed, anecdotal evidence suggests that people with ASD who are incarcerated are more vulnerable due to their gullibility and naïveté. It could be argued that prison, which results in a sensory, social, and often physical assault on the person with autism, constitutes cruel and unusual punishment. It is not the intent of these authors to vilify or patronize people on the autism spectrum. Conversely, it is not our intent to give them a free pass when their behavior reaches the level of criminality. Rather, our aim here is to make the system equitable by highlighting the characteristics of autism that may be implicated in the commission of an offense, and how those characteristics may compromise the constitutional rights of the person with ASD.

• • •

Laurie Sperry, PhD, is an adjunct faculty member at Stanford University, School of Medicine, Department of Psychiatry. Prior to joining Stanford, she was Assistant Clinical Faculty at Yale University, Department of Psychiatry and is a founding member of the Autism Forensics Team there. In addition to a PhD and a degree in forensic psychology and criminology, she is a board-certified Behavior Analyst–Doctoral Level.

In 2006, she was added to the Fulbright Scholarship's Senior Specialist Roster for Autism. She moved to Australia in 2010 and worked at Griffith University in the Department of Arts, Education and Law. Her research focuses on people with ASD who come in contact with the criminal justice system, to ensure their humane treatment within the system. She has served as a Special Interest Group Chair at the International Meeting for Autism Research (IMFAR), providing mentoring and leadership in the field of criminality and ASD. She has provided training to secure forensic psychiatric facility staff in England and presented at the International Conference for Offenders with Disabilities. She has published numerous articles and was an expert panelist at the American Academy of Psychiatry and Law conference, where she spoke on risk assessment, management, and ASD. She has completed ADOS (Autism Diagnostic Observation

Schedule) evaluations in prisons, has testified as an expert witness in sentencing hearings, and has written *amicus curiae* briefs and participated in cases that have been considered before the state supreme court. Dr. Sperry can be reached at autismforensics@gmail.com and her website is http://www.asapsperry.com.

Clare Hughes has spent the past seventeen years at the National Autistic Society of the United Kingdom. Since February 2013, she has been working exclusively in the area of autism and the criminal justice system. This has included leading three projects funded by the Ministry of Justice: one about raising awareness of autism within prisons, one working with the National Probation Service in the northwest of England to look at improving support for autistic people, and another one working again with the National Probation Service and five prisons to improve support and outcomes for autistic people. This current project focuses on autistic people who have committed sexual offenses.

Other work has included developing a criminal justice strategy for the organization, sitting on the Ministry of Justice's cross-department group to address the criminal justice actions within England's autism strategy (Think Autism), and delivering a project looking at safeguarding children and young people with autism.

In 2014, Ms. Hughes began working with HMYOI Feltham to develop autism accreditation standards for prisons. Since then, she has worked with colleagues to develop autism accreditation standards for probation services and the police. She was co-author of "Development and Implementation of Autism Standards for Prisons," an article recently published in the *Journal of Intellectual Disabilities and Offending Behaviour*. She wrote the autism section of the Prison Reform Trust, and Think Mental Illness Mental Health publication, *Autism & Learning Disabilities in the Criminal Courts: Information for Magistrates, District Judges and Court Staff*, and contributed to the Advocate's Gateway Autism Toolkit. Ms. Hughes can be reached at clare.hughes@nas.org.uk.

Michael J. Forsee is a retired Supervisory Special Agent of the Federal Bureau of Investigation (FBI). After obtaining a degree in sociology, he graduated from the Indiana Law Enforcement Academy and the FBI Academy. Forsee also completed numerous specialized training courses at the FBI Academy, including Undercover Certification, Computer

Forensics, Informant Handling and Development, Basic SWAT, Rappel Master, Sniper Certification, Advanced Sniper, Evidence Response Team Certification, Explosive Investigation, and Recovery of Human Remains.

Prior to becoming an FBI Special Agent (SA), Forsee was a uniformed police officer for four years and then a detective for five years. During his time as a detective, he was responsible for the investigation and trial of all types of offenses under state law.

Special Agent Forsee began his career as an FBI SA in a two-man office in Beaufort, S.C. During his time in this office, he was responsible for the investigation of all violations of federal law. Forsee left Beaufort after eleven years and transferred to the New York Office of the FBI. While in New York, Forsee was assigned to the Joint Terrorism Task Force to investigate and counter terrorism. Shortly after arriving in New York, Forsee was sent to East Africa in response to the East Africa Embassy bombings in August 1998. Forsee was made one of the case agents for the Embassy bombing case, the largest counterterrorism investigation in the history of the FBI. After the successful indictment of Usama Bin Laden and his co-conspirators, and the arrest and conviction of four of the men responsible for the Embassy bombings, Forsee received the Attorney General's Award for Excellence in Investigation. Forsee left New York in 2011 and was assigned to Kosovo as the FBI and Justice Department representative investigating terrorism and organized crime. Upon completing his six-month assignment in Kosovo, he was sent to Afghanistan to continue the investigation of Al Qaeda. Forsee then acted as an assistant legal attaché at the U.S. Embassy in Ottawa, Canada, where he was responsible for liaising with Canadian authorities in the investigation of counterterrorism matters. Following his time in Ottawa, Forsee was sent to the U.S. Embassy in Nairobi, Kenya, as the legal attaché. This position is the Justice Department's representative for six East African countries, and he served as supervisor of the FBI office there. Forsee met with embassy personnel as well as government officials for these East African countries.

Upon returning to the United States, Forsee was named to President Bush's High Value Detainee (HVD) interview team. Forsee was selected to represent the FBI on this team in interviewing the HVDs recently released from overseas custody and transferred to the U.S. Naval Base at Guantánamo Bay. During this time Forsee interviewed the HVDs to prepare cases for federal court in the United States. Eventually, Forsee was able to take custody of one of the HVDs and present him to the Southern

District of New York; thereafter, Forsee spent the next few years preparing this case for prosecution. This HVD was convicted and sentenced to life without parole. As a result of this investigation, Forsee received his second Attorney General's Award for Excellence in Investigation. Forsee has interviewed hundreds of defendants and thousands of witnesses in preparing cases for prosecution and has testified numerous times in both state and federal court.

Complete citations are available from the authors upon request.

15

Perception of Defendants with ASD by Judges and Juries

Clare S. Allely

Despite the American presumption of innocence and other constitutional pro-tections, people charged with criminal offenses face tremendous obstacles. This is particularly true for people with mental disabilities, including people with ASD. Indeed, misunderstanding and lack of knowledge about ASD may combine to compromise their rights to substantive and procedural justice.

The following chapter by Dr. Clare S. Allely describes the research done regarding attitudes by judges and juries in this area. She also details why strate-gies such as use of an expert are vital in educating judges and juries. Attorneys representing defendants with ASD must acknowledge this general misunder-standing and lack of knowledge and take steps to combat them.

• • •

There are many myths about people with autism spectrum disorders (ASD) (e.g., John, Knott, & Harvey, 2018). Thus, judges and jurors may rely on misperceptions about ASD. This may result in unjust outcomes. For instance, a defendant with ASD may be sentenced to a long prison term when his/her offending appears to be particularly bizarre or dan-gerous, or when he/she appears to have no remorse (e.g., Kristiansson & Sorman, 2008). It has also been highlighted that jurors may have some degree of skepticism toward the information given by expert witnesses. Expert witnesses themselves may lack understanding of and familiarity with ASD, particularly regarding the ways in which different ASD symptomology can contribute to different types of offending behavior (Allely & Cooper, 2017). Therefore, it is of crucial importance that judges and jurors be educated to understand the true nature of ASD and its symptomology. This emphasizes the need for and significance of expert insights into ASD and its related symptomology (Freckelton, 2012; Freckelton & List, 2009).

Defendants with ASD in the Courtroom

There are a number of features of ASD that may be perceived by criminal justice professionals and jurors as being evidence of guilt or lack of remorse. There are also a variety of behaviors that individuals with ASD may exhibit during court proceedings that can make them appear bizarre and be misunderstood. Some of these are discussed in this section.

Lack of Outward Expressions of Empathy

It is well established that many individuals with ASD have an impaired ability to appreciate the subjective experiences of others; this is typically referred to as an impaired theory of mind (ToM). Thus, the individual with ASD may not exhibit any outward expressions of empathy, which may make him/her appear to be cold and calculating. This apparent lack of feeling can be detrimental in court. For instance, jurors may assume that such defendants are guilty. Moreover, the lack of expression by defendants with ASD can negatively affect sentencing. In contrast, some defendants with ASD may display facial expressions that are considered awkward or inappropriate. A defendant with ASD may suddenly start laughing when talking about the victim or when the alleged victim is being questioned during the court proceedings. However, it is important to highlight that many times this outward expression does not reflect what the individual with ASD is truly feeling or thinking.

Unusual Ways of Speaking

It is important to be aware that many individuals with ASD have an odd or pedantic manner of speaking. They may also exhibit sudden and unexpected verbal utterances or unexpectedly speak at an increased volume. Individuals with ASD can exhibit an unusual or odd-sounding prosody. They may speak in a monotonous voice that has no variation in prosodic elements such as speech rate and rhythm, pitch/fundamental frequency, loudness, intensity, duration, or pause/silence (McCann & Peppé, 2003). Impairments also may be demonstrated in the use of gestures, personal space, timing, topic selection, and difficulties understanding nonliteral language, metaphors, irony, sarcasm, or humor.

Eye Contact and Impaired Ability to Recognize Simple Conventions in Conversation

Defendants with ASD may also be perceived as lacking interest in the court proceedings and/or as being arrogant (Archer & Hurley, 2013). Difficulty making and maintaining eye contact occurs in many individuals with ASD. For example, a defendant with ASD may look down at the table in front of him/her during the entire trial, which can lead people to believe that he/she is so ashamed and guilty that he/she cannot even look the alleged victim(s) or the judge or jurors in the eye. However, many individuals with ASD do this because it helps minimize the sensory overload they are receiving, particularly during situations that are distressing and anxiety inducing, such as a trial. Defendants with ASD may also appear to be rude on occasion during court proceeding because of their impairments in recognizing and detecting simple conventions in conversation. For example, during the court proceedings when the lawyer is talking, they may be unable to detect the social cues that are typically used to signal the end of a conversation and may interrupt or not realize that they have been asked a question (Murrie et al., 2002).

Repetitive Interest and/or Particular Obsessions

Repetitive interests and/or particular obsessions that are displayed by the defendant with ASD throughout the court proceedings, or were displayed during the alleged offending behavior(s), may not be understood or could be misinterpreted by jurors and other criminal justice professionals. If jurors lack an understanding of the symptomology of ASD, some defendants with ASD may be perceived as odd or bizarre (Cea, 2014). During the court proceedings, a defendant with ASD may suddenly shift the topic of the court discussions to something that he/she is interested in talking about (which might be one of his/her preoccupations), and such a person can be very difficult to interrupt. Such behavior may make the person appear as if he/she is being evasive. Moreover, when such people are asked a question during the court proceedings, they may respond at length and with significant detail. Their discourse also may be repetitive and revert to their specific preoccupations and interests.

An increasing number of studies have found that nontypical, repetitive, narrow interests are one of the symptoms of ASD frequently associated with offending behavior. For instance, Tietz (2002) described the case of a man who had a fixation on city transit–related activities. He became involved in the criminal justice system after the unauthorized driving of subway trains and buses. He had also directed traffic around New York City Transit Authority construction sites (Tietz, 2002).

Milton and colleagues (2002) described the case of a man who had a fascination with female genitalia. He was particularly fascinated with the image of women being gynecologically examined by a doctor. To pursue his fascination, he would pretend to be a medical researcher on telephone "chat lines" and would ask the female telephone operators to describe their gynecological examination experiences; he would usually masturbate during these calls.

Another case, described by Murrie and colleagues (2002), involved a thirty-three-year-old unmarried male prosecuted for sexual assault against his nine-year-old daughter and one of her peers. The man had spent an extensive amount of time collecting thousands of paper dolls in the five years prior to his offense. He would use these paper dolls in sexual games and would also integrate photos of himself with them.

Another case involved a man who assaulted women due to idiosyncratic reasons. He attacked one woman, using a saw blade, because she was wearing shorts. On another occasion, he stabbed a woman with a screwdriver because she was driving and he disliked women drivers (Mawson, Grounds, & Tantam, 1985).

Importance of Informing the Jury of the Defendant's Diagnosis of ASD

The studies and areas just discussed underline the importance of informing the court of a diagnosis of ASD and the types of behaviors that someone with ASD may exhibit. It is recommended that expert witness testimony be given in order to provide understanding of the behavior and presentation of a defendant with ASD during court proceedings. An expert can help the jury understand the ways in which the ASD diagnosis, in particular the different symptomologies of ASD, may have contributed to the offending behavior. When given this information, a jury may be less likely to misinterpret the defendant's behavior and presentation during court proceedings.

Nonetheless, a number of courts in the United States do not permit psychiatric experts to provide testimony about Asperger's syndrome (AS) or high-functioning ASD (hfASD).

However, it is important to inform the jury of the defendant's ASD diagnosis because it may help the jurors understand why the defendant may present the way he/she does during the court proceedings. If no expert testimony regarding the defendant's ASD diagnosis is provided to the jury, the jury's negative perception of the demeanor and the apparent lack of remorse exhibited by the defendant with ASD may be particularly detrimental and have harmful consequences (e.g., Cea, 2014; Haskins & Silva, 2006) such as longer sentences. It is crucial that a diagnosis of ASD be considered as a potential mitigating factor. For someone with a diagnosis of ASD, a long sentence may be particularly damaging (*see, e.g.*, Cea, 2015).

Investigating Jurors' and/or Judges' Evaluations of Defendants with ASD

Dr. Colleen Berryessa is an assistant professor at the Rutgers University School of Criminal Justice. She is one of the few researchers who has studied the impact of ASD in the courtroom, and she has published the majority of papers in this area.

Impact of Psychiatric Information on Potential Jurors in Evaluating hfASD

Berryessa and colleagues (2015) developed a three-part survey to investigate potential jurors' attitudes to a defendant with a diagnosis of hfASD with respect to "perceptions and decisions surrounding legal and moral responsibility, personal characteristics of the offender, the introduction of psychiatric and genetic information, and the condition's influence on the facts of the case" (Berryessa, Milner, Garrison, & Cho, 2015, p. 140). The sample consisted of 623 jury-eligible United States adults who completed all three parts of the survey.

Part 1 of the survey asked participants to imagine they were a juror on a case. Participants were presented with a fictional criminal case summary involving a defendant (MK) who had been charged with assault of his roommate. This fictional case was based on the real case of *Regina v. Kagan*. The case summary was 330 words long and included facts about the case, the background of the defendant, and the behavior the defendant exhibited during the trial. Participants were given definitions for a range of legal terms, such as "criminal intention," "legal responsibility," "moral responsibility," and "free will." In part 1 of the survey, no psychiatric evidence or testimony was given to the participants. Participants were then asked to rate their opinions for twelve questions using a scale that ranged from 1 to 5 ("strongly agree" to "strongly disagree"). Some examples of the twelve questions include: "There was criminal intention in the actions made by MK," "MK had reason to fear that his roommate would seriously injure him," "I think MK is a dangerous person," "MK's behavior during the trial makes it look like he does not care," and "MK's behavior during the trial makes him look guilty of his crimes."

However, in part 2 of the survey, an additional summary of the psychiatric testimony (330 words) presented during the trial was given to the participants. This psychiatric testimony provided details that MK's hfASD diagnosis would have previously been Asperger's syndrome (before diagnostic changes made in the *Diagnostic and Statistical Manual, Fifth Edition [DSM-5]*). The summary also suggested that MK's diagnosis of hfASD contributed to MK's behavior and the facts of the case. Information regarding hfASD, its diagnostic characteristics, and evidence on the genetic origin of ASD was also provided to the participants. After they had read the new evidence, participants then re-rated their opinions on the same twelve questions that had been given in part 1.

Based on all the information provided in parts 1 and 2 of the survey, participants were asked to respond to forced-ranking and multiple-choice questions on MK in part 3 of the survey. The questions were about his condition, his dangerousness, legal consequences, and his legal and moral responsibility. Part 3 of the survey was independent of the questions that were asked in parts 1 and 2. In part 3, respondents were asked how and why the responses that they gave in part 1 of the survey had changed in part 2 after they were provided with the additional information on psychiatric conditions, the offender's condition, and the genetic propensity of MK's disorder prior to completing part 2. Participants were also given definitions of legal terms at this stage, such as "criminal intention," "legal responsibility," "moral responsibility," and "free will" (Berryessa et al., 2015).

Overall, the findings of the survey by Berryessa and colleagues (2015) indicated that respondents' opinions were significantly affected following their receipt of the additional summary of the psychiatric testimony (containing information about MK's diagnosis of hfASD and how it potentially contributed to his offending behavior) given during part 2 of the survey. The opinions of the majority of respondents were not found to differ with respect to MK's legal responsibility following provision of the additional psychiatric information at part 2 of the survey. Most of the respondents agreed both before (86.4 percent) and after (74.3 percent) the provision of the psychiatric information on MK's diagnosis that he should be considered legally responsible for his charged actions. This difference was found to be significantly statistically different, however. Although statistically significant, most of respondents agreed both before (88.8 percent) and after (80.6 percent) the provision of the psychiatric information on MK's diagnosis that he had committed a criminal action. Nevertheless, the percentage of respondents who agreed that MK had criminal intent in part 1 was decreased significantly after they received the psychiatric information regarding his diagnosis in part 2 (53.9 percent to 31.1 percent, respectively).

Furthermore, compared to the before-and-after questions in parts 1 and 2, in the stand-alone contextualization questions in part 3, similar respondent attitudes with respect to MK's legal responsibility were found. The majority of respondents were not in agreement with the statements "MK is not guilty of any crimes" and "MK does not understand what he did was wrong, and, therefore, should not be held accountable" (75.4 percent and 72.7 percent, respectively). The opinion that MK was competent to stand trial was found in 64.5 percent of the respondents. The percentage of respondents who did not agree with the statement "MK did not have control over the criminal actions he committed because of his condition" was 55.4 percent. The majority of respondents held the opinion that MK was legally responsible, with regard to the punitive consequences for MK's actions. However, despite this, the study found that 46.9 percent did not agree with the statement "MK should be sentenced to prison time," and 45.1 percent were in agreement that imprisonment should be considered a cruel and unusual punishment. The percent of respondents who held the opinion that therapy was an alternative to prison was 57.6.

In the before-and-after questions, some shifts in responses were identified suggesting that after being provided with psychiatric information regarding MK's diagnosis (which was given in part 2), respondents became more lenient in their opinions regarding MK's moral responsibility for his actions. Following the additional psychiatric information given in part 2, the percentage of respondents who believed that MK was morally responsible decreased from 81.5 percent to 62.3 percent. Also, respondents who agreed that MK should feel bad for his actions decreased from 78.8 percent to 67.7 percent. The respondents' perceptions of MK's behavior during the trial were significantly affected by knowledge of his diagnosis. Specifically, the percentage of respondents who held the opinion that MK's behavior during the trial made him seem as if he "did not care" went down from 83.9 percent to 58.6 percent. In addition, the respondents who had the opinion that MK's behavior during the trial made him "look guilty" went down from 41.7 percent to 32.9 percent. Respondents who reported a change in their opinion regarding MK's trial behavior after the additional summary of the psychiatric testimony was given to them in part 2 was 56 percent. Of the 56 percent of respondents who reported this, 96.8 percent reported that after reading the psychiatric information regarding MK they had a more positive response to him.

Even though there were changes in opinion between the responses given in part 1 and those given in part 2, in the stand-alone contextualization questions in part 3, the majority of respondents reported that they believed that MK's hfASD did not have an impact on his legal (64.1 percent) or moral (58.4 percent) responsibility for his offending behavior. However, a number of respondents held the view that MK was less legally and/or morally responsible due to his hfASD (30.8 percent and 35.2 percent, respectively). In 66.3 percent of the respondents, the psychiatric evidence given in part 2 of the survey was reported to only "somewhat change" their original views of the case. It is interesting that 41.1 percent of the respondents believed "MK was genetically predisposed to the behaviors that led to the actions against his roommate." This is in line with the finding that, of the total sample of respondents, just over half (53.1 percent) stated that the fact that MK's condition is genetic was "very or somewhat influential on their views of the case" (Berryessa et al., 2015).

Berryessa and colleagues (2015) note that their study highlights the importance of considering "how information and research on hfASD is presented to jurors, as well as more generally in the media and on other platforms to members of the public who might serve on juries."

Judges' Views on Criminal Behavior and Intention of Offenders with hfASD

Based on semi-structured telephone interviews with twenty-one California Superior Court judges, Berryessa (2014a) explored how they perceived and understood hfASD and also their understanding of how hfASD can affect individuals' ability to "formulate criminal intent" and control their offending behavior. The interview guide consisted of twenty questions and were grouped under three categories: (1) "genetic disorders, both generally and related to criminal offending"; (2) "ASDs and hfASDs, both generally and related to criminal offending"; and (3) "personal experiences with and media portrayal of hfASDs, both generally and in a criminal justice context." Findings from the study showed that the total sample of twenty-one judges reported having had previous experience with hfASD in either a personal or professional capacity. Seven of the twenty-one judges reported prior case experience with defendants with hfASD. Specifically, four judges reported having come across multiple cases in their professional experience. Three of the judges recalled having come across only one case in their professional experience. Personal experience with individuals with hfASDs was reported by eighteen of the judges. Analysis of the judges' interviews revealed three core themes: predisposition to behavior; the offender's view of the world and criminal intention; and the offender's difficulty controlling behavior and lack of impulse control. The main findings of each of these three main themes are detailed here.

First, with respect to the category "predisposition to behavior," thirteen of the total sample of twenty-one judges gave responses that centered around the theme of predisposition to behavior. "Predisposition to behavior" suggests that offenders who have hfASD are predisposed to behave in certain ways as a direct result of their disorder. This group of thirteen judges included six of the seven judges who reported having had previous case experience of defendants with a diagnosis of hfASD. For offenders with hfASD, the majority of the judges reported feelings of uncertainty in understanding and making decisions with regard to the offenders' criminal responsibility and their sentences. One judge who had had experience with multiple cases involving a defendant with ASD reported feeling hesitant about whether hfASD has any impact on the defendant's criminal responsibility (Berryessa, 2014a).

Second, with respect to the category "the offender's view of the world and criminal intent," eight of the twenty-one interviews contained discussions surrounding the way individuals with ASD "view the world" and how this and their hfASD diagnosis affects their criminal intent. Several of the judges reported that knowing offenders with hfASD "view the world" in a different way, compared to offenders with no hfASD diagnosis, makes it a challenge for the judges to completely understand the role of intent in the actions of these individuals and decide exactly how it should influence sentencing decisions. A diagnosis of hfASD was also reported as being a potential mitigating factor by raising questions as to the presence of "intent and a willful criminal act."

Third, in nine of the interviews the theme of "offender's difficulty controlling behaviour and lack of impulse control" was identified (Berryessa, 2014a). These findings by Berryessa (2014a) provide "insight on judicial understandings of hfASDs, the types of issues they identify as potentially challenging or influential when processing and making decisions concerning diagnosed offenders, areas of practice that could be affected, and a starting point for future research." Berryessa suggests that in the future this research "should serve as fundamental insight for expert witnesses and those who run judicial training or educational programmes on ASDs or other mental health issues into some of the areas and types of difficulties judges have assessing information on hfASDs" (Berryessa, 2014a).

Judges' Perceptions of Media Portrayals of Offenders with hfASDs

In another study, Berryessa (2014b) explored judicial perceptions of media portrayals of offenders with hfASD. To do this, Berryessa conducted semi-structured telephone interviews with twenty-one California Superior Court judges, as part of a larger study that explored the ways in which judges perceive and also formulate decisions regarding individuals with hfASDs. The interview guide consisted of twenty semi-structured questions (as reported for the study by Berryessa and colleagues [2014a] discussed in the previous section). The questions in these semi-structured interviews relevant to the focus of the present study were those that explored the judges' opinions about the portrayal of individuals with hfASD in the media. Some examples of the questions included in the interview were: "In your opinion, how does the media usually portray Autistic Spectrum Disorders or Asperger's Syndrome?"; "What has shaped your view of Asperger's Syndrome or other Autistic Spectrum Disorders when it comes to criminal offenders, the legal or the criminal justice systems?"; and "How did the Sandy Hook Elementary School tragedy and its aftermath, or other media stories in the last 1–2 years, change or affect your views on High Functioning Autistic Spectrum Disorders or Asperger's Syndrome?" (Berryessa, 2014b).

Moreover, although a number of judges reported that there are both negative and positive portrayals of hfASDs in the media, the most frequently held opinion was that these portrayals are usually a mixture of the two. Concerns were raised surrounding the focus on the negative features of hfASD in the media. The judges who viewed the portrayal of hfASD as only positive in the media focused on portrayals of the disorder in fiction and how the general public's awareness of ASD increases as a result of the representation of ASD in the media. The rationale of the judges who viewed the media portrayal of hfASD as positive focused on how this exposure increases the understanding and acceptance of hfASD in the general public. In the study, Berryessa (2014) also found that the large majority of judges viewed the media coverage of offending behavior and hfASDs as being misleading and harmful. Judges, by recognizing this negative bias, can aim to mitigate the potential detrimental effects on their opinions and decisions. Judges reported that the media coverage of the Sandy Hook shooting did not affect their personal views. However, the majority of the judges reported that the coverage of the Sandy Hook shooting has had a negative effect on the public (Berryessa, 2014b). Therefore, Berryessa (2014b) recommends the need for additional "research on the public perceptions, as well as the perceptions of other criminal justice actors, of media portrayals of those with ASDs and hfASDs to gauge if the concerns expressed in these findings are warranted."

Judges' Attitudes Regarding the Sentencing of Offenders with hfASD

Berryessa (2016) investigated the attitudes of twenty-one U.S. trial judges for the California Superior Court on the sentencing of offenders with hfASD. Following analysis of the interviews, two main categories were identified: (1) hfASD as a factor in sentencing and (2) sentencing options for offenders with hfASD. For the category "hfASD as a Factor in Sentencing," fifteen judges reported that when making sentencing decisions an individual's diagnosis of hfASD would be an important consideration, and that information about a defendant's hfASD diagnosis may help judges and jurors ascertain whether the disorder played a contributory role in the offending behavior. Twelve of these fifteen judges considered hfASD to be a mitigating or aggravating factor. Nine judges reported that hfASD would be a potential mitigating factor in sentencing. A large majority of judges who viewed hfASD to be a potential mitigating factor questioned whether the actions of an individual with hfASD would be "completely wilful or if his criminal intent would be potentially influenced by the symptoms of the condition." Of the total sample of twenty-one judges, three considered hfASD to be a possible aggravating factor. Regarding the second category, "Sentencing Options for Offenders with hfASD," Berryessa found that a significant majority of judges reported that they would likely want to try to avoid imprisoning individuals with hfASD because the prison environment may be particularly damaging for these individuals. Judges highlighted the need for alternatives to imprisonment for individuals with hfASD. They noted, however, that the criminal justice system may not have the means to offer other diversionary measures as an alternative to imprisonment (Berryessa, 2016).

Recommendations for Questioning Individuals with ASD

Dr. David Murphy is a Chartered Forensic and Clinical Neuropsychologist at Broadmoor Hospital, which is one of only three high-security psychiatric hospitals in the United Kingdom. Murphy (2018) published a paper that provided an insightful discussion of how to interview individuals with ASD in forensic settings. Murphy stresses that "the language and questions directed at an individual with an ASD may require particular attention and preparation" (Murphy, 2018). This has been described in a variety of sources, such as guidance provided by the advocacy services in the United Kingdom (The Advocate's Gateway, 2013). Questions or statements that are potentially ambiguous should be avoided. Other things to avoid in questioning are metaphors, sarcasm, any nonliteral language, and any questions that require some form of inference, insinuation, deduction, or abstractive extrapolation. It is also recommended that questions be direct and that the use of "tags" be avoided entirely (for instance, asking the question "You went to the park, didn't you?"). Questions should also avoid the use of double negatives (for instance, "You would not disagree with that interpretation, David, would you?"). Some individuals with ASD may also experience an impaired autobiographical memory. Therefore, Murphy's paper recommended that questions be framed in the correct tense, which means not referring to a past event as if in the present. An example of such a question to be avoided is: "Now you are in the street and looking at the car" (Murphy, 2018). (*See* Chap. 14, Vulnerabilities of Defendants with ASD and Strategies for Improving Outcomes.)

Conclusions

Understanding how legal professionals, jurors, judges, and other decision makers within the criminal justice system perceive individuals with ASD is crucial (Maras, Marshall, & Sands, 2018). Many defendants with ASD may display odd, bizarre, or inappropriate behavior during court proceedings; this behavior may have a detrimental impact on the jury's perception of their guilt and ultimately the judge's sentencing decisions. The studies discussed in this chapter clearly highlight the importance of identifying ASD and taking this diagnosis into consideration as early as possible in the criminal justice process.

● ● ●

Clare S. Allely, PhD, is a Reader in Forensic Psychology at the University of Salford in Manchester, England, and is an affiliate member of the Gillberg Neuropsychiatry Centre at Gothenburg University, Sweden. She holds a PhD in Psychology from the University of Manchester and has previously graduated with a Master's in Psychology from the University of Glasgow, a Master's in Psychological Research Methods from the University of Strathclyde, and a Master's in Forensic Psychology from Glasgow Caledonian University. Dr. Allely is an Honorary Research Fellow in the College of Medical, Veterinary, and Life Sciences and is affiliated with the Institute of Health and Wellbeing at the University of Glasgow. Her primary research projects and interests include the pathway to intended violence in mass shooters, serial homicide, investigating how autism symptomology can contribute to different types of offending behavior, and autism in the criminal justice system. Dr. Allely's email is C.S.Allely@salford.ac.uk and her website is https://www.researchgate.net/profile/Clare_Alleley/contributors.

Complete citations available from author upon request.

16

ASD and Sex Offenses: A Son's Perspective

Nicolas Dubin

Even when all of the stars are perfectly aligned in a criminal case — a cooperative defendant, a zealous defense lawyer, highly credentialed experts, and supportive parents — things may not work out, or at least not work out as one might hope. The prosecution of Nicolas (Nick) Dubin, the author of the following chapter, is a case in point. His story is at once compelling, touching, jaw-dropping, and educational.

Chapter 17, ASD and Sex Offenses: A Parent's Perspective is written by Nick's father, a law professor. He tells the same story, but from the perspective of a father who watched the prosecution of his son with shock and was dismayed by how the criminal justice system worked, while at the same time marshalling all his energy and resources. Professor Dubin's chapter is an important contribution because, although we often hear from the families of victims, we do not often hear from the families of the accused.

Both Nick and his father have become passionate and effective advocates for people with ASD who are involved with the criminal justice system. They speak widely, have organized conferences, and have written numerous articles and books.

● ● ●

I was born in 1977. My story is similar to those of many other autistics who grew up in an age before Asperger's syndrome or autism spectrum disorder existed as diagnoses. As a result, people like me were often misunderstood and misdiagnosed throughout their lives. All through school, teachers, my parents, and social workers frequently told me I was not trying hard enough, which was confusing because I believed I was trying my best. Over the years, I received a number of diagnoses that never seemed to fit. For many years, I was a puzzle to myself and to my parents. It wasn't until I was twenty-seven years old that the various pieces of the puzzle finally came together and I was diagnosed with Asperger's syndrome.

This diagnosis brought a tremendous amount of clarity to an otherwise confusing life up to that point and explained many of my past problems, such as why I had had so few friends. Why I couldn't tolerate living in a college dorm. Why I had failed at student teaching even though I had received A's in all my coursework. For the first time in my life, things were starting to make sense. Upon receiving this diagnosis, with the help of the neuropsychologist who diagnosed me, I formed a plan for my future. I had recently been accepted to a doctoral program in psychology, and I decided that my goal in that program would be to help others on the autism spectrum lead better lives.

I attacked that goal with a vengeance. Over the next five years, I not only obtained my doctoral degree but also became a national speaker on subjects related to autism. I wrote several books that were published on these topics. After so many years of frustration and confusion, I was flying high and able to manifest my newfound passion. Life felt wonderful and fulfilling.

Shortly after I completed my doctoral degree, at my mother's urging, I applied for a job as a consultant at a school that was forming to meet the needs of high school students on the autism spectrum. To my utter amazement, I was hired. It was my first legitimate job, and I was excited to begin this new pursuit. But two months into the job, my life ended before it could even begin. To my shock and horror, I was arrested and charged with possession of child pornography. At the time of my arrest, neither my parents nor I had any idea that this type of arrest was a common occurrence for those on the autism spectrum. To understand why that is so, I need to go back in time and provide some important background information.

Early Childhood

There is no doubt that if I were three years old today I would be diagnosed with an autism spectrum disorder (ASD). I had all the telltale signs. I was nonverbal, jumped up and down, flapped my arms, was echolalic

(I repeated back everything that was said to me), and had poor gross and fine motor skills. My parents were alarmed by all these symptoms and behaviors and had me evaluated by a psychologist in the public schools. This psychologist recommended I see a speech and language pathologist at a nearby hospital. The speech pathologist diagnosed me with severe expressive and receptive aphasia, meaning I couldn't express myself or comprehend what others were saying to me. It was decided that I would have speech therapy three times a week, as well as receive occupational therapy to address gross and fine motor delays.

In less than a year, I went from being nonverbal to being able to express myself fairly well and to understand most of what others were saying to me. From this very rapid growth, my speech therapist concluded that I might be gifted. However, my problems did not go away. They only intensified. My speech had improved, but my social pragmatic skills had not. I rarely engaged with other children and only participated in "parallel play," meaning I would play alongside other children but not with them directly. On one occasion, my parents took me to the park because my favorite thing to do was go down the slide. I was enthralled with the repetition of going up and down the slide. But the fun of having the slide all to myself was ruined when another boy also wanted to use it. Because I didn't understand that I did not own the slide and it was public property, I had a huge meltdown that involved screaming at this boy and not understanding I was the one in the wrong in this situation. This kind of behavior concerned my parents and sent them on a quest to get more answers and to find a school that would be a good fit for me as I was about to enter first grade.

Every school we visited seemed to pose a problem. A school for gifted children said I needed more structure. A school for those with learning disabilities felt I was too high-functioning for what they offered. The only option left was public school, which my parents dreaded because they couldn't imagine me in a room with thirty other children and only one teacher.

My first two years of elementary school were tortuous. I felt isolated from my classmates and constantly misunderstood by my teachers. I now know I did unusual things that made other kids think I was strange, such as imitating different game show hosts and touching my classmates' heads. Predictably, I was an easy target for bullies, and at that time, teachers did little to address the bullying, probably because they were perplexed about how to deal with me themselves. Only two weeks into the year, my first-grade teacher told my mom that she thought I belonged in a self-contained classroom for the emotionally impaired because I got hysterical when a bee flew into the classroom and I was afraid of being stung. My mom begged and pleaded with the first-grade teacher to give me more time to adjust. She reminded the teacher that I had come from a private school kindergarten class of only ten students and three teachers and needed extra time and a little patience. The teacher finally agreed. I also received Special Education services in the Learning Resource Center: I would leave my classroom for periods of time and go to the LRC for extra help. I hated being the only one in my class who had to go to the LRC.

In third grade, things improved dramatically. My teacher was a recent college graduate who, unlike my first- and second-grade teachers, had not yet reached the burnout phase of her career. She saw I was struggling socially and paired me up with a couple of neighborhood kids with whom I became friends for several years. Unfortunately, those "friends" took advantage of my naïveté and one day handcuffed me to a tree while we were playing in the park. My father came home, discovered this situation, and talked to the boys sternly about what they had done. Those friendships ended that day and left me with a scar that has truly never healed.

Adolescence

Once middle school arrived, life took a dramatic turn for the worse. Instead of being in the same classroom all day, I now had to be in seven different classrooms. I only had a few minutes between classes to go to my locker, which was not sufficient time for me to stay organized and arrive at the next class with the books I needed. The bullying also intensified in middle school. People mocked the way I walked (like Charlie Chaplin) and the way I talked (like a "little professor," which is typical of those with ASD). I remember telling my school counselor that I hated middle school and wished I could go back to being in elementary school. The counselor told my parents she thought I was much younger than my actual chronological age and strongly recommended they put me in a group for teens who were struggling socially. Unfortunately, because the diagnosis of "Asperger's syndrome" (now autism spectrum disorder) didn't exist at that time, this group experience was not successful for me. I didn't want to be in a group of misfits and resisted going each and every week.

Along with all the social and academic stresses I was experiencing, I was also very troubled by something I dared not speak about with anyone.

With the onset of puberty, I began to notice that I was feeling attractions toward other boys, not girls. This was especially upsetting, not only because I didn't know what to make of it but also because I was aware that being "gay" was totally frowned upon by my peers. Thus, I kept that concern to myself for many years.

Sadly, high school was only slightly better than middle school. But miraculously, in spite of having a history of gross motor problems, I somehow became a very good tennis player. Perhaps it was because my grandfather was a great tennis player and I had his "tennis genes." After many years of lessons and constant practice, I was able to play number one singles on my varsity high school tennis team, which diffused some of the bullying I might otherwise have received. However, my social skills were still stunted. Even though I was the captain of the tennis team, my teammates didn't want to be friends with me and I couldn't understand why. I was not invited to parties and didn't hang out with them on the weekends. Often, I would drive home for lunch instead of eating in the cafeteria or going out to lunch with others. Socializing simply didn't appeal to me as much as my parents and professionals thought it should. I was constantly being encouraged to initiate social contact with others, which I refused to do.

Throughout my adolescence and young adulthood, I was seen as a goody-two-shoes who found it difficult to tell even a simple white lie convincingly. I always told the truth and was a strict rule follower, as those with ASD typically are. It would have been unimaginable for anyone who knew me growing up to believe I could have ended up unwittingly committing a felony.

As I have indicated, much of my adolescence and young adulthood was incredibly confusing when it came to sexuality. Frankly, I wasn't sure what my sexual orientation was. One might ask: How could that be if I knew early on I had same-sex attractions? Unfortunately, it wasn't as simple as that.

Sexual Confusion

I first raised the subject of my sexuality to my parents during my freshman year in college. My mom and dad are very liberal, progressive-minded people, but they were worried that I had more than enough challenges in life and didn't want me to be saddled with yet another one. At first, my parents asked me how I could know for sure that I was gay. After all, I had never had any sexual or romantic experiences with another human being. That seemed logical to me. How *could* I really know for sure? I continued to operate with that logic for the next several years and remained totally confused.

Because I had had no social or sexual outlets, the advent of the internet offered the possibility of sexual exploration with a few clicks of the mouse. Looking back, it seems almost inevitable that I would have turned to pornography. Actually, it was my therapist who first suggested that I go to an adult bookstore and view both men and women in pornographic magazines because I was having trouble deciding whether I was gay or straight. The problem with this advice was that, with the internet at my disposal, I didn't need to travel to an adult bookstore to view pornography. It was much easier to go on the internet than drive to a seedy neighborhood far across town.

How "It" Began

In the early days of Google, one could search for the term "free music" and a program called Limewire would pop up in the search results. There was no "dark net" as it exists today. Bad stuff was easy to find. I was looking to see if there was a way to gain free access to songs, and Limewire seemed like a cool way to do it. It required downloading the application onto my desktop computer, but I didn't really think anything of that. It just meant that I could now download free songs.

I learned sooner rather than later that Limewire provides more than just free songs (and I didn't know at the time where those free songs and other things came from). I had no idea that I was downloading anything from someone else's computer; I thought this material simply came from a website. I also didn't realize that once downloaded onto my computer, anyone could download material from my computer without my knowledge. One could also download pornography without having to give one's name, credit card information, or any other identification. It was free, anonymous, and seemed too good to be true.

I started out looking at adult-age pornography. But, as I was searching for young adult males, I began to receive search results that involved even younger-looking individuals. Curiosity got the better of me and I began to look at some of these pictures. The pictures (or at least the ones I searched for) never involved children having sex with adults, nor did they involve violence or sadomasochism. Although I now totally understand the exploitative nature of child pornography and why it is morally wrong, at the time I didn't understand the true nature of what I was doing—and will forever be remorseful for what I did.

The Nightmare Unfolds

When my apartment was raided in predawn style by the FBI on October 6, 2010, it was the last thing in the world I thought would ever happen to me. Being struck by lightning or buying a winning Lotto ticket would have seemed a more likely possibility.

In order for me to fall asleep, I use several sound machines all at the same time to block out noise. So, by the time I realized there were actually people in my apartment unit, it was only just before they entered my bedroom. I assumed I was being burglarized, and in my mind, I was preparing to die. My dog, Sadie, had woken up around at 6:30 in the morning, which was unusual for her. I told her to go back to sleep, but then I heard loud noises coming from outside my bedroom and I could see flashlights through the heating and cooling vent. Before I knew it, about eight men came in, blinding me with the light from their flashlights, threw me out of bed, and pushed me against the wall. I repeatedly asked who they were: Could they be the local fire department? They wouldn't answer. They just said, "We'll tell you in a minute." I kept asking: "Who are you? What are you doing in my apartment?" I was so scared I barely uttered these words above a whimper. I felt that at any moment I was going to be killed.

The next thing I knew, these men had seated me on my living room couch with all the lights turned on. Seeing the letters on their jackets, I realized I was sitting with about eight FBI agents surrounding me. FBI? What could the FBI possibly be doing at my apartment at 6:30 in the morning? I really didn't know. Then two agents sat down directly across from me. One of them said, "Do you want to tell us what is on your computer?" At that moment, I thought the only possible reason they were there was because of the pictures I had been collecting. "You're here because I have the pictures I have on my computer?" I asked with the voice of a frightened child. In that moment, I confessed without even realizing it. I still didn't understand how they could have known I had these pictures, because I hadn't sent them to anyone. However, unbeknownst to me, I *had* sent them. I had no idea what the concept of "file sharing" meant at the time.

A "good-cop, bad-cop" interrogation then began and went on for at least four hours. One agent promised that if I cooperated and told them everything they wanted to know I would probably get a more lenient sentence. I didn't know it then, but this was a lie. FBI agents can make their feelings known about a defendant to a prosecutor and/or judge, but they are not the ones who decide what a defendant's sentence will be. A second agent led me to believe that if I didn't talk my silence would be used against me. I later learned I had not been given my *Miranda* rights because, technically, I was not in custody. Yet there were several police cars outside my apartment in case I decided to "make a run for it," as I was told by the FBI agents, which suggests I *was* in a custodial setting in my own apartment.

My behavior during the interrogation was typical of a person with an autism spectrum disorder. My dad has since spoken to dozens and dozens of parents of adult children who have gone through exactly what I did. Not one of them concealed information from the agents. Not one of them exercised the right to talk to a lawyer and remain silent. Autistic people tend to be very trusting of authority and believe that people will keep their word. Because I had no experience in the criminal justice system on which to base this interaction with the FBI agents, I didn't know that it would have been perfectly legal for law enforcement to lie during an interrogation to extract information. Like almost every other person on the spectrum who is faced with this horrible situation, I complied.

My Lawyer and Parents Go to Work

The day following the raid, I had to appear in a courtroom to be processed and arraigned. I was completely shell-shocked. Fortunately, I had a lawyer who was a very good communicator. He explained what was most likely going to happen and in what order. I can't emphasize how important it is for an ASD person to regain some peace of mind through structured communication. Much of this communication will often be done in the presence of a parent or guardian, assuming the client gives his/her lawyer permission to speak to them (most often, my dad and I have found this to be the case). What must be remembered from a defense lawyer's point of view is that parents of ASD children have been protecting their children all of their lives. From attending Individualized Educational Program meetings, to dealing with bullies, to helping their children obtain jobs, parents of ASD children are used to fighting battles for their sons and daughters. A lawyer defending an autistic client must be willing to allow a little more time out of his/her schedule to communicate with the ASD client and his family. (*See* Chap. 6, The Bond Hearing.)

The first thing my parents did, at my attorney's direction, was to gather up all records relating to my developmental disability, starting from early childhood. These included medical, school, and therapeutic records. This is crucial information to give expert witnesses, who will, one hopes, make an informed determination that the judge can rely on. Then my parents were asked to write a narrative of my development. In my case, my parents, Kitty and Larry Dubin, were well suited for this task, both being educators at the college level. It may not always be possible for a parent or parents to do this if they don't have competent writing skills or the necessary education to do so. It may be necessary to seek out other family members, such as aunts or uncles, who can help fill in the blanks.

The document they wrote described in detail my lack of psychosexual development, my early neurological symptoms (jumping, flapping, echolalia, speech delay), and severe social problems as I grew up (lack of friends, trouble living away from home, lack of employment, and—most important—no social or dating experience). They knew better than anyone that I had no romantic or sexual experience, and the forensic psychologists who evaluated me found this to be an important link between my diagnosis and my unfortunate behavior.

My lawyer also took the time to do a thorough debriefing with me. He understood early on that I was not going to be a typical client. I needed more reassurance and "hand holding" (so to speak) than most clients. It was clear to my lawyer that somehow my social age did not match my chronological age based upon my needs, and this was before he even learned about what ASD encompassed. I opened up to him rather easily because of his easygoing demeanor.

When he began representing me, he knew very little about ASD. He immersed himself in the subject and spoke to many experts in the field. He had his research assistants learn about it to help inform him so he could provide the most well-informed defense possible.

One of the conditions of my arraignment was placement in a pretrial sex offender group run by a court-appointed therapist. This was unacceptable to my attorney from a Fifth Amendment perspective because I was still innocent until proven guilty. Another reason was that the group was psychologically harmful to someone like myself. Group members were forced to talk about themselves in great detail and were told that if we didn't it would be held against us in our presentence reports, which the judge would factor into his sentence. I didn't feel like I had anything in common with the other group members (many of whom had molested children), and the interpersonal dynamics of these encounters were totally counterproductive to my well-being. My lawyer recognized this immediately and did what a lot of defense attorneys might not otherwise do: He filed a motion for me to work with a private therapist instead. The prosecution did not oppose the motion, and thus I was placed with the therapist I had been working with for the past eight years.

Discussing what happened in therapy immediately made me realize how blind I had been to what I did. The therapist helped me understand that the pictures I looked at were of real people—that they were victims and not just pictures on a screen. This awareness brought me great guilt and mortification. My lawyer thought it was important to explain to the prosecutors that my lack of ability to see the forest for the trees was possible despite my high level of education. He knew this would be a sticking point that the prosecution would focus on: How could someone who was of average intelligence (96 IQ) and possessed of two advanced degrees be so oblivious to something taken for granted as a norm in our society? I certainly couldn't answer this question on my own, and my parents couldn't either. For that, we needed an expert witness.

We had to find a forensic psychologist in our area with expertise in both autism and sexuality. As we soon found out, this was an impossible task. They virtually didn't exist, and we were living in a major city! We could not find an expert who specialized in both sexuality and autism, so eventually we met with a forensic psychologist who had expertise in autism.

Defense Evaluation

I saw this psychologist on four different occasions, and the first time my parents accompanied me. The psychologist administered the Vineland Adaptive Behavior Scales, which measure the personal and social skills of individuals from birth to adulthood. He gave the test to my parents and me separately, and our answers were virtually identical. To my horror, this test placed me with a psychosocial age of a seven- to ten-year-old. This was a humiliating statistic for me to have to come to terms with, but my lawyer was thrilled. He felt it could be used to show the disconnect between my academic accomplishments and my inability to understand the illegality of my behavior. In addition to the Vineland, this forensic psychologist administered a wide battery of other tests. One of them was the Minnesota Multiphasic Personality Inventory (MMPI), which ruled out any anti-social and psychopathic tendencies. (*See* Chap. 9, Testing.)

Probably the most important part of his report was the psychologist's clinical observations regarding the interviews he conducted with me. He asked me some pointed questions that were frankly very difficult to answer. One question in particular was: Why did I look at child pornography? What had motivated me to do that? It was such a difficult question that I really had to take some time to reflect on what the reason was. Because I had spent three months prior talking about this issue with my primary therapist, the answer finally came to me. When I looked at the pictures, I felt the same age as the kids in the photos. I was not looking at the children as if I was an adult, but as if I was another child wanting to be liked by children who were bullying me. I even told the forensic psychologist that the pictures resembled children who bullied me. However, I should point out that the vast majority of what was on my computer was adult pornography.

Mental Illness Versus Developmental Disability?

After my lawyers submitted this psychologist's report to the assistant U.S. attorneys (AUSAs), they responded with another question. How does a developmental disability differ from a mental illness? The prosecutors said they prosecute people with mental illnesses all the time, and many end up going to prison. What differentiated having autism from someone having depression or social anxiety? In response to that question, the forensic psychologist wrote a supplemental report, the gist of which was that autism is a neurological, not a psychological, disability that exists from birth and affects all aspects of development from the day one is born until the day one dies. One can have a genetic predisposition for a mental illness, but the age of onset might not be until late adolescence or early adulthood, meaning that a good portion of many people's early development was not impacted by the mental illness.

Requesting Pretrial Diversion

It's important to note that when my lawyers (and I had two of them by this point) submitted this report they requested pretrial diversion for my adjudication. They made this request for a couple of reasons. First, federal law permits a person who commits the offense of possession of child pornography to receive diversion under appropriate circumstances. Second, they wanted to set the bar high and ask for something they knew they most likely couldn't get, in the hope that it would help with long-term negotiations down the road.

Prosecution Evaluations

The AUSAs weren't going to agree to diversion right off the bat, but neither were they hell-bent on a prison term. My lawyers found this extremely encouraging. The prosecutor's first offer was for me to plead to possession, with no insistence on prison at sentencing. That would be left up to the judge. Still, I would have to register as a sex offender. Although my lawyers were encouraged, they were also unsatisfied with this offer. They asked that I be evaluated by an expert of the prosecutor's own choosing. The prosecutors then selected the head of the Victim Assistance Unit for the FBI, who was a neuropsychologist, to do this next evaluation. I was to meet him at the J. Edgar Hoover building in Washington, D.C. This meeting was risky, but we agreed because my lawyers believed in me and my case and felt I should get diversion, and they thought this might be the only way to achieve that goal. They believed that if I was forthright in the same way I had been with the defense expert it would be hard to repudiate or argue against giving me diversion.

And that's exactly what happened. After my seven-hour interview in Washington, D.C., the government expert found nothing in the defense expert's report to disagree with and said he would be OK with diversion. We were elated! That elation immediately turned to despondence when, in spite of the government expert being OK with diversion, the prosecution was unwilling to change their offer.

Now feeling somewhat desperate, my lawyers made another pitch to the U.S. Attorney in our district, who then decided I needed to be evaluated by yet another prosecution expert. The thought of another evaluation nearly sent me over the edge, but my parents and my lawyers felt it was our last hope. Thus, I went through another six-hour interview, after which this psychologist also opined that I was a low-risk individual and did not see me as needing sex offender registration. Once again, it made no difference. The AUSA's final offer was the same as their first offer: take it or leave it. I had no choice but to take it.

Aftermath

I was extremely lucky not to have to spend time in a federal prison, but as of this writing, I am still a registered sex offender and have been for approximately seven years. Even almost ten years after my arrest, there is an air of unreality to that statement. Being labeled a registered sex offender is in no way in keeping with who I am as a person. I might as well be labeled a terrorist or an alcoholic, both of which are utterly untrue.

Suggestions for Lawyers

Representing someone on the autism spectrum can be a rewarding opportunity for a defense attorney, but before taking on such a case, it is essential that the lawyer do the necessary research on how the client's autism may have contributed to the charges against the client. I remember reading an appellate court case not long ago in which a judge opined that because the defendant with ASD was able to drive a car he understood the nature and consequences of his actions. This attitude reflects a common misconception among judges and prosecutors and does not take into account the uneven development individuals with autism display. For example, an autistic savant may be able to play Rachmaninoff's Third Piano Concerto blindfolded but still not be able to tie his shoes. That is an extreme example, but to some extent, all persons with autism display uneven skills in their overall profiles. How to explain this? By understanding that these "splinter skills" are compartmentalized and isolated from one's overall general ability. A judge or a prosecutor may try to isolate these splinter skills, such as college degrees, being able to drive a car, or other accomplishments, and try to hold them against the ASD defendant when establishing competence, criminal responsibility, or even mitigation.

A defense lawyer must, at all costs, try to avoid a sentence that includes incarceration for an ASD client. Most autistic individuals are fragile, gentle, and hypersensitive beings. The thought of them being incarcerated is unfathomable. It may sound like a platitude, but prison environments for ASD individuals could easily constitute cruel and unusual punishment.

I strongly advise defense attorneys to sit in with the ASD client when he/she meets with the probation officer for the presentence report interview. Judges rely heavily on this report. Not every lawyer chooses to go to these meetings, but it really is a "must." A probation officer not trained in autism may interpret certain behaviors as being disrespectful, rude, or not taking responsibility for the crime. It is essential to be there as the client's interpreter, to avoid misunderstandings or having an inaccuracy make its way into the presentence report.

There may be times where communication breaks down between pretrial services and the client and, heaven forbid, the client is incarcerated before trial for not having made bail. It would be crucial at a bail hearing to demonstrate that an autistic person, who is typically very rule-oriented, will be extremely compliant and unlikely to flee. If keeping the client out of jail is not possible, it will be critical to inform the client exactly how to behave in jail. The client must be clearly educated about the charges against him/her, encouraged to remain respectful to other incarcerated individuals and guards, and not to look (or stare) at people intently (as this can be viewed as a sign of aggression).

If an ASD client is sent to prison, there is no question that it will be difficult, if not impossible, for him/her to survive. Keep in mind that navigating daily life outside of prison has been a constant challenge for this person's entire life. It can be assumed that an autistic client will lack the necessary social skills to intuitively know or learn how to stay out of trouble in a custodial setting. It would be most helpful if a lawyer could have some discussion with the custodial staff prior to the defendant surrendering. I have heard many tragic stories of autistic people who have spent long periods of time in solitary confinement or taken their own lives because they simply were not able to function in prison. (*See* Chap. 13, Prison Accommodations.)

Although I strongly encourage defense lawyers to educate judges about autism, there are a couple of risks in doing so. Judges may interpret the diagnosis as an aggravating factor if they feel it indicates that the defendant has less volitional control. Autism should always be seen as a mitigating factor if the defense lawyers are doing their job correctly. There is also a slight chance, especially with sex offenses, that autism could be used against a defendant at the end of a criminal sentence as a basis for civil commitment. That, too, is unacceptable. In the case of civil commitment, the lawyer's role will probably have ended, as that usually happens years into one's prison sentence. The bottom line is that lawyers should at least be mindful of this possibility, and also of the fact that prosecutors love to use what should be mitigating factors as aggravating ones.

Last, the sex offender registry is a civil disability that expels one from civic participation and a normal quality of life. Autism is enough of a disability by itself. This should be carefully explained to the judge and the prosecutor to get them to return with a charge that would make the defendant eligible for a nonregistrable offense in the plea negotiations.

It is my hope that by sharing the worst experience of my life and a few things I have learned along the way, I will have helped members of the criminal justice system better understand and deal appropriately and compassionately with ASD defendants.

● ● ●

Nicolas (Nick) Dubin, PsyD, was diagnosed with autism spectrum disorder in 2004.

He holds a bachelor's degree in Communications from Oakland University, a master's degree in Learning Disabilities from the University of Detroit Mercy, and a specialist degree in Psychology and PsyD from the Michigan School of Professional Psychology. He has authored many books on autism spectrum disorders, including *Asperger Syndrome and Anxiety* (Jessica Kingsley Publishers). He has served on the board of directors of several autism organizations and was a columnist for the *Autism-Asperger's Digest*. He is dedicated to helping those individuals on the autism spectrum receive due process and justice within the criminal justice system. Dr. Dubin can be reached at nweild77@gmail.com.

17

ASD and Sex Offenses: A Parent's Perspective

Lawrence A. Dubin

On October 6, 2010, my thirty-three-year-old son Nick, who had been diagnosed on the autism spectrum at age twenty-seven, was charged in federal court with having illegal images on his computer. (*See* Chap. 16, ASD and Sex Offenses: A Son's Perspective.) After this nightmare, I have come away with a different perception of the criminal justice than the one I had during my more than five decades of being a lawyer. Men on the autism spectrum are mistreated and misunderstood by those who operate our criminal justice system. My intent in writing this chapter is to create a more fair and just system for men like my son.

I graduated from the University of Michigan Law School in 1966. After practicing law for almost ten years, including work as a criminal defense lawyer, I embarked on a career change and have been a law professor for the past forty-four years, attaining the status of professor emeritus at the University of Detroit Mercy School of Law. My teaching and publication interests are in the areas of legal ethics and litigation; I have written books on professional responsibility, trial practice, and evidence as well as numerous law review articles.

I have received a number of awards from the State Bar of Michigan that have reflected my interest and belief in the importance of the pursuit of justice within the criminal justice system, as well as in the ethical practice of lawyers who operate that system. One of the awards was for a public television documentary that I made, *Legal Heroes*, which profiled three lawyers who represented the type of lawyers we should all strive to be. One lawyer I selected was Fred Gray, who represented Rosa Parks from the time of her arrest in 1955 for refusing to give up her seat on a Montgomery bus. I had the privilege of interviewing Ms. Parks in my home. I kept my son home from school that day so that he could meet this legendary and historical person. My interview with Fred Gray was a highlight of making that program.

Fred Gray was denied admission to the University of Alabama Law School because of his race, but the state paid his tuition to attend Western Reserve Law School in Cleveland. His purpose for becoming a lawyer was to return to Alabama and desegregate everything that legally separated the races, from the hospitals where babies are born to the cemeteries where people are buried, and everything about life in between. After graduation, he went back to Alabama as a lawyer but couldn't attend bar functions or eat in restaurants. As a twenty-three-year-old lawyer, he would often have lunch with his friend Rosa Parks. At the time of her arrest, she immediately called Fred Gray, who went on to represent her, successfully challenge the bus policies in the U.S. Supreme Court, and go on to strike down segregation laws at all levels of education in the state of Alabama. He also helped select Dr. Martin Luther King Jr. as the community spokesman during the bus boycott and represented Dr. King during later times when he was arrested.

For me, Fred Gray personified my belief that the legal system has the potential to overcome great injustices and to self-correct when an intelligent voice of reason presents the case for change. I carried that belief in the capacity of our legal system, aspiring to achieve justice even if it takes time for the "arc" to bend in the right direction. That belief nurtured me as a law professor, feeding my hope of opening the minds of future students to their importance in working toward principles of justice.

To achieve my purpose in writing this chapter, I want to state that I believe a competent and ethically sensitive criminal defense lawyer needs to understand autism as a developmental disability. This understanding is essential in order to be an ethically competent lawyer. This knowledge will assist the defense lawyer in properly communicating with disabled clients and their parents or guardians. The defense lawyer will then be able to help educate prosecutors and judges about how autism is related to the crime charged and how justice can best be achieved under the circumstances. The competent defense lawyer then assists the prosecutor—who is not only an advocate but also, as stated in our ethics rules, a "minister of justice"—to agree to a resolution reflecting that high ethical responsibility, which transcends a prosecutor's more limited version of the job as just securing guilty pleas.

I write this chapter as a parent who has experienced the nightmare of having a child on the autism spectrum charged with a criminal offense. I also write this chapter as a lawyer who understands the ethical and constitutional expectations that a lawyer must fulfill in order to successfully prosecute or provide representation under these circumstances. I intend to provide the perspectives of both the parent of the autistic child who is prosecuted for a crime and a lawyer who believes that all the participants in the criminal justice system (defense lawyer, prosecutor, and judge) should seek justice.

Nick's Childhood and Early Adult Years

In many ways, my son is typical of a child with high-functioning autism. His condition used to be referred to as Asperger's syndrome. After he was able to walk, he started jumping and flapping. At three years of age, his language was limited to a few unclearly stated words, and he lacked the ability to speak sentences. In essence, he was nonverbal. At a local hospital's speech and language department, he was diagnosed with both inability to speak (aphasia) and an inability to comprehend what others were stating; he simply repeated what he heard others say (echolalia). He was placed in a Special Education unit in our local school district. These events all occurred before Asperger's was a recognized diagnosis. My wife and I were very worried about his future intellectual development because no specific diagnosis, other than general learning disabilities, had been made. Testing also showed that he had deficits in gross and fine motor skills. He was extremely nonathletic. He also did not like to socialize with other children.

My wife and I felt great anxiety about his potential future development and a tremendous responsibility to help our son traverse the problems and roadblocks he was encountering at that time and as he grew older. Many of the problems he faced centered on interactions with other children and teachers. His social difficulties caused him great anxiety. Making friends was very difficult for him. As he got older, other kids severely bullied him. Some teachers were very insensitive to his limitations. His art teacher once held up his poor artwork in front of the entire class and informed the other students that this was how their work should *not* be done. Another time, two kids he thought were friends handcuffed him to a playground swing and rode their bikes in circles around him, laughing while he cried and screamed for help. I was home at the time and saw the incident from my window. I ran out of the house and freed him while sternly informing his tormentors that their behavior was unacceptable. On a regular basis, I had to go to his school to request that he be protected from bullies and to offer suggestions to his teachers, based on what other experts had advised us, about how to better understand and relate to him. They tended to think he was just being lazy and not trying hard enough.

In spite of all of his problems, here is what has always amazed me about my son: What was a deficit at one time could become a strength. When he was nonverbal, he started speech therapy. Within months, his verbal skills became one of his strengths. At age ten, he tried out to play baseball. Ten minutes into the tryout, he ran off the field. He did not have the skills that would have helped him catch or throw a ball, let alone get a hit. Out of desperation to involve him in some athletic endeavor, I signed him up to take a tennis lesson. After this final attempt to get him involved in a sport, I expected to call it quits. My son proved me wrong and took to the sport from his first lesson.

By the time he was in high school, he was the number-one ranked tennis player in southeast Michigan, was highly ranked in our six-state region, played number-one singles on his highly competitive high school tennis team for four years, and was designated as an all-state tennis player by the state tennis coaches. It seemed like a miracle. Yet what didn't change was his inability to interact socially with his peers. While they went out after tennis matches and engaged in normal social ways, he remained socially isolated, lacking any of the normal social and sexual experimentation of adolescence.

After high school graduation, my son wanted to go away to college because that's what most students in his class were doing. He wanted to be like everyone else, even though he had different needs. He learned later on why that was so. He attended a state university about 150 miles from our home. When my wife and I dropped him off at his dorm on the first day, his discomfort level seemed so high that we thought he would call us later that night to say that he was going to come home. When he did call, he said his roommate was unfriendly and the dorm was very noisy. A few weeks later, he called and said he was dropping out. He couldn't sleep well, his roommate was coming in at all hours of the night, the music was always loud, and he couldn't think or study. Not wanting him to fail so early in his college experience, I went to his college the next day and got permission for him to leave his dorm and live in the basement of a home off campus. He never liked living there, but the change in the environment was helpful in keeping him in school long enough to finish the year.

Although he played number-one singles on the tennis team, he made no friends and drove home almost every Friday, leaving to go back to college every Sunday night. It was apparent that his high achievement in some areas of his life coexisted with very low development in other areas of his life. As parents, we never could find an explanation for his uneven development.

The next year he decided to stay home and attend a local university. He went on to graduate with a BA in Communications (speaking was now a strength). He then worked toward a master's degree in Learning Disabilities. His goal was to help young students with learning disabilities, a desire springing from the problems he had experienced in his Special Education courses. He spent the next four years getting a joint degree in elementary education and learning disabilities. He received very good grades in all his courses. However, when he began his student teaching in a second-grade classroom, it only took a few weeks for him and his supervising teacher to realize that he would not be able to finish because the multitasking necessary to teach a second-grade class overwhelmed his ability to function. He couldn't understand how he could do well academically but be unable to perform in the classroom, as he would have to in order to obtain the teaching certificate necessary for his future employment.

My son was distressed, unable to understand why he was so different from other people. None of the many experts he had seen during the course of his life could explain the social and educational difficulties he had experienced. He became very depressed. He felt he was at a dead end regarding his future. Then he discovered that with his BA and MA degrees he qualified for a doctorate program at a well-respected independent college of psychology. While taking the undergraduate courses necessary for his admission to this doctoral program, in an abnormal psychology class about Asperger's syndrome, he learned and was certain that this term described him. The description explained so much that he had not understood about himself before. He went to a neuropsychologist who specialized in autism, and after much testing and evaluation, he received a clear diagnosis that he had Asperger's. With that diagnosis, he decided to work toward his doctorate in psychology specializing in autism so he could help people on the autism spectrum better understand themselves and avoid some of the suffering he had experienced in his life. The only accommodation he received while earning his doctoral degree was that he was permitted to spend 2,000 hours working at a nonprofit that provided assistance to people on the autism spectrum or at a university where he could do research, writing, and speaking.

Once again, my son amazed me by obtaining his doctorate and, in the process of doing so, he wrote books for people with autism that addressed the anxiety and depression often experienced by this population. He became a recognized speaker at national autism conferences all over the country, providing helpful information based on his research.

The pride that I felt in my son's accomplishments made all of the pain that he had experienced in life and all of the support and love that we gave him seem worth it. He truly was an amazing person. He went from a young child who seemed to lack the skills to ever become educated to a highly intelligent professional whose main goal in life was to help others. However, the one clear residual effect of his being on the autism spectrum was that he had not undergone normal maturational development as a social, sexual adult.

Criminal Charges

October 6, 2010, was the day of my personal Pearl Harbor, when a bomb dropped on my world. I was driving on my way to teach my law classes. I was enjoying a lovely sunny fall day when my cell phone rang. A male voice said that he was an FBI agent. In the past I have received calls from these agents, usually asking for information about some former law students who used me as a reference for a job. Rather than hearing what I had anticipated, the agent told me that my son's living quarters, pursuant to a warrant, were being searched. He said that my son was in very bad emotional shape and that I should come there immediately.

I was in an absolute state of shock. My mind turned to mush. I had to concentrate on how to get to my son's apartment. When I arrived, it looked like a scene out of a movie where Al Capone's residence was being raided. There were multiple police and FBI vehicles. FBI agents walked freely in and out of his apartment. My son was in a fetal position on his couch with his head buried under a pillow. Although I am a reality-based person, I nevertheless found myself having an out-of-body experience. I do remember immediately going over to my son, finding his cheek and giving him a kiss, and whispering in his ear, "I love you."

Why was I shocked to find out that my son was under FBI scrutiny? Being on the autism spectrum, my son always knew he was different and didn't easily fit in with his peers. He felt most comfortable spending time by himself watching videos, listening to music, and so on. He was polite and respectful to everyone. He was a rule follower, not a rule breaker. He had never hurt anyone or expressed a desire to do so. In short, he was the last person I ever thought would become a defendant in a criminal case.

I received a call later that afternoon from an assistant U.S. attorney (AUSA). He informed me that my son was to be arraigned before a federal magistrate the following afternoon. I was told that the charges involved distributing, receiving, and possessing illegal images on his computer. He also mentioned that these charges could result in a sentence of more than a decade in a federal prison. This experience went from surreal to bizarre. Without trying to be overly dramatic, every cell of my body felt under attack. I had a feeling that my life had changed forever—that my family's very survival was being challenged.

In looking back with a calmer head, I remember being flabbergasted that my son was charged with very serious sex crimes, albeit of a noncontact nature. He had never really expressed an interest in sex. During his adolescent years, I would bring up the subject of sex, but he would brush me off, reflecting a desire to not have a discussion of that topic. I wasn't bothered by his attitude because there were always enough other issues in his life that required attention. If he lacked an interest in sex, that seemed acceptable. One less thing to worry about.

I needed a lawyer to represent my son the next afternoon. What did I learn at this time from the position of being a client—or, more accurately, a parent of a child on the autism spectrum who is technically the client? My belief in our criminal justice system was clashing with the fear I was experiencing. My overly innocent and unworldly son, who was born with a developmental disability, was now facing a lengthy prison sentence for viewing illegal images in the privacy of his room without any thoughts or intent of hurting anyone and without any understanding that he was violating a federal law. The legal system that I believed in and had spent my entire adult life teaching my students about was now the same legal system that threatened my son's very existence. I knew he could never survive in prison. He couldn't even survive in a college dorm.

I contacted a lawyer I knew. I had great respect for his competence, advocacy, and ethics. I knew he had handled cases before the United States Supreme Court. I called him and he agreed to meet me and my son the next afternoon outside the federal magistrate's courtroom. My son appeared to be suffering from the trauma of the day before, when a dozen FBI agents broke into his apartment at six in the morning. They'd woken him from a deep sleep and gotten him out of bed, then handcuffed his wrists behind his back. When I arrived at his apartment, he seemed to be in a vegetative state.

After the brief arraignment, my son and I got on an elevator going up to Pretrial Services. A television reporter for one of our local stations who had interviewed me about legal matters in the past was on the elevator and assumed I was there representing a client. She said hello to me. I felt like I was in a bottle and that everyone from my former life was out of reach. The meaning of my life had changed. I was no longer a respected lawyer in town but a father whose sole mission in life was to try to save the life of my son. My family and my life seemed doomed.

My son's lawyer was calm, and he assured us that he would do everything in his power to help my son. We met him the next day in his office. He told me that he had no prior experience in representing anyone on the autism spectrum but that he had already started the process of learning everything he could about the subject. His law clerk had printed a lot of information for him to read. He had calls in to a number of federal defenders around the country to get as much information as possible about their experiences in representing clients on the autism spectrum who faced similar charges. His willingness to acknowledge that he had to learn all he could about the developmental disability of autism spectrum disorders is essential for any lawyer undertaking the representation of a person on the autism spectrum.

I also knew that our lawyer had a good reputation for being honest, ethical, and zealous in representing clients. He made it very clear that he would defend the case and not simply try to get the best plea deal he could.

I was not an easy parent of a client. I woke up every day with many questions and strategic points that I wanted to communicate to the lawyer. I constantly bombarded him with questions and my opinions on what needed to be done. He was patient but firm in letting me know that he was the lawyer and couldn't surrender his own independent judgment. I appreciated the fact that he knew his objectivity was needed and couldn't be clouded by my fear. My confidence that he was going to do everything possible to defend my son was very reassuring.

I was also impressed with how he dealt with experts. He retained three experts who evaluated my son. One was a local forensic expert psychologist who specialized in autism. Another was a world-renowned expert in autism from Yale University. The third was a psychologist who was an expert in evaluating risk assessment. His job was to determine my son's likelihood of either recidivism or actually harming someone. All three experts agreed that my son fell into the lowest risk category. He had nothing in his background that demonstrated a lack of respect for the law. It was also readily apparent that there was a significant gap between his level of intelligence and his social and sexual development that was related to his developmental disability.

Our lawyer viewed the initial report of each expert as a draft. He would then go over each report with the expert to clarify exactly what he felt needed to be explained more clearly. His ability to communicate this process to us was very helpful in understanding what he was trying to accomplish: educate the prosecutors about the relationship of my son's life history to the charged crime. The final reports convinced our lawyer that justice demanded that my son receive diversion, which would place him on probation with Pretrial Services for eighteen months, after which he would not have a criminal record and would not have to register as a sex offender. These reports were sent to the U.S. Attorneys' Office, whose agents were prosecuting our son. After their review, which took months, they were still unwilling to agree to diversion. Having confidence in the honest opinions expressed in the expert reports, our lawyer asked the AUSA if any prosecution expert had reviewed those reports. When the answer received was "no," he asked if that step could be taken.

A few months later, our attorney called and said the AUSA had informed him that an FBI neuropsychologist at the FBI building in Washington, D.C., would evaluate my son. We went to Washington and met this FBI neuropsychologist, who had read my son's complete life history, from early speech therapy through all his years in special education to reports from many therapists.

My son spent an entire day being examined by this neuropsychologist, who clearly understood autism. He also was aware that while my son was on the internet he never went into a chat room and never tried to make any contact with a minor. He seemed to understand the naïve observation opportunities that free pornographic images on the internet offered to a person on the autism spectrum who possessed a lack of intent or danger of harming others. At the end of the day, he stated to me and my son that he would promptly get a report out to the U.S. Attorney.

Four months later, our attorney called and said the AUSA had told him that the FBI psychologist agreed with all of our experts and also felt that diversion was the appropriate way to resolve the case. I took a deep breath. Then he said, "But their position hasn't changed."

My sense of justice felt trampled on. Why send my son to Washington to undergo that type of intensive examination if they only wanted a finding to justify their idea that he shouldn't get diversion? What further outraged me was that the AUSA apparently told the FBI psychologist that he didn't have to write a report.

Again, our attorney was not willing to concede his position. He went to see the U.S. Attorney for our district. After that meeting, the AUSA requested that my son undergo examination by yet another forensic psychologist, who wrote a lengthy report after spending eight hours evaluating him. He ended the report by giving the following advice to the U.S. Attorney: "In fact, there does not appear to be any basis for concluding that Nick is at any particular risk of sex offending. . . . What he is accused of doing . . . is not sex offending in any case. . . . Nick faces substantial challenges in making his way in the world, achieving a greater level of social connectedness and independence, and finding ways to cope with the depression and anxiety that his developmental disorder has produced. . . . It is worthwhile, from all points of view, for him to continue without the imposition of new impediments, particularly ones that would limit his access to social support and opportunities for social learning. His path is hard enough as it is."

I viewed this report as a strong argument for *not* sending Nick to prison, *not* making him a convicted felon, and *not* forcing him to register as a sex offender.

And yet, after five experts seemed to agree that justice in this case meant giving my son diversion, the final plea that was offered was to one count of possession of child pornography, five years of supervised release, and no prison. On one hand, I was grateful that my son didn't go to prison, which could easily have ended his life. On the other hand, my son becoming a convicted felon and a registered sex offender deeply offended my notion of justice. I knew I would never again feel as good about being a lawyer as I had before the FBI knocked on my son's door.

I did greatly appreciate our lawyer. He worked hard to gain a competent understanding of autism; he communicated effectively with my family; he helped the experts address the important issues in their reports; he was articulate in his spoken and written words; and he conducted himself without compromise until there was nothing further that he could do. A less skilled attorney could have caused my son to have been sentenced to prison. On the other side of the scale, a fair-minded United States Attorney would have concluded, based on all of the experts' opinions and reports, that it was an injustice to require my son to be a convicted federal felon for life and a registrant under the state sex offender registration act for fifteen years.

I hope lawyers reading this chapter can extrapolate and appreciate the special attention that must be given to the representation of a client on the autism spectrum. Had his lawyer not done so, it is highly likely my son would be in a federal prison, or perhaps dead.

I have lost my enthusiasm for being a part of this profession. When prosecutors care more about obtaining convictions than seeking justice, notions of compassion and redemption become meaningless. When my family's life was on the line, I know that the criminal justice system dealt us an injustice. I feel like the doctor who believes in modern medicine only to have a family member die as a result of medical malpractice. I am aware of the broad brush I am using in expressing my feelings toward the criminal justice system, yet it is difficult for me to maintain my enthusiasm for a system that destructively and unnecessarily is ruining the lives of many people on the autism spectrum and their families.

As much as I have enjoyed my career as a law professor, my family's experience has colored my perspective to such an extent that it is better for me to step aside and let someone who doesn't have this baggage take my place in the classroom. I will spend my time trying to change laws and helping other families with a child on the autism spectrum who has been swept into the criminal justice system. In doing so, I will use my First Amendment right to speak, write, and edit others on this topic. I have written a book with Emily Horowitz, PhD, titled *Caught in the Web of the Criminal Justice System: Autism, Developmental Disabilities, and Sex Crimes* (Jessica Kingsley Publishers, 2017).

The irony is that at the end of 2018, at the annual meeting of the State Bar of Michigan, I was the recipient of the John Reed Legacy Award, which is given to a legal educator "who has made a significant contribution to the practice of law." I was honored to receive this prestigious award, but I know that my significant contribution remains as a future challenge rather than one earned by my past efforts.

The fates placed me in the role of a parent of a client needing the services of a competent lawyer to save my son from imprisonment, which would likely have been a death sentence. From that experience, I can summarize what I believe to be the attributes of a lawyer well suited to representing a client on the autism spectrum:

- Become an expert in understanding autism and how it relates to the charged crime.
- Know where to find an effective mental health expert who can perform an evaluation to confirm a prior diagnosis of autism or to make the diagnosis, and then be able to show the relationship between autism and the crime charged to establish lack of criminal intent.
- Be experienced in negotiating pleas.
- Consider an expert's report as a draft to be discussed and improved upon for the purpose of educating prosecutors about the desired outcome (diversion). If at all possible, do not under any circumstances accept a plea requiring incarceration.
- Bring any preliminary motions necessary, such as lack of capacity to stand trial or to have understood or appreciated the nature and consequences of the charged criminal acts.
- Understand the time commitment necessary to communicate with a client on the autism spectrum.
- Recognize and welcome parents, guardians, and others to help the client process important information about the case, including whether a plea has been offered, the consequences therefrom, and the recommendations; include these people in a discussion if sex offender registry will be required.
- Show care and concern about the well-being of the client and family. They will all be in a state of shock and will need comforting as well as a game plan.

* * *

Professor Lawrence A. Dubin is a Professor Emeritus at the University of Detroit Mercy School of Law, where he taught courses in legal ethics and litigation. He was appointed by the Michigan Supreme Court to be a member of the Michigan Attorney Grievance Commission from 1978 to 1986, serving at times as its chair. Professor Dubin served for many years on the State Bar of Michigan's Standing Committee on Grievance, as well as acting as co-chair for the state bar's Lawyers and Judges Assistance Committee. He has authored books on the subjects of legal ethics, evidence, and trial practice, and has written many articles on the subject of legal ethics. The State Bar of Michigan has twice awarded him the Wade H. McCree Jr. Award for the Advancement of Justice for his public television programs. In 2018, the state bar awarded him the John W. Reed Michigan Lawyer Legacy Award, which is given to an educator from a Michigan law school whose influence on lawyers has elevated the quality of legal practice in the state.

Professor Dubin's advocacy for people on the autism spectrum who are brought into the criminal justice system is reflected in his recent book, *Caught in the Web of the Criminal Justice System: Autism, Developmental Disabilities and Sex Offenses* (co-edited with Emily Horowitz) (London: Jessica Kingsley Publishers, 2017).

Professor Dubin's email is ladonlaw@aol.com.

Suggested Works

The following list of suggested works is arranged according to chapter order. These categories are not airtight, and some resources listed in one chapter may be relevant to another. In addition to exploring the works cited in individual chapters, readers are encouraged to explore the articles and books written by the various chapter authors, many of whom are prolific writers.

The Intersection of Autism Spectrum Disorders and the Criminal Justice System

John Donovan and Caren Zucker. *In a Different Key: The Story of Autism* (Broadway Books, 2016).

Ana and Curt Warner. *The Warner Boys: Our Family's Story of Autism and Hope* (Little A, 2018).

The Arc. Criminal Justice Initiative. https://thearc.org/our-initiatives/criminal-justice/.

Competency

Simon Baron-Cohen. *The Science of Evil: On Empathy and the Origins of Cruelty* (Little Brown, 2011).

Howard Gardner. *Frames of Mind: The Theory of Multiple Intelligences* (Basic Books, 1983).

Steven K. Hoge, Richard Bonnie, Norman G. Poythress, and John Monahan. *The MacArthur Competence Assessment Tool—Criminal Adjudication (MacCAT-CA)* (PAR, 1999).

Justin Kruger and David Dunning. "Unskilled and Unaware of It: How Difficulties in Recognizing One's Own Incompetence Lead to Inflated Self-Assessment." *Journal of Personality and Social Psychology* 77, 121–134 (1999).

Michael Rutter. "Incidence of Autism Spectrum Disorders: Changes Over Time and Their Meaning." *Acta Paediatrica* 94, 2–15 (2005).

Criminal Responsibility

Tessa Grant, Rosaria Furlano, Layla Hall, and Elizabeth Kelley. "Criminal Responsibility in Autism Spectrum Disorder: A Critical Review Examining Empathy and Moral Reasoning." *Canadian Psychology/Psychologie Canadienne* 59(1), 65–75 (2018).

Marianne Kristiansson and Karolina Sorman. "Autism Spectrum Disorders—Legal and Forensic Psychiatric Aspects and Reflections." *Clinical Neuropsychiatry* 5(1), 55–61 (2008).

Heather A. Strickland, "Autism and Crime: Should Autistic Individuals Be Afforded the Use of an 'Autism Defense?'" *UDS/DCSL Law Review* 14 (2011).

Stephan G. White, J. Reid Meloy, Kris Mohandie, and Kristine Kienlen. "Autism Spectrum Disorder and Violence: Threat Assessment Issues." *Journal of Threat Assessment Issues* 4(3), 144–163 (2017).

Co-Occurring Disorders
Lauren Bishop-Fitzpatrick and Eric Rubenstein. "The Physical and Mental Health of Middle Aged and Older Adults on the Autism Spectrum and the Impact of Intellectual Disability." *Research in Autism Spectrum Disorders* 63, 34–41 (2019).

Jill C. Fodstad. "Special Issue on Mental Health Issues in Autism Spectrum Disorder." *Review Journal of Autism and Developmental Disorders* 6(3), 243–245 (2019).

Maya G. Mosner, Jessica L. Kinard, Jasmine S. Shah, Sean McWeeny, Rachel K. Greene, Sara C. Lowery, Carla A. Mazefsky, and Gabrielle S. Dichter. "Rates of Co-Occurring Psychiatric Disorders in Autism Spectrum Disorder Using the Mini International Neuropsychiatric Interview." *Journal of Autism and Developmental Disorders* 49(9), 3819–3832 (2019).

Stewart S. Newman and Mohammad Ghaziuddin. "Violent Crime in Asperger Syndrome: The Role of Psychiatric Comorbidity." *Journal of Autism and Developmental Disorders* 38(10), 1848–1852 (2008).

Tamara E. Rosen, Carla A. Mazefsky, Roma A. Vasa, and Matthew D. Lerner. "Co-Occurring Psychiatric Conditions in Autism Spectrum Disorder." *International Review of Psychiatry* 30(1), 40–62 (2018).

Adults with ASD
The Asperger/Autism Network. https://www.aane.org.

Stephen Mark Shore, Ed.D. http://www.autismasperger.net.

Temple Grandin, Ph.D. https://www.templegrandin.com.

The Bond Hearing
Christine N. Cea. "Autism and the Criminal Defendant." *St. John's Law Review* 88, 495 (2014).

The National Autism Association. "Meet the Police: A Guide to Introducing Children and Adults with ASD to Local Law Enforcement." 2017.

Working with the Expert: An Attorney's Perspective
A resource by and for autistic women. http://www.spectrumwomen.com.

Monique Chiacchia. "Autism Spectrum Disorder and the Criminal Justice System." https://www.purdueglobal.edu/blog/criminal-justice/autism-and-the-criminal-justice-system/ (April 5, 2016).

Individuals with Autism in the Criminal Justice System. http://www.autismsocietyofindiana.org/individuals-autism-criminal-justice-system.

Marc Woodbury-Smith and Kalpana Dein. "Autism Spectrum Disorder (ASD) and Unlawful Behavior: Where Do We Go from Here?" *Journal of Autism and Developmental Disorders* 44, 2734–2741 (2014).

Working with the Expert: An Expert's Perspective

Tony Attwood, Isabelle Henault, and Nick Dubin. *The Autism Spectrum, Sexuality, and the Law: What Every Parent and Professional Needs to Know* (Jessica Kingsley Publishers, 2014).

Ian Freckelton and David List. "Asperger's Disorder, Criminal Responsibility and Criminal Culpability." *Psychiatry, Psychology, and Law* 16(1), 16–40 (2009).

Testing

Simon Baron-Cohen, Rosa Hoekstra, Rebecca Knickmeyer, and Sally Wheelwright. "The Autism-Spectrum Quotient (AQ)—Adolescent Version." *Journal of Autism and Developmental Disorders* 36, 343–350 (2006). https://doi.org/10.1007/s10803-006-0073-6.

Katherine Gotham, Susan Risi, Andrew Pickles, and Catherine Lord. "The Autism Diagnostic Observation Schedule: Revised Algorithms for Improved Diagnostic Validity." *Journal of Autism and Developmental Disorders* 37, 613–627 (2007). https://www.ncbi.nlm.nih.gov/pmc/articles/PMC3057666/.

Marisela Huerta and Catherine Lord. "Diagnostic Evaluation of Autism Spectrum Disorders." *Pediatric Clinics of North America* 59(1), 103–111 (2012). https://www.ncbi.nlm.nih.gov/pmc/articles/PMC3269006/.

Catherine Lord, Michael Rutter, and Ann LeCouteur. "Autism Diagnostic Interview-Revised: A Revised Version of a Diagnostic Interview for Caregivers of Individuals with Possible Pervasive Developmental Disorders." *Journal of Autism and Developmental Disorders* 24(5), 659–685 (1994).

Sara S. Sparrow, Dominic V. Cichetti, and David A. Balla. *Vineland Adaptive Behavior Scales 2d Edition* (NCS Pearson, 2015).

Risk of Violence for People with ASD

Clare Sarah Allely, Phillip Wilson, Helen Minnis, Lucy Thompson, Enzo Yaksie, and Christopher Gillberg. "Violence Is Rare in Autism: When It Does Occur, Is It Sometimes Extreme?" *Journal of Psychology* 151, 49–68 (2016).

David S. Im. "Template to Perpetrate: An Update on Violence in Autism Spectrum Disorder." *Harvard Review of Psychiatry* 24, 14–35 (2016).

David S. Im. "Trauma as a Contributor to Violence in Autism Spectrum Disorder." *Journal of American Academy of Psychiatry and Law* 44(2), 184–192 (2016).

J. Reid Meloy, Anthony G. Hempill, Thomas Gray, Mohandie Kris, Andrew Shiva, and Thomas Richards. "A Comparative Analysis of North American Adolescent and Adult Mass Murderers." *Behavioral Sciences and the Law* 22, 291–309 (2004).

Bryan Vossekuil, Robert A. Fein, Marisa Reddy, Rady Borum, and William Modzeleski. *The Final Report and Findings of the Safe School Initiative: Implications for the Prevention of School Attacks in the United States* (U.S. Secret Service and U.S. Department of Education, 2002).

Creative Mitigation

Jodi Picoult. *House Rules* (Washington Square Press, 2010).

John Elder Robinson. *Look Me in the Eye* (Three Rivers Press, 2008).

Steve Silberman. *Neurotribes: The Legacy of Autism and the Future of Neurodiversity* (Penguin/Random House, 2015).

Graeme Simson. *The Rosie Project* (Simon & Schuster, 2013).

Mitigation Using Community Resources

Equal Justice Talks Webinar Series, The Arc of New Jersey Criminal Justice Advocacy Program (n.d.). https://www.arcnj.org/programs/criminal-justice-advocacy-program/#stq=Mitigation%3A%20Designing%20a%20Plan%20for%20People%20with%20ASD%20Using%20Community%20Resources&stp=1.

Dorothy Griffiths, Kendra Thomason, Stephanie Ioannou, Jordan Heath, and Robin Wilson. *Sex Offending Behavior of Persons with an Intellectual Disability: A Multi-Component Applied Behavior Analytic Approach* (NADD Press, 2018).

Barbara Haskins and Arturo Silva. "Asperger's Disorder and Criminal Behavior: Forensic-Psychiatric Considerations." *Journal of Psychiatry and Law* 34(3), 374–384 (2006).

Mark Mahoney. "Asperger's Syndrome and the Criminal Law: A Special Case of Child Pornography." Available from the author at http://www.harringtonmahoney.com.

Ohio Department of Developmental Disabilities-Sex Offender Workgroup. *Considerations for Developing Relapse Prevention for Individuals with Developmental Disabilities Who Have Been Convicted of a Sex Offense* at http://www.oacbdd.org/clientuploads/Docs/2014/140827-JenkinsSex Offenderpress.pdf (May 2014).

Prison Accommodations

Autism Society. "Autism Information for Advocates, Attorneys, and Judges." https://www.autism-society.org/wp-content/uploads/2014/04/Advocates_Attorneys_and_Judges.pdf.

Autism Speaks. https://www.autismspeaks.org/judicial-system.

CorrectionalOfficer.org. "Overseeing Inmates with Autism." http://www.correction-alofficer.org/overseeing-inmates-with-autism.

Sheryl Dicker and Robert Marion. "Judicial Spectrum Primer: What Judges Need to Know About Children with Autism Spectrum Disorders." *Juvenile Family Court Journal* (Spring 2012). https://www.aucd.org/docs/lend/judicial_primer_judges_need_to_know_about_asd.pdf.

Isabella Michna and Robert Trestman. "Correctional Management and Treatment of Autism Spectrum Disorder." *Journal of the American Academy of Psychiatry and the Law* 44(2), 253–258 (June 2016). http://jaapl.org/content/44/2/253.

Vulnerabilities of Defendants with ASD and Strategies for Improving Outcomes

Alexis Apel and James Diller. "Prison as Punishment: A Behavior-Analytic Evaluation of Incarceration." *The Behavior Analyst* 40(1), (2017).

Tony Charman, Andrew Pickles, Emily Simonoff, Susie Chandler, Tom Loucas, and Gillian Baird. "IQ in Children with Autism Spectrum Disorders: Data from the Special Needs and Autism Project (SNAP)." *PsycholoMed* 41(3), 619–627 (2011).

Matthew R. Durose, Alexa D. Cooper, and Howard N. Snyder. "Recidivism of Prisoners Released in 30 States in 2005: Patterns from 2005 to 2010." Bureau of Justice Statistics Special Report, NCJ 244205 (2014).

Leo Kanner. "Autistic Disturbances of Affective Contact." *Nervous Child* 2, 217–250 (1943).

The National Autistic Society (UK). http://www.autism.org.uk/cjs.aspx.

Rebecca Vallas. *Disabled Behind Bars: The Mass Incarceration of People with Disabilities in America's Jails and Prisons* (Center for American Progress, 2016).

Perception of Defendants with ASD by Judges and Juries

Colleen M. Berryessa. "Judiciary Views on Criminal Behavior and Intention of Offenders with High-Functioning Autism." *Journal of Intellectual Disabilities and Offending Behavior* 5(2), 96–107 (2014).

Colleen M. Berryessa, Lauren C. Milner, Nanibaa A. Garrison, and Mildred K. Cho. "Impact of Psychiatric Information on Potential Jurors in Evaluating High-Functioning Autism Spectrum Disorder (hfASD)." *Journal of Mental Health Research in Intellectual Disabilities* 8(3), 140–167 (2015).

Penny Cooper and Clare Allely. "You Can't Judge a Book by Its Cover: Evolving Professional Responsibilities, Liabilities and Judgecraft when a Party Has Asperger's Syndrome." *Northern Ireland Legal Quarterly* 69, 35–58 (2017).

Ian Freckelton. "Forensic Issues in Autism Spectrum Disorder: Learning from Court Decisions." In *Recent Advances in Autism Spectrum Disorders—Volume II* (InTech, 2013). https://www.intechopen.com/books/recent-advances-in-autism-spectrum-disorders-volume-ii/forensic-issues-in-autism-spectrum-disorder-learning-from-court-decisions.

ASD and Sex Offenses: A Son's Perspective
Does v. Snyder, 834 F.3d 696 (6th Cir. 2016).

Legal Reform for the Intellectually and Developmentally Disabled. http://www.lridd.org.

ASD and Sex Offenses: A Parent's Perspective
Alissa R. Ackerman and Marshall Burns. "Bad Data: How Government Agencies Distort Statistics on Sex-Crime Recidivism." *Justice Policy Journal* 13(1) (Spring 2016).

Nancy G. Calleja. "Deconstructing a Puzzling Relationship: Sex Offender Legislation, the Crimes That Inspired It and Sustained Moral Panic." *Justice Policy Journal* 13(1) (Spring 2016).

David Feige. "When Junk Science About Sex Offenders Infects the Supreme Court." *New York Times* (September 12, 2017). https://www.nytimes.com/2017/09/12/opinion/when-junk-science-about-sex-offenders-infects-the-supreme-court.html.

Melissa Hamilton. "The Child Pornography Crusade and Its Net-Widening Effect." *Cardozo Law Review* 33(1), (2012).

Adam Liptak. "Did the Supreme Court Base a Ruling on a Myth?" *New York Times* (March 6, 2017). https://www.nytimes.com/2017/03/06/us/politics/supreme-court-repeat-sex-offenders.html.